Immigrants
and
Their Church

MAKERS OF THE CATHOLIC COMMUNITY

The Bicentennial History of the Catholic Church in America
Authorized by the National Conference of Catholic Bishops

Gerald P. Fogarty, S.J., ed. *Patterns of Episcopal Leadership*

Joseph P. Chinnici, O.F.M. *Living Stones: The History and Structure of Catholic Spiritual Life in the United States*

Margaret Mary Reher. *Catholic Intellectual Life in America: A Historical Study of Persons and Movements*

Dolores Liptak, R.S.M. *Immigrants and Their Church*

David O'Brien. *Public Catholicism*

Karen Kennelly, C.S.J., ed. *American Catholic Women: A Historical Exploration*

Immigrants and Their Church

Dolores Liptak, R.S.M.

The Bicentennial History of the Catholic Church in America
Authorized by the National Conference of Catholic Bishops
Christopher J. Kauffman, General Editor

MACMILLAN PUBLISHING COMPANY
NEW YORK

Collier Macmillan Publishers
LONDON

Macmillan Publishing Company
866 Third Avenue, New York, NY 10022

Collier Macmillan Canada, Inc.

Library of Congress Catalog Card Number: 88-18109

Printed in the United States of America

printing number
1 2 3 4 5 6 7 8 9 10

Library of Congress Cataloging-in-Publication Data

Liptak, Dolores Ann.
    Immigrants and their church / Dolores Liptak.
        p.   cm. — (The Bicentennial history of the Catholic Church in America)
    ISBN 0-02-919231-5
    1. Immigrants—United States—Religion. 2. Catholic Church—United States—Membership. 3. United States—Emigration and immigration. 4. Catholic Church—United States—History. 5. United States—Church history.   I. Title.   II. Series.
BX1407.I45L57 1989
282′.73—dc19   88-18109
                                                              CIP

Contents

General Editor's Preface

The Second Vatican Council developed a new apologetic, a fresh articulation of faith suitable to the diverse peoples of the world. The Council also marked the turn from the atemporal transcendental character of the neoscholastic theological synthesis to a historical approach to the role of culture in the development of dogma, an approach influenced by the historical-literary methodology fostered by Catholic biblical exegetes. Implicit in the Council Fathers' call to discern the "signs of the times" is the need of the historian to provide a lens to improve our vision of the signs of past times. New models of the church, such as the "pilgrim people" or the "people of God," stressed not the institutional structures but rather the people's religious experiences.

Concurrent with these general trends in apologetics, systematic theology, and ecclesiology was the dramatic rise in consciousness of the ethnic particularities throughout the world. Just as the movements in the Catholic church were based upon a dynamic of historical consciousness, so the rise in ethnic awareness was steeped in the historical dynamic of national and regional identities.

Of all the students of American Catholicism, James Hennesey, S.J., stands out for his singular contribution to the dialogue between theologians and historians. In several studies he has focused on the role of the Christian historian in the process of discerning the authentic tradition of the church. To sharpen our focus on that tradition he juxtaposes a quotation from John Henry Newman with a text from the conciliar decree on Divine Revelation.

Newman in 1859:

> I think I am right in saying that the tradition of the Apostles, committed
> to the whole Church in its various constituents and functions *per modum*

unius [as one unit], manifests itself variously at various times, sometimes by the mouth of the episcopacy, sometimes by the doctors, sometimes by the people, sometimes by liturgies, rites, ceremonies and customs, by events, disputes, movements, and all those other phenomena which are comprised under the name of history. It follows that none of these channels of tradition may be treated with disrespect; granting at the same time fully that the gift of discerning, discriminating, defining, promulgating, and enforcing any portion of that tradition resides solely in the Ecclesia Docens [the teaching Church].

The Council Fathers in 1965:

What was handed on by the apostles [the tradition] comprises everything that serves to make the People of God live their lives in holiness and increase their faith. In this way the Church in her doctrine, life and worship, perpetuates and transmits to every generation all that she herself is, all that she believes.

Of course this implied religious task of the church historian must be grounded in the rigorous principles and scholarly methodology of the profession. Writing religious history is by its very nature different from writing, say, economic history. Both must avoid a priori reasoning and evaluate the sources of their discipline with a precise analysis. Just as the economic historian must be conscious of the biases embedded in her or his social-class perspective, so the church historian must explore her or his place at the intersection of faith and culture. Without such a hermeneutical exercise of self-exploration one can neither adequately struggle against biases nor develop clear principles for understanding the past. During several group meetings with the six primary contributors to this work such a hermeneutical process developed. Since all of us have been influenced by recent trends in ecclesiology and historiography, each has a sense of her or his place at the intersection of faith and culture. Though some focus on the institutional church and others analyze the movement of peoples, all are professionally trained historians and are sensitive to Newman's notion of the diverse manifestations of tradition.

We conceived this topical approach of the six-volume history as the most effective means of dealing with an enormous amount of material. In a sense this project was an attempt to weave the American fabric of tradition into distinctive patterns. Although I designed the overall project, each of the primary contributors, either author or editor-author, was responsible for the particular design of his or her book. We seven historians met several times over a three-year period. In this case the term "community of scholars" is no exaggeration; a remarkable climate of honesty, candor, civility, and humor prevailed in our discussions. Though each volume stands on its own, the six

achieve an unusual unity. There is a common beginning in most of
the books. Commemorating the bicentennial of the appointment of
John Carroll, each of the books opens during the federal period when
Catholics achieved some semblance of ecclesiastical organization. We
anticipate that a fresh synthesis of colonial Catholic history will be
published at the quincentennial in 1992 of Columbus's arrival in the
New World.

Throughout these volumes one reads about the persistent need for
Catholics to forge their religious identities within the ethos of the
new nation. In its origins the nation tended toward enlightenment
and toleration; Catholics in Maryland and Pennsylvania reflected an
open cosmopolitanism symbolized by the leadership of John Carroll.
There was a conscious effort to embrace religious liberty and pluralism as positive factors; a denominational civility characterized the
era. Subsequently, periodic outbursts of militant anti-Catholicism and
nativism during the periods of immigration led Catholics to identify
their loyalty to the United States in terms of good citizenship, but
they retreated from the culture into ethnic enclaves; these were the
preservationists who nurtured their particular Old World cultures in
defense against this hostility. Isaac Hecker and the Americanists, such
as John Ireland, forged a transformationist identity, one that was derived from the Carroll era and was based upon the spiritual compatibility of Catholicism and American culture.

Preservationist and transformationist are more appropriate concepts than ideological terms such as conservative and liberal because
they are rooted in the religious and social contexts. Though today the
lines are blurred between these identities, they are still viable con-
ceptually. Today's preservationists are defensive against what they
perceive as the antireligious tendencies of the culture and are searching for a wholeness in their view of the past. Transformationists tend
to mediate religion in the terms of the culture and, like Isaac Hecker,
see the movement of the Spirit not in opposition to modern society
but within strands of the larger national ethos.

The "Romanness" of the American Catholic identity has seldom
been a problem. During periods of conflict and controversy leaders
in both camps have appealed to Rome as symbolic of their general
loyalty to the papacy. American notions of religious liberty, denom-
inationalism, pluralism, and voluntarism were not legitimated by
Rome until the Second Vatican Council. While many Americans have
consistently held that this attitude by the Vatican represents the inherent conflict between Roman authority and American democracy,
Catholics have tended to consider the assumption that there is such
a conflict to be another malicious manifestation of the anti-Catholic
animus. While very loyal to Rome, Catholics have shared with other

Americans a pragmatic sense, a sense that Martin E. Marty refers to as a kind of experimentalism. While Catholics articulated a loyalty to Rome as the center of their changeless religion, paradoxically many had derived from their American experience a spirituality and a religious worldview that accept change as a fact of life. Marty quotes Jacques Maritain on American experimentalism: "Americans seem to be in their own land as pilgrims, prodded by a dream! They are always on the move—available for new tasks, prepared for the possible loss of what they have. They are not settled, installed. . . . In this sense of becoming and impermanence one may discern a feeling of evangelical origin which has been projected into temporal activity." In a sense this Catholic insistence on changeless faith, while their religious behavior is protean, allowed many leaders to hold to an Americanist vision and even a modernist methodology (applied not to Scripture but to evangelization) after the condemnations of Americanism and modernism.

Catholic identities derived from race, gender, and non-European ethnic groups are distinctive from the Roman, transformationist, and preservationist identities. Black Catholics were so marginalized that there was no sizable number of black clergy until the mid-twentieth century. The general periodization, particularly "immigrant church," is simply meaningless to their experience. The racism of the vast majority of people was reflected in the church. Many black Catholics now identify with Afro-American culture and the exodus experience basic to liberation theology. French Canadians and many Hispanic people also have developed their distinctive identities. Their non-European origins marginalized them in a church dominated by assimilationists of the more affluent classes. As with the black Catholics, their identities are deeply influenced by their historically rooted outsider status.

These six volumes struggled against exclusivism based on race, ethnicity, and gender. While chapters in these books deal with race and major non-European ethnic groups, an entire volume focuses on gender. I consulted with several Catholic feminists before deciding on a separate book on women in the Catholic community. Some might ask why not each of the other five books deals with this subject. Because there are so few secondary works on Catholic women and because not each historian could do ground-breaking research in women's studies, it became evident that an entire book should be devoted to this topic. As a consequence of a corollary decision, specialists in particular areas wrote separate chapters in the book because one author could not do justice to a general history of Catholic women. Of course, many Catholic women were drawn into the issues discussed in the other five volumes, but many behaved in a countercultural manner and opposed the dominant ecclesiastical identity represented by the conventional notion of the "ideal Catholic woman." In the shadow of patriarchy many women formed spiritual identities that did not fit religious and social categories.

Dolores Liptak, R.S.M., and Karen Kennelly, C.S.J., help us to understand the varieties of ethnic and female identities; David O'Brien and Gerald P. Fogarty, S.J., elaborate on the public forms of Catholicism and episcopal leadership; Margaret Mary Reher and Joseph P. Chinnici, O.F.M., locate various Catholic identities on the intellectual, spiritual, and devotional planes.

These six historians have been sensitive to regional variations, to differing contexts of urban development, and to the need to expand beyond the boundary of the stated theme of each volume into such frontiers as the micro-history of neighborhoods and parishes, the rural Catholic experience, meanings of the Catholic rites of passage and of Catholic "habits of the heart." The design of the project and the bicentennial deadlines limited the historians' range to the broad national contours of their topics. Though there is unavoidable overlapping in the treatment of persons and movements, the particular points of view preclude redundancy. More significantly, these books focus on the distinctive character of the American aspect of the Catholic community and represent various blends of original research and a unique rendering of topics derived from secondary literature.

From design to production I have had the good fortune to work with excellent historians and other fine people. To Justus George Lawler, the literary editor, to Charles Buggé, our liaison with the United States Catholic Conference, to Elly Dickason and Charles E. Smith of Macmillan Publishing Company, to Virgil C. Dechant and the late John M. Murphy of the Knights of Columbus, to Archbishop William D. Borders of Baltimore and Archbishop Oscar H. Lipscomb of Mobile, chairmen of the bicentennial committees of the National Conference of Catholic Bishops, and to John Bowen, S.S., Sulpician archivist and consultant, I am exceedingly grateful for their participation in making this six-volume set an appropriate tribute to John Carroll and to all those people who formed the Catholic tradition in the United States. I am particularly indebted to the inspiration of John Tracy Ellis in this the fifty-first year of his priesthood. May we always cherish his tradition of scholarship, honesty, and civility.

Christopher J. Kauffman

Acknowledgments

The National Conference of Catholic Bishops in 1981 established an ad hoc committee to plan for an appropriate observance of the 200th anniversary of the appointment in 1789 of John Carroll of Baltimore as the first Roman Catholic bishop for the United States of America. It was quickly determined that an important component of that observance should be a serious and substantial effort to shed added light on the growth and development of the Catholic church in Carroll's native land for these two hundred years. A subcommittee for publications was formed and the six volumes, *Makers of the Catholic Community,* are the result of its initiatives.

Grateful acknowledgment is made to the Knights of Columbus and their Supreme Knight, Virgil C. Dechant, who provided a generous grant that underwrote the scholarly efforts necessary to such a venture. For more than a century the work of the Knights of Columbus has epitomized much of the Catholic life that fills these volumes just as their presence and spirit have given discernible form to the faith and external witness of the Catholic church in the United States.

The Order has a rich tradition of fostering historical studies. In 1921 the Fourth Degree established the K of C Historical Commission. It presented its awards to Samuel Flagg Bemis and Allan Nevins, historians who later became notable figures. The commission also sponsored the publication of the K of C Racial Contribution Series: W. E. B. DuBois, *The Gift of the Black Folk;* George W. Cohen, *The Jews in the Making of America;* and Frederick F. Schrader, *The Germans in the Making of America.* Coincidentally, these books were also published by Macmillan. The K of C microfilm collection of the manuscripts of the Vatican archives, which resides at Saint Louis University, is a remarkable testimony to the Knights' promotion of scholarship. In 1982 a scholarly history of the Order, *Faith and Fraternalism,* by

Christopher J. Kauffman, was published, a book that has been widely noted as a solid contribution to social and religious history. Hence, *Makers of the Catholic Community* is a significant mark on the long continuum of the Knights' role in historical scholarship.

For six years the NCCB Ad Hoc Committee for the Bicentennial of the U.S. Hierarchy has given consistent and affirmative support for this series, and the Subcommittee for Publications has provided the technical insights and guidance that were necessary to the finished work. All who have thus contributed time and talent deserve recognition and gratitude. The members of the committee were: Archbishop William D. Borders, chairman; Archbishops Eugene A. Marino, S.S.J., Theodore E. McCarrick, and Robert F. Sanchez; and Bishops John S. Cummins, F. Joseph Gossman, Raymond W. Lucker, and Sylvester W. Treinen. The staff consisted of Rev. Robert Lynch and Mr. Richard Hirsch. Members of the subcommittee were: Rev. William A. Au, Ph.D.; Msgr. John Tracy Ellis, Ph.D.; Sister Alice Gallin, O.S.U., Ph.D.; Msgr. James Gaffey, Ph.D.; Rev. James Hennesey, S.J., Ph.D.; and Msgr. Francis J. Lally.

> Most Reverend Oscar H. Lipscomb
> *Chairman*, Subcommittee for Publications

Foreword

Ethnicity may be viewed through the lens of the sociologist, anthropologist, or historian. Timothy L. Smith's work on religion and ethnicity, based upon a synthesis of the views of each of these disciplines, distinguishes ethnicity from nationality and states that the essence of ethnicity is "a sense of peoplehood." In its nineteenth-century manifestation this sense reflected so strongly the influence of religion that the particular faith-tradition became its basis.

Dolores Liptak focuses on the particular Catholic ground on which a wide variety of ethnic groups have developed their sense of peoplehood, from the time of John Carroll to the present. A full understanding of the central period of the immigrant church requires an examination of both frontier and urban Catholic communities, as well as consideration of the effects of the predominance of the Irish in the church hierarchy. Liptak's study is not an ethnic or immigrant history but rather a church history, one that recounts the interaction between immigrants and their church.

In her exploration of the ethnic factor in American church history, Liptak delineates the shifting cultural boundaries within the ecclesiastical topography. Many Catholics still refer to the German, Polish, French, or Italian churches within their dioceses. These national parishes are the legacy of episcopal accommodation to ethnic particularism. An expert on the history of these parishes, Liptak describes them as religious and social centers where the language and culture of the old world were seen as essential to the preservation of the faith. From the Irish-American episcopal point of view, these parishes were way stations on the road to the full Americanization of all immigrant groups. To the particular ethnic groups they were islands of faith in uncharted waters.

As the book clearly illustrates, the American Catholic people possess a multitude of identities, derived not only from their varying ethnic and religious backgrounds but also from the particular circumstances of their settlement in the United States. Though it is beyond the scope of this work to depict the differences between an ethnic parish in Philadelphia and its counterpart in San Francisco, regional specificity is a distinctive feature of immigrant Catholic communities. This is also true of racial Catholic identity—as seen, for instance, in differences between the cultures of black Catholics in Louisiana and Maryland. Time is as important a determinant as place. Whether settlement in the United States came during a period of impassioned nativism and anti-Catholicism, or during an economic depression, certainly had an impact upon the development of a particular group's sense of belonging.

This ethnic complexity is a very positive mark of the protean Catholic development in the United States. The complexity helps to explain the origins of Catholic separatism—understood not only as the development by American Catholics of their institutions, such as the Catholic professional societies, but also as the growth of separate ethnic enclaves within the Catholic community. The so-called Catholic ghetto was composed of many ethnic ghettos.

Despite the collapse of Catholic separatism, concurrent with the Second Vatican Council, ethnicity is still a strong factor in the life of contemporary American Catholics. Though church leaders cherish the pluriform character of American Catholicism, Hispanic, Vietnamese, and other ethnic groups still struggle to maintain their traditions, just as did their predecessors who formed the first national parishes.

Christopher J. Kauffman

Preface

As the ethnic historian Moses Rischin has commented, U.S. Catholicism absorbed an "almost unique cosmopolitan sweep" of American people over its two hundred years of official history. Sociologist Harold J. Abramson has also taken note of the ethnic factor in the shaping of American Catholic church. Impressed by the variety of social and cultural values that have motivated members of diverse ethnic groups to practice their faith and to style their lives according to cherished religious traditions, he has devoted much research to assessing the significance of ethnic diversity upon generations and across ethnic groups. Defining ethnicity broadly as the intrinsic quality that symbolically and literally sets the boundaries between people on the basis of language, nationality, and culture, both scholars I am citing have challenged Catholics to devote more serious study to the ethnic factor in American Catholicism.[1]

Catholic historians and sociologists have also examined the American Catholic church along ethnic lines. Important monographs and articles have appeared as a result of these investigations. Most have detailed one ethnic group that, through parish, diocesan, or, occasionally, national involvement has interacted with the institutional church as a whole. These specialized studies have made impressive contributions to American Catholic historiography.[2] The aim of the present book is to synthesize the conclusions of these studies and to analyze the ways in which the phenomenon of ethnicity has shaped the overall development of the American Catholic church. It attempts to probe the degree to which the ethnic factor has affected all Catholics in every aspect of church life and has occasioned a uniqueness *vis-à-vis* the world church. Most importantly, this work tries to consider each immigrant group from its own perspective, in order to discern the ways in which each particular group sought to be part of the church and to contribute to its identity.

Given the complexity of studying the two-hundred-year growth of the church along the cosmopolitan lines Rischin described, however, I recognize that this study is but a modest first step along the path of synthesis and analysis. It has limited itself to several major questions. How, for example, have the contours of the immigrant church developed? What has accounted for the transition from immigrant church to the present institution, with its continuing need to develop strategies for the incorporation of new Catholics? How has the interplay among ethnic groups explicitly affected the kind of church that American Catholicism has become? Why did episodes of divisiveness occur? What role have clergy and laity played in the making of the church along each stage of development? What are the implications of continuing Catholic immigration?

In the attempt to answer these questions, the lives and ministries of immigrant Catholics have been considered with a view to evaluating those who built their church in a new land, first as missionaries among diverse populations and then, more particularly, as a Catholic people trying to preserve their separate ethnic identities. In examining the church with respect to its ethnic manifestations I do not, of course, suggest that the Catholic church has been the only American church affected by the ethnic diversity of its membership. Protestant denominations were also initiated into the complex problems created by ethnic difference. But, since it is the very nature of Protestantism to reestablish and reorganize on the basis of difference, the crisis caused by immigration was more simply handled, as developments among the Scandinavian and German Lutheran or the various Hungarian Reformed churches readily testify. For the Catholic church—which aims to be a universal, all-encompassing church—diversity has always been viewed from a very different perspective. In fact, it is seen as an essential mark of the church, one for which leaders must find accommodation. Thus, the Catholic challenge has meant finding ways to resolve the problem of incorporating, into one body, "other Catholics." For this reason, the way in which Catholic leaders have managed to safeguard unity amid diversity becomes a question especially pertinent to Catholic historiography.

Today, the ethnic contours shaped by immigrant Catholics remain apparent. Irish-Americans continue to dominate many aspects of church life; yet church authority has begun to be shared by a new generation less interested in determining policy or practice on the basis of ethnicity. What this new direction will mean to the development of the church in the third century can be understood only in the context of the immigrant experience. Therefore, this study has much to say to those who are planning for the future of the church. Yet it raises its own set of questions. Will the roles that the various ethnic groups have assumed continue to serve? Will the new forces of assimilation require new solutions or will the lessons of history provide a blueprint sufficient for future practice? What changes should be anticipated as new ethnic minorities press for incorporation?

Clearly, the challenge of incorporating new members of the American Catholic church remains. Yet this study should provide some insight toward the making of the third-century church. Out of many lands, a new and vibrant Catholic people was created and given strength. Those of former generations knew and appreciated the work of the giants of the church who took charge during the previous crisis of ethnic growth and who established churches for immigrants in such a way that they sensed belonging, were sustained in their individual Catholic culture, and were able to inspire the next generation in their vocational choices. That world was one in which ethnicity loomed very large yet seldom became oppressive. For most Catholics the separate world of ethnic Catholicism has ended. Yet the rationale behind it remains. There is nothing to indicate that the U.S. Catholic church in the next century will not continue to embrace such diversity even while it develops new ways of allowing the next generations of ethnic Catholics to survive in a postimmigrant church.

PART ONE

The Early Immigrant Church, 1790–1860

In his introduction to *The Story of American Catholicism*, published in 1941, the historian Theodore Maynard repeated the words of Peter Guilday, to whom he referred as "the leading ecclesiastical historian": "What genius indeed could in a few broad strokes of his brush on the canvas give even the highlights of all that has been accomplished by the Church?"[1] The story of American Catholicism is kaleidoscopic. Told over the years by such notable historians as John Gilmary Shea, Peter Guilday, Thomas Maynard, Thomas McAvoy, and John Tracy Ellis, and more recently by James Hennesey, S. J., and Jay P. Dolan, it waits to be told again and again. Fresh perspectives emerge as new ideas and experiences occur; they add color, shape, and form to the basic story. In this way, the framework holds firm: the church's institutional development and dimensions, the major details of growth, the episodes and personalities that gave it a social identity and context—all these become the fabric of the tale.

Now we are two hundred years into the telling of this story. In this bicentennial year, which commemorates, on November 6, 1989, the appointment of John Carroll as bishop of Baltimore, the time is appropriate to review American Catholicism's history and, in an effort to understand the direction the church should take for the future, to introduce the factor of ethnicity and investigate its place in the familiar pattern of the story.

1

CHAPTER
1
Identification and Structure of the Immigrant Church

꘏꘎

*T*he Catholic church in the United States had its official beginnings as an American institution in 1789 when John Carroll (1735–1815) was appointed its first bishop. Once consecrated in England, on August 15, 1790, Carroll would set to work developing the organizational structure of the church, designating parishes and dioceses, and recruiting personnel. Under him, the status of American Catholics would be formalized within the Roman Catholic church and informally ratified within an American setting. With him, Catholic leaders and ordinary church members joined in building an institution that could meet the challenges posed by a new social context requiring separate allegiances to church and state.

Not that it was the task of Carroll or other contemporary Catholics to introduce the church within the American setting. In fact, as John Gilmary Shea has pointed out, "The Catholic church is the oldest organization in the United States and the only one that has retained the same life and polity and forms through each succeeding age."[1] Long before the establishment of the United States, the outlines of the American Catholic church were being drawn by missionary journeys throughout lands now part of the United States. During the days of the Spanish exploration, for example, the Floridas, together with southern and western continental areas that would later comprise Louisiana, Texas, New Mexico, Arizona, and California, formed an arc of Spanish missions. These had been founded by Jesuits, Franciscans, Carmelites, Capuchins, Augustinians, and other clergy. The

Catholic faith was firmly planted in this arc land by zeal and even martyrdom. A Catholic culture had developed westward from the peninsula mission of Nombre de Dios at St. Augustine, Florida (1565). Mexican foundations had been established in 1629 in the western regions of the continent; later missions, such as San Antonio de Valero, were added. After the mid-1700s, twenty-one California missions had been developed by the friar Junipero Serra and his Franciscan successors; these were spaced a day's journey from one another along a corridor reaching from San Diego to the northern territory claimed by Russia. Far to the north, French missionaries were accomplishing similar feats on behalf of religion. There as well, not a cape was turned, nor a river entered, without the presence of missionary priests. Maine, the upper Mississippi regions, and the area of the Great Lakes witnessed the evangelization of the native tribes. Eight clerical missionaries, six of whom were priests of the Society of Jesus, and two lay missionaries laid down their lives within the same decade (the 1640s) in the service of the church; they would be canonized as the North American Martyrs in 1930. By the time that independence had been achieved by England's thirteen mainland American colonies in 1783, a crescent of Catholic influence to the north, south, and west had come to surround the new nation.

For all that, the Roman Catholic church was perceived in a very different light within the newly created confederation of states. For the two centuries of British colonial development, Catholics had led scattered, tentative lives throughout the thirteen colonies, deliberately living anonymous existences—unless their imminent deaths gave them courage to declare their faith. Thus, Boston's Goody Glover, judged by Cotton Mather to be hanged as a witch, was reported to have announced before she went to her death in 1688, "I die a Catholic."[2] Only for brief intervals in Maryland and New York, and consistently only in the colony of Pennsylvania—where the Quaker descendants of William Penn strictly upheld principles of toleration and brotherly love—was it possible for Catholics to express publicly their religious affiliation. After the grant of religious liberty, evoked in the Declaration of Independence, had finally been incorporated in several state constitutions, Catholics were, for the first time, able to practice their religion without political reprisal. Still, in a world flooded by the language of bigotry, in which Rome was perceived as Babylon and where *Foxe's Book of Martyrs* remained a favored text, the small band of American Catholics was not inclined to declare its official existence, especially its explicit Roman ties. Catholic development in the United States had to proceed with caution.

John Carroll's appointment as bishop and the establishment of the first episcopal see in 1789 illustrates the degree to which Catholics had already been adversely influenced by Protestant attitudes. These two milestones of Catholic history occurred only after Carroll and his fellow priests felt that Rome's plan to inaugurate a church in the United States would be found generally acceptable among Americans. Especially through the first half-century of the American Republic, Catholics continued to be dubious about their place among Protestants. For one thing, the taint of being immigrants professing a "foreign religion" seemed indelible. Carroll himself worried about this. He described Catholic membership, which numbered approximately 23,000 in 1785, as being constantly added to by immigrants who poured "in upon us in large numbers from the various European countries."[3] From Carroll's time on, the ethnic character of the new membership would become an inescapable concern. Further, an impressive network of Congregational, Presbyterian, Baptist, Methodist, and Episcopal churches, as well as rapidly growing fundamentalist Protestant denominations, covered the American landscape. In such a setting, Catholic leaders had great difficulty holding their own.

At the same time, their identification as a "despised minority" for religious and ethnic reasons tended to produce in Catholics an inner tension. From the beginning, Catholic development in the United States would reflect this unresolved ambivalence: on the one hand, Catholics attempted to become associated with the dominant culture and to downplay their ethnic diversity; on the other, they manifested as strong a need to project a Catholic identification with their own ethno-cultural traditions and to criticize the overpowering nature of the Protestant presence. This complex tension, in fact, would retard the development of a clear Catholic identity throughout the history of the American Catholic church.

If Carroll's major responsibility as the first bishop of Baltimore was to establish the necessary institutions of the church and to recruit personnel, it was his concern with achieving Catholic respectability that was to become a primary preoccupation. His attempt to present the Catholic church as American was to meet with only marginal success. Circumstances continually worked against this goal. When, for example, he was asked to name bishops to head new dioceses, he hoped to use the opportunity to emphasize the American aspects of the church. Despite his intentions to find clergy who clearly were representative of "American" ideals, however, he had no American-born candidates to choose from when the first four dioceses were erected in 1808. Two of the candidates he ultimately suggested to fill these new posts were French emigrés; the two others had been born in Ireland. When Carroll looked for other personnel to convey the message of Americanism, he sought in vain. Instead, throughout his tenure, he had to rely heavily upon European communities, especially the Sulpicians, and an immigrant clergy to staff his seminaries and to help evangelize his church.

Throughout his episcopacy, moreover, Carroll was also required to remain sensitive to the ethnic component of Catholic life in general. The Germans were only the first to document their insecurities as foreign-language-speaking Catholics. Everywhere, circumstances compelled Carroll to recognize that most of the church's membership were recent European immigrants, outcasts from their own lands for either political or economic reasons. Despite all the indications that the church he headed could not neatly be characterized as an American organization, Carroll tried to develop institutions that would parallel American models. Among the early American institutions that he sponsored were orphanages, schools, colleges, and seminaries. Thus, Georgetown University in Washington, D.C., and Saint Mary Seminary in Baltimore, both founded in 1791, and the beginnings of the parochial school system, started under Elizabeth Bayley Seton in Maryland in 1808, can be attributed to Carroll's administrative foresight. As a rule, however, those who first joined these institutions were from abroad, and those they served were overwhelmingly of immigrant background. The Frenchman Stephen Badin and the Russian Demetrius Gallitzin, for example, were among the first graduates of Carroll's seminary, while the children of immigrants were the first to fill the orphanages and become students at the free schools he encouraged. Even Mother Seton's American heritage was almost immediately submerged within a congregation of Sisters of Charity that rapidly became a magnet for Irish-American young women.

But what particularly bothered Carroll in the formative years of Catholic development was the occasional negative publicity directed against the ethnicity of the church's membership. That this might interfere with the normal operation of his church, or that its immigrant nature would in any way suggest to others that the Catholic Church was not fully an American institution, was a constant cause of concern and stress. Of some French merchants who practiced their religion in Baltimore, Carroll himself wrote that most were a scandal whose contempt for the church and disregard of religious practice were perverting other French Catholics. His unpleasant encounters with Germans in Philadelphia and Baltimore were demoralizing to the Germans and personally humbling to Carroll. With regard to one Boston congregation whose problems were not ameliorated until 1792, a wiser Carroll expressed the wish that "all would lay aside national distinctions & attachments & strive to form not Irish, or English, or French Congregations & Churches, but Catholic-American Congregations and Churches."[4]

But disharmony among members did not excessively disturb the rapid growth of the nation or the church. Immigration and annexation continued to enlarge the nation. Their effect upon the Catholic church was especially remarkable. Under Carroll's successors, Catholic population soared. In 1825, for example, there was already at least a sevenfold increase over the numbers Carroll had reported when he was first superior of the Mission in 1785. To a great extent, the new total of approximately 195,000 Catholics could be attributed to the annexations of the territories of Louisiana in 1803 and Florida in 1819. But approximately 77,000 of the new membership were immigrants from Germany and Ireland. By 1850, there were one and a half million American Catholics, spread from Galveston, Texas, to Charleston, South Carolina, from Portland, Maine, to the far-western lands at Oregon City and Monterey. Serving this widespread community were approximately two thousand priests, one-third of whom were of Irish descent, and an episcopacy that showed clear signs of becoming predominantly Irish. Ten years later, Catholic population would reach an astounding 3,103,000, giving the Catholic Church the numerical majority among denominations. To the dozen dioceses or archdioceses that had been established before 1830, another thirty-five had been added by 1860. By this time, too, the pattern of Catholic growth more clearly reflected the multiethnic composition of the American church. Since most of the newest immigrants had been forced to the United States through economic dislocation, the figure revealed a second social reality: the added Catholic membership came from the most destitute segment of the European population. Revolutionary industrial developments in the United States became a constant lure, especially for German or Irish workers and farmers whose dreams of a secure future were being ruined by the effect of modernization.

The rapid increase of the Catholic immigrant population exacerbated the problems of Catholic identity in a new nation. Efforts to organize membership within parishes or dioceses constantly faltered because of the sheer increase in numbers and the problems that strangers in a new land had to encounter. More personnel were recruited and new dioceses were created, often so quickly that complaints reached Rome over the mistaken notion Europeans had of American geography. Some dioceses were even forced to relocate: Bardstown, for example, was transferred to Louisville, Kentucky, in 1841. Although both were established in 1843, the future of the dioceses of Little Rock, Arkansas, and Hartford, Connecticut, hung in the balance until population increases and economic improvements stabilized them. Despite the need for planning and organization in the midst of such hectic growth, however, no invitation to convoke a national meeting of the bishops was issued—perhaps for reasons related to ethnic preferences. It was widely understood that most of the bishops preferred to keep matters as they were. But the growing need to define common problems led some to search for "one settled plan of operations" and to "pull to-gether," as Boston's Benedict J. Fenwick (1782–1846) suggested should be done.[5] In 1829 the first provincial council to be called since Carroll's time was convened. From 1829 to 1866, there would be seven provincial and two plenary councils. In these meetings, many of the most difficult aspects of church organization and polity were addressed, and some attention was given to the question of unity in the American Catholic church.

Problems related to ethnic difference continued to trouble the church, but they did not yet shape policy in these formative years preceding the Civil War. This occurred despite the admission of ethnic bias by Catholic leaders themselves. Bishops often publicly commented upon the implications of cultural differences; their letters sometimes bristled with remarks concerning an ethno-cultural rivalry that could produce rancorous interactions. The French-born archbishop of Baltimore, Ambrose Maréchal (1764–1828), was not above referring to the Irish as *la canaille irlandaise;* he even petitioned Rome against "having more Irish bishops." His successor, James Whitfield (1770–1834), referred to two of his contemporary bishops as "both warm headed Irishmen," who "have, it seems, a strong Irish predilection in favor of Irish Bishops and Irish discipline for the United States."[6] Such ethnically based concerns found reciprocation among Whitfield's colleagues who worried instead about the pervasive French influence. Lay Catholics shared similar sentiments; fearing loss of cultural identity or religious expression, they were often disturbed about certain episcopal appointments or parochial developments. Trustees in Norfolk, Virginia, for example, implied that they were entitled to special treatment not so much because, as Catholic laymen, they should share authority with the clergy but rather because, precisely as Irish Catholics, they should have more say in the appointment of clergy. The conflicts initiated by trustees in Philadelphia, Charleston, New York, and New Orleans that pitted bishops against elements within local parishes can also be seen as involving ethnic differences between parishioners and assigned personnel as much as questions of authority per se. And the struggles that Pittsburgh's Benedictine, Redemptorist, and Notre Dame communities early experienced are in part traceable to the cultural differences emphasized by their bishop, Michael O'Connor (1810–1872) and other Irish leaders.

Still, evangelization and organization remained the explicit preoccupations of early church leaders. The call to mission, whether in the wilderness or in the more settled urban environment, lasted as long as there were new people to evangelize or new areas to be explored and populated. If at first most of the early church personnel had come as émigrés or exiles from nations unfriendly to the Catholic religion, the newer immigrant clergy and religious came to serve the expanding, urbanizing church. European seminarians and clergy had heard the universal appeal to evangelize as it was related in stories disseminated by mission organizations, from visiting American bishops who requested their assistance, or in letters from America. Somehow those who immigrated instinctively knew that they must help to build an American church. Biographies reveal the original expectations of the early missionaries. The vocation of John Nepomucene Neumann (1811–1860), for example, provides evidence of this church-building desire. Although remembered as an apostle among German immigrants and the first builder of the Archdiocese of Philadelphia, Neumann had not intended that he would make the care of immigrants his prior apostolate. Instead, he came with the desire to convert the Indians; his chance reading of letters sent to his seminary in Budweis by the well-known pioneer missionary Frederic Baraga (1797–1868) provided the initial spark. After his arrival in the United States, however, Neumann's dream of working among the Indians rudely halted. Adopted almost immediately by the immigrant John Dubois (1764–1842), who was then bishop of New York, he was asked to work among destitute Germans upstate. From that point on, Neumann's ambitions were redirected. Instead of the Indian languages he had wanted to use to convert the Indian, he would spend his years learning and speaking the languages of immigrants, anticipating their needs and organizing their activities. Instead of converting Indians, Neumann spread the gospel in at least eight modern languages, including several Slavic languages and even the Gaelic of Western Ireland's most recent newcomers.

Like Neumann, other immigrant priests and religious also saw their missionary aims totally altered by the pressing needs of America's Catholic immigrants. Although the missionary apostolate to the Indians had beckoned them and the vigorous challenge of its stark, unrelenting roughness still commanded their imagination, these missionaries seemed able to divert their fascination for the land and for its people to respond to other needs of the new American society. For them, the United States was the ready soil for Catholicism; they were willing to take any role in the invigorating Catholic experiment. When the spiritual and physical needs of their fellow immigrants became apparent, most adapted quickly, recognizing the importance of directing their efforts toward building a strong Catholic base in the new land. While cooperating in the process of building the essential structures of the American Catholic church, however, most remained committed to the missionary aspects of their work, whether they were engaged in city or frontier apostolates.

Literally from coast to coast, pioneer missionaries worked to gather the Catholic diaspora, regardless of racial or ethnic background, and develop an American church. Together, missionaries and a Catholic people built monuments to Catholic faith. The first log cabin, frame, or adobe buildings would eventually become brick-structure churches. The makeshift, one-room learning centers grew into substantial grade schools, academies, or colleges. Immigrants found enough resources to send their children for educations that sometimes utilized the most progressive pedagogical principles developed abroad. Even Indians and blacks benefited from the missionary approach; newly recruited religious congregations from Central America and Europe made the education and care of minorities their particular apostolate. Printing presses, orphanages, boarding schools, and hospitals were raised on the frontier or established in the city; each stood as a remarkable reminder of the ever-growing Catholic presence. Above all, close-knit communities, headed by enthusiastic, energetic men and women, conveyed the unmistakable message of Catholic strength. Providing for the simple corporal and spiritual needs of their brothers and sisters in Christ, they often turned their hard-pressed efforts into great accomplishments and adventures.

Evangelization and organization were to remain the essential tasks of nineteenth century Catholic church builders. But John Carroll's insistence that the church identify itself as American remained a crucial factor influencing the shape that the U.S. Catholic Church was to take during the first hundred years of its development. The concern for an American identity was symbolically reiterated by the joint bishops' action in 1840, when they legislated that only priests who were citizens of the United States should be considered for the episcopate. As the background of the bishops shifted more and more to include Irish-Americans, this viewpoint was especially championed by the immigrants from Ireland. Charleston's John England (1786–1842) consistently advocated the compatibility of American republicanism with Catholic thought; he was, moreover, the first Catholic priest to address Congress, in 1816, one month before he received his final citizenship papers. New York's John Hughes (1797–1864) mounted a spirited defense of Catholicism against Protestant clergymen, using their newspapers and a Protestant pseudonym, to illustrate how unfounded their prejudices against the church could be, and he, too, cultivated Protestant, "American" friends in high places of government. Pittsburgh's Michael O'Connor (1810–1872) supported many of John England's liberal views about church polity and demonstrated concern over the ethnic bias of the Germans of his diocese. Hartford's Bernard O'Reilly (1803–1856) rose to the defense of Providence Catholics through articles submitted to local newspapers under the pseudonym of the quintessential American, Roger Williams.

If attentiveness to American values shaped the church during the antebellum period, it did so mainly through the insistence of Irish immigrant bishops and other leaders who championed republican views. A church that had originally attempted to prove its Americanism on the basis of its Anglo-Catholic origins or its French sympathies turned to Gaelic-Americans to counter the arguments of Protestants and show how the philosophy and practice of the church could be compatible with American institutions. Dominating the wide variety of nationalities, a cadre of Irish immigrant leaders developed an American bias that became more and more distinct after mid-century. As the bishops met in provincial and plenary councils, in fact, they consistently expressed their desire to be seen as American. "We do not acknowledge any civil or political supremacy, or power over us," they stated during the first plenary council in 1837, or "any foreign potentate or power, though that potentate might be the chief pastor of our church."[7]

There were, of course, some negative reasons that helped to reinforce this kind of public statement by the bishops. Strong bouts of anti-Catholicism had racked the church from colonial times and continued to cause both physical and psychological damage. In 1834, the citizens of Charlestown, Massachusetts, had unleashed their prejudices, torching a Catholic academy and forcing the Ursuline Sisters to withdraw from their Boston-area apostolate. The inspiration for this had come from the New England preacher Lyman Beecher; his famous plea "for the west" sounded the warning to his fellow Protestants of the Catholic threat. By the 1840s, Catholics in the newly populated frontier areas had become the targets of anti-Catholic attack. Ten years later, Philadelphia was the scene of death, destruction, and arson; uneasy quiet did not come until scores of Irish shanties, two churches, and one seminary were destroyed and thirteen people had died in three days of rioting. By this time, state political parties had been formed, culminating in the Know-Nothing Party that took over several state legislatures during the mid-1850s. A crescendo of violence reverberated from the East to the Middle West. In Providence, Rhode Island, a confrontation between an immigrant bishop, Bernard O'Reilly, and a mob in search of a missing girl allegedly being detained at a Catholic academy was defused only at the last hour. Ill will triggered even worse outbursts of destruction and rioting in New York, Buffalo, Cincinnati, and St. Louis. Some of the rioting was inspired by anti-Catholic lectures, such as those that pointed to "awful disclosures" of practices in convents or commented on the unfortunately timed visit of a papal legate. Whatever prompted the disturbances, a rising anti-Catholic sentiment, which included the desire to rid the nation of the Catholic menace, served notice nationwide that Catholics were still perceived as outsiders. Generally, wherever they attempted either to improve themselves culturally or economically or to exert some influence over American hospital or educational systems, Catholics could anticipate the same kind of swift or violent resistance from a firmly established Protestant majority.

Thus, fearing overt Roman ties and understandably anxious to be accepted by Americans, Catholic leaders in the United States attempted to build their church. Through the confusions of rejection and misunderstanding, they still expressed respect for the conciliar and collegial traditions that had developed since Carroll's time. Their writings, sermons, and, especially, their pastoral letters pointed to a continuing ambiguity. This interplay between American and ethnic traditions eventually resulted in a strengthening of resolve on the part of America's bishops at the eve of the Civil War. Then the church in the United States could, at least, prove its loyalty to the American cause—whether Union or Confederate. Then, the whole diverse community of Catholics—Irish and German immigrants, native-born Americans who had been received into the church, and clusters of free blacks, slaves, or Indians—proved its Americanism by responding bravely to arms. In the postwar euphoria, American bishops continued to acknowlege publicly their desire to be perceived as upholders of American republicanism. Competition among Americans in general or within the church between German, Irish, and French leaders might linger. But so would the expectation that "the cordial union which, notwithstanding the diversity or origin, customs, and language, reigns throughout the whole Catholic body in this vast country" be strengthened through both cooperation and discipline.[8]

During the years 1790–1860, American Catholics had never given up their dreams to be identified as Americans—or to evangelize their neighbors. Thus, despite the multiethnic roots of the church, a certain mutuality of aims bonded Catholics. Any explicit moves to demand special treatment remained isolated instances—albeit significant to the participants themselves—within certain ethnic enclaves. As the American nation itself struggled with problems of national identity and constantly grew in population and territory, American Catholics maintained a cautious openness to adaptation and integration. The ethnic factor that would shape the church along separatist lines more dramatically in the second century of Catholic development remained a minor hindrance amid the more unitive developments that allowed Catholicism in the first period of strong growth within the American environment.

CHAPTER
2
Frontier Evangelizing and Organizing

❦

*A*merican Catholics have always been characterized as a diverse people. They are identified as a people whose ethnicity has particularly marked them with an unmistakable quality of difference. For the most part this view is based upon the phenomenon of growth that began during the church's first years of establishment after 1790 and that continued in the following years with an ever growing and amazingly diverse stream of immigrants from many European lands. In many ways, the American Catholic church became the outstanding example in modern times of a catholic, or universal, church. Without the benefit of foresight, however, the early leaders of the church in the United States simply assumed the challenge before them: their main desire was to establish a religious institution that would be as legitimate and attractive to Americans as any to which the new republic gave birth.

Together with those who answered his call, John Carroll faced the initial challenge of legitimizing the place of the U.S. Catholic church within the religious fabric of the American republic. At this early stage of institutional development, therefore, Carroll and his associates spent much of their time attempting to develop a congenial climate in which both Catholics and other Americans felt comfortable with one another. Cooperation in missionizing and lively competition in terms of organization and building became both logical and normative for all concerned in the enterprise of creating the American Catholic church. In this regard, American Catholics were simply imitating

13

Americans in general: they not only welcomed the steady stream of immigrants but foresaw the rapid creation of a "new" American population created from immigrant stock.

In these early stages of American Catholic development, the moves toward separatism, the ethnic alignments, were local affairs, depending greatly upon whether Catholic immigrants expected special consideration from bishops or pastors. Apart from some German congregations that did ask for separate parishes in Pennsylvania, New York, and Maryland, most Catholics seemed to have a broader view with regard to ethnic preferment in the American Catholic church. Thus, even the German parishes begun during the 1830s and 1840s in Cincinnati and St. Louis seemed open to change. Moreover, episcopal overtures that were sympathetic to separate accommodations were viewed as exceptions to the general pattern; their function seemed to involve the defusing of tense situations that ethnic rivalry had occasioned.

Yet, inexorably during the pre–Civil War years, the multiethnic character of the U.S. Catholic church did gradually develop. Apart from a core of Anglo- or Irish-Americans mostly from Maryland or Pennsylvania, Catholics became identified as an immigrant people— albeit mostly Irish or German. The European background of their leadership confirmed the reality. As dioceses and parishes developed, the commingling of peoples was obvious, to be sure, but distinct needs were joined in the common effort to advance the faith as amicably as possible. Through the skills, insights, and attitudes that were mutually developed in this process, the social fabric of the American Catholic community was gracefully woven. Under a zealous band of clergy, a frontier church was evangelized and early organizational efforts shaped. A missionary zeal prompted the Catholic errand into the wilderness and permeated the indomitable spirit of the early Catholic church—a sense of mission that would inevitably become the loom on which the many diverse strands of Catholic culture would be woven into a unity of purpose and institutional existence in the new American environment.

For the American people, the years 1790–1860 were a confusing, boisterous, optimistic, dynamic, purposeful, and even dangerous time. Population soared, doubling in the twenty years between 1830 and 1850 to reach more than a quarter million residents. Westward migrations and the rush for gold pushed the frontier toward the Pacific, while the Northeast continued its rapid industrialization and population increase. Despite the temporary setbacks of panics or unfulfilled dreams, the burgeoning American economy beckoned even more workers to the United States. This bustling energy was memorialized by foreign visitors, like Alexis de Tocqueville, and fueled the ambitions of immigrants with names like de Crèvecoeur, Steinmeyer, and Gallitzin. The excitement and dynamism provided the first bursts of Catholic activity. For pioneers who sought to recreate their church here, the time seemed right to shape a bulwark of Catholicism by identifying their hopes with other Christian, albeit Protestant, dreams. Not only had this been John Carroll's aim and that of the few Anglo-American priests who served Catholics in the years immediately following the establishment of religious liberty, but it energized the first French émigré priests and other European missionaries at the turn of the century. Further, it continued to animate an increasing number of like-minded European clergy as the Catholic population of the nation expanded. Evangelizing the frontier and organizing became two of the primary tasks for those who wished to be part of the creation of the American Catholic church.

Well into the nineteenth century, the missionary spirit prevailed. It was a time for heroes and heroines, an expansive and generous time, one conducive to accepting the challenge of planting and sustaining the faith in a new land. Especially on the frontier, Catholic and Protestant seemed on equal footing, fueling Catholic optimism. Whatever was to be done in the name of the Catholic religion was somehow understood as for the sake of the new nation as well. Across the vast territories, French Sulpicians, Irish or Italian Dominicans, Slovenian or Belgian missionaries, German Jesuits or Redemptorists, as well as Italian Vincentians, commanded the respect of Americans in general. A new Catholic people was to emerge—baptized in the one, true faith, to be sure, yet fully integrated into the American social fabric. By no means was it a time to dwell upon the superficial cultural differences of the European past.

The roster of early missionaries, evident in the lists of those who attended the first synod called by Carroll in 1790, revealed the ethnic variety of those caught up in the Americanizing spirit of the frontier. Eighty percent were foreign-born. Three-fifths of the first graduates of the seminary begun by Carroll in Baltimore were also foreign-born. The first to be ordained by Carroll, the French-born Stephen Badin, moved immediately to missionary work in the Kentucky and Indiana territories. And the first candidate to be both educated for the priesthood and ordained in the United States was Prince Demetrius Augustine Gallitzin, the son of a Russian ambassador to The Hague and a Prussian countess; he would spend his life on the frontier, creating before his death an extraordinary Catholic community in the western wilderness of Pennsylvania. Years before a native-born clergy was able to develop, other European immigrants, especially those of German, Irish, and Belgian background, shared the honors of being the church's first evangelizers.

Forty years after the establishment of the American Catholic church, more than one half of the church's 232 clergy were still from abroad—Ireland, France, Belgium, and Germany claiming the largest numbers. Many of these had heard the call to serve the American church while studying in their native lands—either from conversations with or lectures by recruiting American bishops or from advertisements placed judiciously in the foreign press, beckoning the courageous to the excitement of the new world. Many a young European seminarian or priest ventured forth to spread the good news after feeling the challenge of words such as these: "We offer you: No Salary; No Recompense; No Holidays; No Pension. But: Much Hard Work; a Poor Dwelling; Few Consolations; Many Disappointments; Frequent Sickness; A Violent or Lonely Death; An Unknown Grave."[1] Carroll may have wanted a native clergy, accustomed to "our climate, and acquainted with the tempers, manners and government of the people, to whom they are to dispense the ministry of salvation," but what he got was a foreign-born phalanx equally capable and dedicated to the same missionary task.[2] Even the first leaders of the church came to be chosen from foreign ranks. This expedient continued well beyond the time that Carroll would have deemed it necessary. The decade after Carroll's death in 1815, in fact, five of the six presiding bishops were French-born clergy, but they were as intent upon converting the nation, spreading the gospel news, and creating a national American church as Carroll could ever have been. Of twenty-three bishops sent to western dioceses or territories in the first half of the nineteenth century, moreover, eleven were from France, three were Irish-born, two each were Belgian, German, and Italian. Although some of the clergy, especially the Sulpicians and Jesuits, may have expressed concern over American institutions or ideas, most were more exhilarated by the prospects of religious conversion here, especially on the frontier. To Samuel Mazzuchelli, an Italian Dominican who began his service to the American church in 1828, for example, Catholicism seemed "hardly yet born." No wonder that he would speak of the thrill of venturing forth, still "trembling" with the challenge and his expectation of a spiritual harvest.[3]

During the first half of the nineteenth century, therefore, European clergy provided a powerful example of Catholic solidarity for the sake of mission. From the early decades, when the American church had extended its mission with the creation of the first frontier diocese at Bardstown, Kentucky, to well past mid-century, this trend would continue. The French-born Benedict Joseph Flaget (1763–1850), a veteran of the mission at Vincennes (Indiana), who was named to head the new diocese, would quintessentially convey the image of the "New World collective personality," a leader who was once described by his friend Henry Clay as one royally bred but without a crown. The premier organizer of the frontier church, Bishop Flaget's early round of experiences at Vincennes and in Havana prepared him for thirty-nine years of rigorous administration that involved the continuing task of building new institutions and that even brought him to the point of having to relocate his cathedral city, as the frontier's path moved toward Louisville.

Both the cosmopolitan European training of the immigrant clergy and the democratic mentality that they developed here seemed assets and incentives in designing the new American Catholic church. The real task before them was establishing the faith on equal terms with the faith of other American denominations. Baltimore's third archbishop, Ambrose Maréchal (1764–1828), cited the effects of this uncomplicated Catholic approach in his report to the Propaganda in 1818 with these words: "The Catholic church has vindicated for herself general veneration and the Protestants turn their eyes toward her." If his confreres spoke the language haltingly, he added, it was a forgivable flaw, for "they do announce the word of God in a manner that is not displeasing to Americans." Moreover, he concluded, it was not those who appeared as outsiders because of their broken English who had called attention to what might divide Catholics, but rather certain of the clergy (his bias led him to designate the Irish) whose drunkenness and ambition were obviously doing the real damage to the Catholic image. To early churchmen like Maréchal and Flaget, being foreign was not in itself an obstacle to the advancement of the frontier American Catholic church.[4]

Many elements conspired to help the missionary church remain united in purpose, collaborative in style, and unself-conscious with regard to ethnic difference during the early decades of the nineteenth century. The beginnings in Kentucky are only one example of the early singleness of purpose. From the start, the need to work together to overcome the hazards of the wilderness and to band together for spiritual and psychological support brought European-born clergy from many nations together with those more accustomed to American ways. Thus, the boat that ferried Flaget, fellow Sulpician John Baptist Mary David, and several students down the Ohio to Bardstown in 1811 became their ethnic "cradle"; there a sense of comradeship, inspired by shared prayer, study, and church affairs, bonded the original group, albeit from diverse backgrounds, to forge a future model for the church. In the first, arduous years on the frontier, this collaboration encouraged the Belgian Charles Nerinckx, the Frenchman John David, the native-born Edward Fenwick, and various members of the Kentucky Dominican order, to call upon Americans to join them in their labors. New congregations were formed. Native-born women, such as Catherine Spalding and Mary Rhodes, quickly filled the ranks of the Sisters of Charity of Nazareth, the Sisters of Loretto at the Foot of the Cross, and the Carmelites, or Third Order Dominicans. All relied upon European spiritualities in the service of an American church, but the common pursuit was missionary building.[5]

Apostolic zeal overflowed in other missionary areas during the formative frontier years. For most, the desire to convert the Indian was soon deflected into more obvious apostolic concerns as they quickly adjusted to the reality that the new white settlers on the frontier—even the Catholic blacks from the Caribbean who stayed closer to the ports of entry—could easily become their common preoccupation. Priests and sisters initiated the move; the faith of the people sustained it. After their arrival from Lyons, France, in the 1830s, for example, the Sisters of Saint Joseph thought that their work would be simply to "convert the savages, instructing the little ones." Soon they shared work with clergy and laity, giving themselves to all the works of mercy. In the midst of the most mundane of chores, such as "shaking snow from the boarders' beds in the middle of the night" at their log cabin school in Carondelet, for example, they provided a Catholic witness to Americans in general. Extolled as "excellent catechists, good nurses for the sick, perfect sacristans, zealous teachers," they "were ready for anything."[6]

Desire to assist free blacks and slaves had prompted apostolic commitment on the part of immigrant clergy and religious as well. If no prophetic voices were raised to address the moral issues of the slave system, at least these missionaries understood that practical action was essential. In Maryland and Louisiana, black congregations were formed. In Baltimore, the Sulpicians provided chaplains and a chapel. One religious congregation was also established, sponsored by the Sulpician Jacques Joubert de la Muraille and begun with the cooperation of Elizabeth Lange and three other black women of Haitian descent. Known as the Oblate Sisters of Providence, this community was among the first religious congregations founded in America. Later these Oblate Sisters, who sought to provide education and social services to fellow blacks, would have a second start under the patronage of another immigrant, John Nepomucene Neumann, who was then the Redemptorist Superior in Baltimore. In Louisiana, during the 1840s, a second congregation of black women was started. The Holy Family Sisters ministered to the slaves and poor blacks of New Orleans by teaching slave children, conducting an orphanage, and founding a school for girls from free black families. The Irish immigrant bishop John England also played an important role in finding personnel to help educate the blacks of South Carolina.

The Sulpician Gabriel Richard, who ministered to the outpost territories north and west of Ohio from 1792 until 1832, fits the model of a flexible French-born missionary prepared for the multitude of challenges of American frontier life. His first assignment after fleeing the anticlerical French Revolutionary government was working among the Indians of Illinois and Michigan. Yet, among the goals he developed as he labored in the Detroit area was the education of the city's Catholic immigrants. By 1804 he was vicar-general of the area; he established an elementary school in 1802 and helped to open his first "college or clergy school." Although this school did not flourish because of the "scarcity of scholars," Richard continued to search out ways of developing educational options. Amid building schools, hospitals and churches, he returned to his dream of providing higher education. Together with some of Detroit's most prominent citizens, who decided to lend their endorsement to his plan, he managed to found what would later become the University of Michigan at Ann Arbor. Richard also founded a unique lay "sisterhood" for the education of girls, attempted to interest the federal government in Indian education, and tried to provide education for the deaf. In addition, he is credited with starting the first printing press in the Michigan territory and publishing the first Catholic newspaper there.

Richard's belief in the promise of America not only led him to become involved in educational and political matters but also helped him develop a reputation as polemicist and politician (after his becoming a citizen in 1823, Michigan territory voters elected him to serve as a representative to Congress), as well as an acknowledged leader of the American Catholic church. In the eyes of one immigrant Catholic admirer, Richard possessed what were the best qualities of any missionary. His description of what Richard represented for other Catholic missionaries helps explain why his fellow citizens considered him so remarkable a churchman and American:

> This ecclesiastic is, moreover, thoroughly estimable on account of his regularity, of the variety of his knowledge, and especially of any activity of which it is difficult to form an idea. He has the talent of doing, almost simultaneously, ten entirely different things. Provided with newspapers, well informed on all political matters, ever ready to argue on religion when the occasion presents itself, and thoroughly learned in theology, he reaps his hay, gathers the fruits of his garden, manages a fishery fronting his lot, teaches . . . devotes time to mental prayer, . . . confesses all his people, imports carding and spinning wheels and looms to teach the women of his parish how to work, leaves not a single act of his parochial register unwritten . . . goes on sick calls . . . writes letters, preaches every

> Sunday and holyday . . . and is in good health, as fresh and able at the
> age of fifty as one usually is at thirty.[7]

Richard's concerns were American Catholic and universal to the end.

Still another of these vigorous French-born missionaries who served the frontier church was John Dubois (1764–1842). Already ordained when he entered the port of Norfolk, Virginia, in 1791, he was, like the other French émigrés, a person scarred by the experience of the French Revolution. Carrying a letter of introduction from the Marquis de Lafayette, Dubois had come to the United States with his own personal convictions about the opportunities available here. Although his heavy French accent always provided others with a glimpse into his foreign background (he was supposed to have learned his English from Patrick Henry), he nevertheless worked to persuade his American hosts that his major goal was to be identified as a self-reliant, republican, entrepreneurial American. If willing to be an owner of slaves, Dubois still parted ideological company with his southern hosts on their neat distinctions concerning the socioeconomic merits of the slave system. Noting that his fellow Frenchmen tended to impose their culture upon Americans, while the Germans formed exclusive ghettos and the Irish grew abusive in their demands for equal and immediate acceptance, Dubois preferred instead to win respect as a churchman who valued the options that being an American allowed.

In 1807 Dubois bought and developed property in Emmitsburg, Maryland, for a seminary-college to be known as Mount Saint Mary. A few years later, he befriended Elizabeth Bayley Seton, welcomed her to Emmitsburg, and assisted her both in the establishment of her religious congregation and in the development of free and boarding schools. Practical, pragmatic, and exceedingly hard-working, he quickly gained a reputation as a talented businessman. Particularly because he had started the college and helped found schools and orphanages, and also because he had assisted in forming a community of women, he became in 1826 a preferred candidate to be named bishop of New York. From the time of his appointment, however, Dubois was to endure the ill will of many of the immigrant Irish clergy and laity of the diocese who had already made clear that they would have preferred a bishop of their own ethnic heritage.

Until his death, in fact, Dubois was to be continually reminded that he had failed to present the kind of American image upon which his fellow New York Catholics, as Irish-Americans, prided themselves. "Why should a Frenchman govern an Irish congregation?" was a question constantly addressed to him. What the Irish-Americans failed to see in their complaints, however, was their own overbearing ethnic ways. Dubois realized this and tried to make it clear from the start. His first attempt, a pastoral letter, was actually refused publication by *The Truth Teller*, the Irish-controlled New York Catholic journal. Subsequently published in another Catholic newspaper, his letter persuasively pointed out the narrowmindedness of his accusers. "Who are those who object to our foreign birth?" he asked, "Are they not in the same sense foreigners themselves? For the question is not why an American had not been appointed but why was not an Irishman."[8] His conclusion began with a plea "to those dear exiles of Ireland whom we took to our bosom and educated at Mount Saint Mary's when they were fatherless and friendless." Then he asked his most pointed series of questions:

> Were the apostles natives of the countries to which they were sent to preach? Is St. Patrick less the patron of Ireland for having been born in Gaul? In this city there are Americans, Irish, English, French, Spanish, and German Catholics. Is each nation to have a bishop of its own? When formerly we watched over the couch of our sick Americans, Irish, or German brethren; when for thirty-five years we rode nights and days to afford them the sweet comforts of religion, did they ever inquire where we were born?[9]

Dubois's questions were, of course, rhetorical. And as the years went on Dubois found, furthermore, that he could never expect to be relieved of the ethnic pressures exerted by his majority Irish constituents. Nor was he given much support in his own efforts to develop his rapidly expanding diocese according to his own plans. Still he persisted as a leader who not only refused to do battle on ethnic grounds but also publicly begged his people not to enter into public debate either with regard to such concerns or with respect to the nativist protests of the state's Protestant majority. So harried was Dubois by his fellow Catholics, especially during one long-lasting nativist debate, that even an anti-Catholic newsletter, *The Downfall of Babylon*, chose to defend him for not following the political tactics of the Irish. "Bishop Dubois is a Frenchman," they wrote on July 4, 1835, "and we have ever looked upon him as a pure man and sincere Christian. He, we are confident, has in no way interfered in our elections though it is within our knowledge that he has reason to lecture the Irish priests under his charge upon the impropriety of their meddling with politics."[10] It was an ironic commendation.

Dubois's last years were among his most difficult. Attempting to remain apart from the mounting Protestant–Catholic debate, Dubois increased his missionary pace, circuit-riding within his huge diocese and traveling to both Europe and Ireland for new recruits. In fact, he kept the needs of his "frontier church" sharply in focus. There was one bright note during these dreary years. When one "ill-organized and adventurous" Bohemian seminarian arrived at his rectory in the spring of 1836, Dubois immediately encouraged his vocation. His support of this immigrant proved valuable to German immigrants in New York state and especially fortuitous for the American church. His Bohemian prospect was John Nepomucene Neumann, a future Redemptorist superior, later bishop of Philadelphia, and now a canonized saint. When ill health finally forced Dubois into retirement—and even greater insignificance—he would, however, begin to believe he was a total failure. Thus, his final pessimistic request to be buried "where the people will walk over me in death as they wished to do in life."[11] It was one request that his coadjutor and former student John Hughes seemed to honor; the Irishman whom Dubois had once attempted to befriend did not even preach at his mentor's funeral. Thus, to his death in 1842, Dubois was to bear the telltale marks of a missionary plagued by an ethnic narrowness that he himself eschewed.

Demetrius Gallitzin was clearly cut from the same missionary cloth as both Gabriel Richard and John Dubois; he was even more interested in the pursuit of the promise that was America. Both Richard and Dubois had arrived in the United States already prepared for ministry; Gallitzin came merely to visit and to complete his secular education. Still, all three would go on to devote years of service in the northeastern United States; Dubois and Gallitzin died just two years apart in the early 1840s. For this young prince, the journey had been motivated by the desire to discover a new land. But with his sojourn to the United States, his life took a dramatic new direction. The new land not only converted him to "Mr. Smith," the name under which he travelled and that he used during his seminary and early priesthood years, but also provided him with a vocational direction.

Ordained in 1795—the first American candidate, in fact, to receive all his priestly training in the United States—Gallitzin was allowed to choose his own missionary field. Under the name of Augustine Smith, he settled in the Allegheny mountain region of central Pennsylvania in 1799. At Cambria County, he founded a Catholic settlement, again with the permission of Carroll, and was given ecclesiastical jurisdiction over an area with a hundred-mile radius. From the Loretto community he served a backwoods area, giving of himself unstintingly, developing a kind of utopian world—this several decades before the utopian movement developed elsewhere in the United States. Some of the land that served as his parish setting he resold at one fourth its value to Catholics of the area. On other parcels, he put up a tannery, a flour mill, and a sawmill. There he remained his entire life, as pastor and strict shepherd of the flock. A cultured European and an effective apologist, he could pronounce stern moral principles in tones highly compatible with his fellow American ministers of the frontier.

Like Richard, Gallitzin remained an apologist who consistently appealed for dialogue with the Protestant public. His important defense of Catholic principles, published in Pittsburgh in 1816, became the model of polemical literature for decades. Like Richard as well, he enjoyed the admiration of civil authorities who celebrated his memory by naming projects in his honor. But for many, from those to whom he taught the art of swordsmanship during the War of 1812 to those who became generous promoters in the cause of perpetuating his memory, he remained a fascinating, unique representative of the early missionary church, a supporter of Catholic truths, a European in intellectual and spiritual matters, but a first-class American frontier apostle in every other respect. In his senior years, the "Prince" may have appeared to some as simply a cantankerous old cripple whose missionary style, like Dubois's, seemed no longer relevant to the bustling, institutionalizing American Catholic church. Yet, like Dubois and Richard, Gallitzin could not be so lightly dismissed. He had accepted the challenge of the frontier missionary, his efforts had transformed Loretto and the surrounding area from a wilderness to a flourishing community. He had striven to be American. His choice of name, his circle of important friends in high places, and his vigorous and graceful gift of prose were all symbolic ways of indicating that desire. In every respect, he had pursued both the social and economic opportunities that America provided. He had successfully entered into dialogue with those who already claimed to own the Christian dream: his aim was to reinterpret it in Catholic terms.

A second generation of immigrant clergy took up the challenge of the frontier as it reached beyond the Alleghenies and the Mississippi, especially in the second quarter of the nineteenth century. Midland America, with its fresh, mobile, energetic, and flexible society, became both the source of inspiration and the destination for many of those who embarked on this next round of rough beginnings. Mission societies, such as Lyons's Propagation of the Faith (1803), Vienna's Leopoldine Stiftung (1812), and Munich's Ludwigs Verein (1838), provided the financial backing for these American ventures. But these societies had come into existence because of the recommendations of earlier American missionary-bishops, such as Louis William Valentine DuBourg (1766–1833) and John Frederic Résé (1791–1871), who sustained the missionary momentum through their visits to various European seminaries in search of recruits. French and Belgian missionaries, with help from donations of the societies, made the most remarkable contributions of the period. From the start, the desire of both recruiting bishops and the men and the women who responded to their invitation was to build a new American Catholic church.

The first bishops of Cincinnati, Edward Fenwick (1768–1832) and his successor John B. Purcell (1800–1883), were among the early church leaders whose task it was to encourage Europe's clergy to join in the work of building the American church. Both succeeded in making their dioceses important staging grounds for ministry. Because of their efforts, names like Lamy, Machebeuf, Mazzuchelli, and Segale would be remembered as among the more important missionary greats who brought the faith to Indian lands and rocky wildernesses and who established the Catholic church in some of the most remote corners of the continent.

When the missionary Projectus Joseph Machebeuf (1812–1889) volunteered for service in the United States at the invitation of Purcell in 1839, for example, he was immediately sent to the Ohio frontier. So quickly was Machebeuf moved to the farming community of Tiffin, Ohio, that he had to learn "to lisp" his English under the tutelage of his pious, but very sickly, pastor, James MacNamee. The rigors of his life in Tiffin provided him with many happy moments as well as the needed experience for his future frontier assignments. As Purcell had hoped, it confirmed his missionary call. "These are the things which console and recompense us for the long journey we have to make to visit our Catholics," Machebeuf wrote to his sister in 1840. "I assure you," he continued, "that I have found many very edifying things on these visits—such, for instance, as when elderly and highly respectable appearing people come to throw themselves on their knees before a young priest to ask his blessing."[12] Enduring the hardship of the penetrating cold that sometimes forced him to run beside his horse in order to get warm, he could match his distress with the reward of "seeing the faith, the eagerness, and the devotion of the greater part of our Catholics." This was the lot of the frontier missionary, and the frontier was the place to learn the task of building American Catholicism. Machebeuf's experience in Ohio was only a prelude to his greater service to the American church in the Southwest and West. First as vicar-general of the diocese of Santa Fe, where he worked closely with his good friend John Baptist Lamy, then as the first vicar-apostolic to the Colorado and Utah territories from 1868–1887 and finally, for the last two years of his life, as bishop of Denver, he would spend his remaining years leading those who had become part of the remote and primitive church there.

Farther to the north of Machebeuf's Colorado domain, missionary work was extended by like-minded clergy who had also first heard of the needs of the American mission in the quiet atmosphere of their European seminaries. One such impressionable candidate was the

Dominican student Samuel Mazzuchelli. This Milanese native, who answered the call that his fellow Dominican, Bishop Fenwick of Cincinnati, preached at the Dominican House of Studies in Rome, would go on to remarkable ministerial work among both Indians and settlers in the sometimes frozen lands of Upper Michigan, Wisconsin, and the frontier wilderness of Iowa. In Archbishop Ireland's words, Mazzuchelli might represent, from the time he came to the United States in 1828 until his death in 1864, "a foreigner by birth" who "was an American to the tip of his finger."[13] In fact, Mazzuchelli was preoccupied by the challenge provided by both native and immigrant Americans. For Indians and whites Mazzuchelli preached the same message of repentance for sin and salvation; for both he became the model for living the Christian life in the midst of hardship and poverty; on behalf of both he worked to establish schools for Christian education, even institutions of higher learning; and because of both he became an advocate for justice before government agencies, the president, and the Congress.

Appointed by Fenwick a "missionary apostolic" to the vast areas of his Cincinnati diocese, Mazzuchelli began his priestly career on Mackinac Island, in the upper regions of Lake Michigan, a land successfully prepared a century and a half before by the Jesuit missionary Père Marquette. His first work was primarily with the Winnebago Indians, whose language he quickly mastered and for whom he translated and printed prayers books. But his efforts were soon turned in the direction of the white settlers who had been streaming into the northwestern territories during the 1830s. For the remainder of his missionary service the needs of both Indians and whites would preoccupy him. An impoverished chapel of mats laid over poles was often his setting for divine services. He would travel by snowshoe, canoe, or horseback between the rugged outposts and the more civilized centers. He conducted vespers or liturgies under the roofs of simple churches built from his own plans and with his own hands. Both city and frontier supplied the appropriate setting for the gathering of the Christian community. Chippewa and Menominee Indians, American, Irish, French-Canadian, and German immigrants—all were subjects of his apostolate.

Once Mazzuchelli was able to center his activities in more developed areas, such as Galena, Illinois, or Dubuque, Iowa, he increased his role as advocate for Catholic and missionary causes. As chaplain of the Wisconsin legislature and, later, in his association with the Iowa state senate, he remained in the public arena, maintaining cooperative relations between Protestants and Catholics, especially whenever mutual suspicions grew. Sessions of the Iowa legislature even transpired at a church that he was in the process of constructing.

Serious illnesses beset him after 1843; Dominican priests and sisters came to continue his work in the three-state area; the Sinsinawa Dominicans, a community of women that he cofounded, became one of the most impressive monuments to his legacy. To the end, American identity remained his personal aim. Even when he came to be called "Father Matthew Kelly" by Americans who misheard his Italian surname, he could easily assent to the ethnic confusion. He had, after all, come to serve the American Catholic church.[14]

The Cincinnati diocese also became the destination for one of the most unusual migrations of European clergy anxious to serve an American church. This group was from Slovenia (present-day Yugoslavia), and by the turn of the twentieth century they would number almost one hundred missionaries. Their achievements, especially among the Indians of the Northwest, represent one of the most unusual services that the early church offered to the American frontier. John Frederic Résé, at that time Cincinnati's vicar-general, who was closely connected with the founding of Vienna's Leopoldine Association in 1829, had been responsible for initiating the request among the Slovenians. It was Résé who accepted the application of the first of these missionaries, Frederic Baraga (1797–1868).

In December of 1830, the youthful Baraga arrived to begin his apostolate in the upper Midwest. From that time, a steady stream of Slovenian missionaries, most of whom had been recruited from the diocesan clergy, followed his lead. Sharing Baraga's missionary zeal and commitment, they also had to contend with the unique problems that he had earlier faced. What made their situation particularly difficult was that, for the most part, they lacked the national or religious sponsorship that many of their contemporary missionaries could count upon. Moreover, the frontier dioceses in these remote areas, which were in the greatest need of their services, were not able to provide more than minimal financial or material support. Finally, since there were few of their countrymen in the areas to which their ministry directed them, they could find little initial financial assistance among the people they served. Thus, from the start these Slovenian missionaries were forced to rely on personal resources or on the occasional contributions of their countrymen if they chose to build churches or provide for schools. Although they were able to make direct appeals to the three European organizations that were interested in the North American missions, they often had to use their own funds even to help clothe and feed the Indians among whom they preferred to work. In such straitened circumstances, the Slovenian missionaries embarked on what may be considered the most selfless endeavor pursued by any immigrant group.

Frederic Baraga clearly exemplifies the special call of these missionaries. His foremost interest had been in bringing the good news to the Indians. In his application to Cincinnati he wrote, "I speak German, Illyrian, Latin, French, Italian, and English"; it was his way of pointing out the contributions his language abilities could make in his hoped-for apostolate. Well into his sixties, Baraga was still at the task. By then he had mastered several more languages; he was particularly fluent in the Ojibway tongue. He thought nothing of snowshoe treks to his mission outposts to visit his people, supervise the building of churches or schools, or personally erect living quarters. Respecting the customs and appreciative of the languages of the Indians, he saw to the publishing of their own religious materials, including grammars and dictionaries in Indian dialect. Because of his language skills, moreover, he was able to become an important interpreter and intermediary with the federal government, and often the Indians' advocate as well. Little wonder that Baraga succeeded in establishing permanent Indian missions or that before his death there were over twenty-five thousand Catholic Indians under his care. Not surprising, either, that in 1838 Baraga would be appointed vicar-general for the territory of Wisconsin, in 1850, be named bishop of Marquette, and three years later, become first bishop of Sault Ste. Marie.

Other Slovenians quickly arrived to continue Baraga's work. Francis Pirc came in 1835. Then fifty years of age, he was prepared to offer his special horticultural talents, if not his youth. For a dozen years, Pirc worked among the Ottawa Indians of Michigan. At one time he personally inoculated every one of the inhabitants of the Arbre Croche mission against smallpox; a few years later he did the same against cholera. An accomplished gardener who had written on the topic in Europe, Pirc applied his knowledge to frontier conditions— growing fruit trees and garden produce—and subsequently taught the Indians how to increase farm yields. A keen observer of Indian lore and of the American natural environment, Pirc extended his talents by becoming versed in Indian-inspired homeopathic medicines, dispensing remedies and medical attention to both Indians and white settlers. All this was the fruitful backdrop to his primary ministry of preaching the gospel. By 1852, he would move to the newly established diocese of St. Paul, where he was soon appointed director of all Indian missions north of the Mississippi. Because of his articles and reports, printed in German-language newspapers in the United States and in Europe, caravans of German settlers began to settle in the areas that he had so glowingly described. Because of this Slovenian missionary, the German-American character of the territory was more firmly established.

Later Slovenian missionaries modeled themselves after both Baraga and Pirc, as preachers, teachers, Indian advocates to presidents, government officials, and promoters of the Northwest territories. Settling at first along the northern shores of Lake Michigan and Lake Superior, then moving on to the Dakota territories or Minnesota, they made a remarkably positive impact upon Indians and white settlers— though often becoming thorns in the sides of government officials or Protestant missionaries. In fact, many Slovenian missionaries moved on to positions of prominence within Catholic circles. Here, as opposed to any other region where the church had been established, for example, non-Irish bishops began to predominate. Five Slovenians headed dioceses after 1850, an extremely high proportion relative to Slovenian Catholic membership. Besides Baraga, there was Ignatius Mrak, who became second bishop of Marquette in 1869. He was succeeded by Joseph Vertin. Later in the century, James Trobec would head the Saint Cloud, Minnesota, diocese from 1897 to 1914, and John Stariha became the first bishop of Lead, South Dakota, in 1902. Others would be elected to monastic positions or receive other church honors. Branching out from missionary and advocacy roles, the Slovenian missionaries achieved more visibility in important church circles than any other Catholic minority of the area. Yet their aim had simply been to build the American church.[15]

A major way station for frontier evangelization, similar in this respect to Cincinnati, was Saint Louis, Missouri, founded in 1826 under Bishop Dubourg of New Orleans. Under Dubourg and his successor, Joseph Rosati (1789–1843), who was a Vincentian from Naples, Saint Louis became an important gateway to Indian lands and immigrant settlements. Under them, important moves were made, especially toward the building of the American Catholic church west of the Mississippi. After settling in Saint Louis in 1818, Dubourg had founded a seminary and encouraged the establishment of a college. The latter, under the Jesuits, became the first university west of the Mississippi. From Missouri, as well, began the career of a remarkable Jesuit, the Belgian Pierre DeSmet, who became known as the Apostle to Kansas, Oregon, and the Rockies. Besides establishing missions in Iowa and Montana, he recruited missionaries and was personally responsible for bringing the Sisters of Notre Dame de Namur to Oregon. Soon more involved in administration and in serving as government peace commissioner, DeSmet gained importance as a chronicler and publicist through such writings as *Letters and Sketches*, which appeared in 1843, *Oregon Missions and Travels* (1847), *Western Missions and Missionaries* (1859), and *New Indian Sketches* (1863).

Other outstanding groups also began their missionary work in Missouri. A religious of the Sacred Heart and American cofounder of the French-based congregation, Sister Rose Philippine Duchesne (canonized in 1988) early accepted the responsibility of educating young women (including Indian women) and helped begin six houses along the Mississippi by 1828. At age seventy-one she still considered missionary work in the plains of Kansas and beyond. From Saint Louis, too, the Congregation of the Mission (Vincentians), encouraged by its American founder, Father Felix DeAndreis, began its extensive ministry in the midwestern states. Communities that were also quickly attracted to the diocese were the Ursulines, the Daughters of Charity, and the Sisters of Saint Joseph, whose first American foundation was made at nearby Carondelet. Most seemed to be responding to a challenge presented by DeSmet: "Believe me, you will never succeed in this country till you draw down on your work the blessing of God by founding an establishment among the savages."[16]

By the 1840s, Saint Louis had become largely populated by immigrant Catholics; more than sixty-five churches and seventy-four Indian missions served the needs of its Catholic inhabitants. The frontier mission call, as it emanated from Saint Louis, moreover, provided a twofold advantage for the U.S. Catholic Church: it built up the more populated area and became a staging ground for the continuing ministry. Once again, reference to Saint Rose Philippine Duchesne can illustrate this point. When her own obligations to the church of Saint Louis were fulfilled, Mother Duchesne finally attempted to answer the call that had originally brought her to the territory. Although unable to learn the Potawatomi language because of her advanced years, she nevertheless volunteered for the mission at Sugar Creek and attempted to begin a school for the Indians there. Valued as "the woman who prays always" by the Indians, she stayed on for four long and ultimately frustrating years. Symbolically, however, she had underscored the point that animated early American Catholics on the frontier and enabled them to be almost single-minded in their aims.

A cosmopolitan zeal seemed to radiate to the North, the Southwest, and the West—its missionary proponents often accompanying the first white traders, trappers, and settlers. Under Canadians François N. Blanchet and his brother, Magliore, the mission to the Oregon Territory was begun, the dioceses of Nesqually, Walla Walla, and Oregon City (later Seattle and Portland archdioceses) were established, and the first college, Saint Joseph, and hospitals, missions, and schools for Indians were founded. Both brothers are considered apostles of the Indians, and François was a forerunner in the creation of the Catholic Indian Commission in Washington, D.C., which was organized by the American bishops. The same zeal developed Vincennes as still another frontier outpost in western Indiana. There migrant Catholic missionaries early sought to bring the faith. Established as a diocese in 1834, Vincennes's first bishop was Simon Bruté de Remur (1779–1839), yet another Sulpician and a close friend of Kentucky's Bishop Flaget. In the spirit of his contemporaries, Bruté exchanged his studious environment at Mount Saint Mary in Maryland for leadership of the new diocese, then a land of Indians, hunters, and trappers. His zeal would attract a hardy lot of missionaries. For example, he was able to send Benjamin Marie Petit as missionary among the Potawatomi. When these Indians were forced to relocate to Sugar Creek in 1838, Petit accompanied them on pony, celebrating mass along the way, tending the dying, baptizing the newborn. Bruté and Petit agonized over the injustice and understood the impact of the exile to which the Indians had been subjected. Their only recourse was to continue their ministry with the Indians and marvel at the faith they witnessed.

An American foundress of the Congregation of the Sisters of Providence, Mother Theodore Guérin, was another Vincennes recruit. She amply described the process by which her own community had come to work in Bruté's land. Instead of an "exotic country populated by savages," which she admitted that her community members had romantically anticipated, they had found a "wild, uncultivated" world that "seemed to be in its cradle." They immediately opened an academy for girls, the first in Indiana, and prepared to approach settlers as well as Indians in this "immense field for evangelization and education."[17] Before her death in 1856, the motherhouse of the sisters, at Saint Mary-of-the-Woods, Indiana, and ten schools had been established. The Brothers of the Congregation of Holy Cross began with similar hopes, expecting merely to evangelize or to help the new settlers as they sought to develop the area. Slowly, however, under Father Edward Sorin and his Holy Cross successors, from beginnings in a log cabin grew a vast Catholic ministry, including the University of Notre Dame du Lac, founded in 1842. Once again, an American Catholic church was created in a frontier environment.

Finally, these early immigrant missionaries were responsible for bringing the faith to southwestern and western United States—even in the years before the Civil War. In fact, as soon as the Southwest became part of the United States, priests who had gained experience from their years of service in other areas of the American frontier found themselves assigned as bishops: John M. Odin (1801–1861) was named to Texas; Joseph Sadoc Alemany, O.P. (1814–1888), to California, and John Baptist Lamy (1814–1888), to New Mexico. All three, fully understanding the enormity of their apostolates, immediately set out in search of fellow missionaries. Odin might have been awed by the vast prairies and pasturage of his territory, which stretched four hundred thousand square miles; but he was as amazed by the faith of the few remaining Christian Indians, and he was quick to find priests, sisters, and brothers to help him met the needs of the small Catholic population scattered in the Protestant environment. Lamy immediately requested the assistance of Joseph Machebeuf, his friend and fellow missionary, to assist him as he began his New Mexican apostolate. Before long he had also persuaded several communities of religious women, including the Sisters of Charity and the Sisters of Loretto, to assist him. If his Romanesque-styled cathedral in Santa Fe suggested that Lamy wished to Europeanize his diocese, there is other convincing evidence that his stronger desire was to bring the Catholic church of the Southwest within the physical and pyscho-logical boundaries of the American Catholic church.

Alemany repeated the pattern. His earlier years of missionary service in Ohio and Tennessee had prepared him for the new challenge. As a later historian of San Francisco would say of him: "No man was better qualified than he to be the connecting link between the old and the new." He was a Spaniard by birth who was revered by the Mexican people, but he was also a loyal American. Not only was he a naturalized citizen, but "he was in full sympathy with American ideas and principles."[18] When Alemany's petition that his California diocese be split between San Francisco and Monterey was accepted, he took charge of San Francisco, delighted that this more concentrated population was "so white for the harvest." Then he too set out on recruitment tours. Already counting forty-one priests and a Belgian congregation of Sisters of Notre Dame de Namur among his personnel, he was able to obtain the Daughters of Charity from Emmitsburg in 1852, the Sisters of Mercy and the Presentation Sisters from Ireland, and additional Jesuits to continue the process of building an American Catholic church.

Thus the mission of the church was begun and rapidly extended to willing hands, often those of other immigrants, the members of congregations of priests, brothers, or sisters. Together, bishops and coworkers brought Catholicism to the farthest reaches of their vast dioceses—albeit in a manner sometimes embellished with distinctly European style and ceremony. The fascinating stories of founding sisters like Mother Baptist Russell, who was part of the first Mercy group to respond to Alemany's call for missionaries in San Francisco, illustrates the adaptability of each immigrant community to American circumstances. Within a year, Mercy sisters were making visitations to the sick poor, to the county hospital and jail; from that beginning they expanded their work to include other fields of social service. Elsewhere they would work with the Choctaws or Cherokees of Arkansas, the Abenaki of Maine, and the Indians of Oregon. There were the Washington missionaries, the Sisters of Providence, who braved a forty-five-day journey over land and water from their motherhouse in Montreal and who would produce similar feats of missionary zeal and courage. As the years passed, Italian Jesuits and Franciscans, Irish Trappists, Dominican priests and sisters, Sisters of Charity of the Blessed Virgin Mary, Sisters of the Incarnate Word, Immaculate Heart of Mary Sisters, and others developed their missionary style as they built a Catholic church that was acceptable to Americans.

CHAPTER
3
Organizational Strategies
for the Urban Church

$\mathcal{F}$rontier evangelization had originally motivated pioneer Catholic bishops, clergy, and religious men and women. Certainly John Carroll thought of the expansion of the American church in terms of the frontier. Thus, in 1808, he had seen to it that a diocese to serve Catholics in the wildernesses of Kentucky and beyond was named along with the new metropolitan dioceses of Baltimore, Philadelphia, and New York. So premature was his decision with respect to Bardstown, however, that its primacy in the Kentucky frontier was soon subsumed by the realities of American expansion: in 1841 the diocese of Bardstown was transferred to the prospering commercial hub at Louisville. Later bishops at first saw their newly formed dioceses of New Orleans, Cincinnati, or Vincennes primarily as staging grounds for evangelizing the vast territories within their jurisdiction. But, from the start, another aspect of the development of the pre–Civil War church was gaining influence over the creation of American Catholicism and forced the Catholic leaders to rethink their earlier emphasis on the evangelization of the frontier.

As more and more Irish and German immigrants arrived at the major port areas of the United States, the urban dimension of American Catholicism became more distinct. The rapid increase of immigrant Catholics within the bounds of city limits diverted the original agenda of bishops, clergy, and religious. By the early nineteenth century, the more realistic considerations became those involving the need to supply the basic physical amenities of life to an often impoverished people who were required to practice their religion in the midst of Protestant strongholds. As the century matured, it became clear that a different church was being created in the American setting and that different tactics were needed to develop this urban church. Just as with frontier evangelization and development, this aspect of American Catholic growth was led by an immigrant clergy, with the cooperation of religious men and women and with the financial and moral support of an immigrant people themselves.

By 1860, there were forty-three dioceses and 1,606,000 Catholics, the majority of whom remained in the crowded cities and towns of eastern and midwestern United States. As a consequence of the rapid urban expansion of the church, a somewhat different emphasis concerning church growth had emerged. Now the task of the missionary—typically still a European clergy originally motivated to evangelize Indians—was directed toward liturgical and sacramental leadership in city parishes and helping newcomers keep the faith through the more routine functions of religious activity—hearing confessions, blessing marriages, and burying the dead. In their work among people enduring difficult lives within crowded ghettos, moreover, urban missionaries had to become concerned with the realities of disease, the temptations of city life, and the threat of industrial accidents. In the midst of established Protestantism, they had to exercise caution lest their public expression of religion appear intentionally antagonistic. Those who were assigned to work in these urban settings began to realize that their ministry would involve the more routine aspects of pastoral ministry—planning for the parish and developing strategies of accommodation within American society.

Pastoral letters indicate that immigrant bishops and clergy who had once been inclined to concentrate on the conversion of the Indians changed their focus, becoming concerned with finding ways to make their religion compatible with the dominant Protestantism. In joint letters written in 1837 and 1843, for example, these European-born clergy wrote hopefully that the "days of perfect unity may not be far distant."[1] To their fellow Catholics, they reported the many hopeful signs of conversion that were emanating from the Oxford Movement in England and that were bearing fruit in the United States. Despite their own European backgrounds and the occasional outbursts of nativism with which they had to contend in Boston, Providence, Cincinnati, or Saint Louis, the bishops could state boldly, and with pride: "We know of no other portion of the Church in any region of the world, where in one sense, the words of the apostle, 'who planteth a vineyard and eateth not of the fruit thereof,' would be so properly applicable as in the United States."[2] And they quietly thrilled to the conversions they helped to effect; some even cautioned prudence over too facile a response to questions concerning conversion. Conversions among important Protestant and Episcopal families like the Barbers, Tylers, Bayleys, as well as of writers and philosophers such as Orestes Brownson or Isaac Hecker, sustained their patience and their zeal. "To be well on the way to complete acceptance in Protestant American Society" was a hope often in the mind of Catholics and sometimes on the lips of Protestant observers even in the pre–Civil War era.[3] As the first century of U.S. Catholic development proceeded, clergy and laity reminded one another that defending the faith in this Protestant world was "in no way inconsistent with your civil allegiance, your social duties as citizens, or your rights as men."[4] Even if their style of leadership and their models of spirituality continued to reflect certain European Catholic habits, they hoped to effect an American change of heart. As urban missionaries, they counted on the possibility that theological perspectives could redirect the emphasis of the general religious awakening and bring it back to the Church of Rome. Nothing was more important to these early immigrant missionaries who ministered in the Protestant strongholds of the nation's cities, however, than to have their church identified as equally American and as appealing to those of other religious denominations.

In whatever area in which immigrant church leaders initially worked, there were necessary restraints on their urban missionary thrust. The one unavoidable reality that confronted them throughout the pre–Civil War era was the dire poverty of the immigrants which intensified moral temptations for those trying to escape its effects. Earlier, Carroll had been aware of the need to protect Catholics from the worst aspects of this urban curse. He expressed concern over the plight of all those living in poverty in remote areas, from New Jersey and New York to the Mississippi, who were "entirely destitute of spiritual succours." But his special sympathies went to those in the crowded port cities and towns where poverty and temptation were overwhelming realities. Certain obstacles to the practice of faith were stressed: the seduction of "dancing and other such things," or the cheap thrills of novels that Catholic youth might read with "unbelievable eagerness." These had to be countered in structured ways.[5] In finding a response to this constant barrage of threats to the faith, urban missionaries had their work cut out for them. What disturbed Carroll throughout his administration would also deeply concern later immigrant bishops, such as Philadelphia's Neumann or Cincinnati's Purcell.

There was also ignorance of the faith, exacerbated by the foreign backgrounds of the newcomers, that needed to be combated. This required finding new ways of evangelizing within the urban setting. Thus, the dissemination of information through Catholic publications,

such as books and newspapers, and through the establishment of literary societies became an important aim. From the Philadelphia press
of the immigrant Catholic layman Matthew Carey came a Catholic
version of the Bible; it was first distributed for instruction in the 1790s.
From his press, too, many English editions of European prayer books
and catechisms were distributed. For the twenty years of Carey's
apostolate of the press, in fact, missionaries could expect a constant
stream of catechisms and religious texts. In Detroit, Catholic books
or articles were distributed by another immigrant missionary, Father
Gabriel Richard. By the late 1820s, moroever, several Catholic newspapers had begun publication. The first of these, *The Catholic Miscellany* of Charleston (1822) and Boston's *Pilot* (1836), had long-lasting
effects upon Catholic journalism; more importantly, they helped to
strengthen the faith of a people whose Catholic traditions could be
jeopardized by a hostile religious environment. Others, like the short-
lived *Catholic Press* (1829) of Hartford, Connecticut, appealed to clusters of Catholics in localized urban areas. These catechetical means,
coupled with the many opportunities for dialogue between educated
Catholics and fellow Americans within the urban setting, made the
goals of the missionary all the more realizable.

Especially after the 1830s, the specific details of organizing the
church through developing parochial and diocesan structures had to
be attended to by an immigrant clergy, who were thus required to
learn the American way of doing business. Following the example of
Protestant leaders, they applied the lessons of American capitalism,
becoming the bricks-and-mortar builders of the new Catholic Jerusalem. It was more than a sense of business competitiveness, of course,
that impelled them to this task. Catholic schools, hospitals, orphanages, and homes for the needy simply had to be fostered in a society
in which public money was available for the Protestant pursuit of
the same goals. The faith of immigrant Catholics needed to be safeguarded through institutional means. In this way, the future of the
church was strengthed within an unfriendly and seemingly unre-
sponsive society; missionary aims were redirected toward more complex evangelization choices, and prejudicial and discriminatory patterns were monitored or even countered. At the same time, new ways
to handle church governance, including the ownership of land in a
democratic environment, were developed. All this had to be accomplished by bishops and pastors whose foreign background seemed to
belie their ability to create such an American Catholic church.

With each succeeding decade of the nineteenth century, then, as
the Catholic population expanded both within the boundaries of important American cities and outward to other urban areas—stretching
always to the west—the task of satisfactorily building urban insti-

tutions and developing perspectives to serve urban Catholics became
the primary concern, especially among Catholic bishops and clergy.
If Benedict Joseph Flaget had proved that, despite natural hazards
and hardships, a French émigré priest could build an amazingly vibrant church in the first of the western frontiers, two other Frenchmen,
Jean Louis Anne Madeleine Lefebvre de Cheverus (1768–1836), who
became bishop of Boston in 1808, and his close friend and associate
in the diocese, Francis Anthony Matignon, early provided testimony
that charismatic leadership in the heart of one of New England's most
prestigious cities might likewise produce unanticipated and favorable
results for the American Catholic church. They were the first of many
outstanding early-nineteenth-century clergy whose efforts to establish
Catholicism in the Protestant urban setting had constructive implications for the church.

Arriving in Boston in 1796, the future bishop of Boston had, for
example, almost immediately attempted to dispel the notion that his
foreign background should deter any proper Bostonian from recognizing that the Catholic church had much to contribute to the culture
and politics of the American society. Anglicizing his rather formidable
name to the simple "John Cheverus" was but one of the steps he took
to adapt himself to the popular democratic spirit. So great was the
good impression Cheverus made through such overtures that, after
only three years' residence, he was able to negotiate, at moderate
cost, the purchase of a prime plot of land from a Protestant businessman in order to build Boston's first Catholic church. Beyond that,
among Boston Brahmins his brilliance was readily acknowledged; in
particular, his ability to acquire languages was found remarkable.
Eloquent in his extemporaneous sermons and homilies, Cheverus
chose to persuade through recourse to sound judgment and quiet wisdom. As one observer commented: "When assailed by croaking bigotry
or assuming ignorance, he replied by putting some questions far beyond the depth of the interrogator; or if crowded by good natured
curiousity [sic], he got rid of the subject by some adroit evasion which
gave no offence."[6] Especially through his verbal skills, therefore,
Cheverus communicated the essential message: that the Catholic
church must be taken seriously by his Protestant contemporaries.
Clearly an intellectual match for his fellow Christians, he became a
living admonition of the need to rethink ancient prejudices. Why else
would so many a Protestant gentleman, among whom would be "the
most respected and beloved president of the United States, John Adams," liberally subscribe to Cheverus' fund-raising project for the
building of the first Catholic church of Boston? With a grace and gift-
edness that would easily produce accord, this French-American would
serve the Boston church for almost twenty years.[7]

Although both Cheverus and Matignon attempted to find others to assist them in their task of creating an acceptable church in Yankee Boston, most of their years of service found them the sole communicators of Catholic truth. Only in 1817 would the first priest, Dennis Ryan, be ordained specifically for Boston. From time to time, itinerant missionaries, including the convert John Thayer, also served the diocese, and, in 1820, the first congregation of religious women, the Ursulines, were added to the diocese's personnel. The academy that this community directed was, for more than a decade, considered an important Catholic symbol of belonging: a finishing school that the daughters of Boston's most proper citizens felt privileged to attend. By the time new personnel had arrived, however, Matignon had died, exhausted by his missionary travels and his efforts to dispel prejudice and hatred. By 1823, moreover, Cheverus had resigned his position and returned to serve the church in his native France. Thus the early achievements of both Cheverus and Matignon in expanding the church at Boston may seem to have produced meager results compared to what later bishops would accomplish. But in their own way these two émigré priests had performed a yeoman's task for the American Catholic church. Forced to be part of a society that openly acknowledged that it detested everything Catholic, both Cheverus and Matignon had managed to turn aside the special brand of hatred for papists that had flourished in New England. As one observer commented concerning Matignon's charm in this regard, he was "so gentle and so just . . . that even the censorious forgot to watch him, and the malicious were too cunning to attack one armed so strong in honesty."[8] Indeed, so powerful was the impression Cheverus made upon his fellow Bostonians that when he chose to return to Europe, many Protestants joined those who formally petitioned church officials not to accept his resignation.

Because of the steady direction provided by both Cheverus and Matignon, the second bishop of Boston, Benedict J. Fenwick (1782–1846) found a firmly established diocese that was prepared to meet the demands of American society. In his memoirs, Fenwick wrote of the great mental strength and effective ministry of both men; he was also deeply impressed with their refined European ways, which he recognized as having "wrought marvelous concessions" for the Catholics of New England. The two had taken on a fiercely Protestant stronghold that Carroll had earlier described as a place where "a Popish priest was thought to be the greatest monster in creation" and in which a later missionary would experience being "hooted and occasionally stoned by urchins who had imbibed the prejudices of their parents."[9] In the process they had been able to address some of the most crucial problems confronting those whose task it was to develop the Catholic church in the urban setting. They set the stage for other equally able immigrant bishops and clergy whose evenness of temperament and American style also dispelled the prejudices of opponents and eased the way for the institutional development of the U.S. Catholic church.

During their first twenty years, the churches of both New York and Philadelphia lacked the kind of leadership that the first bishop of Boston had offered. Both appeared to serve merely as way stations for immigrant leaders and their Catholic people. Occasionally they benefited from the presence of lay men and women who contributed money and service to the development of nascent Catholic congregations. It was well into the 1830s before a middle-class Irish Catholic community became noticeable within each diocese and, finally, both came under the leadership of able bishops who seemed intent upon advancing the interests of the American Catholic Church. The bishops who were to provide the coherent, American-oriented direction were both immigrants. One was the Irish-born John Hughes (1797–1864), once a student at John Dubois's seminary in Emmitsburg and later his coadjutor in New York; the other, the Bohemian John Nepomucene Neumann (1811–1860), who had early been befriended by the same Dubois. Hughes, who had originally been assigned to the Philadelphia church, was to give outstanding service to the diocese of New York as its bishop from 1837 until 1864; Neumann, who had first been assigned to the New York frontier, was to serve as the bishop and builder of the church of Philadelphia from 1852–1860. The improved stature that New York's Catholics achieved under Hughes or that Philadelphia Catholics could experience because of Neumann's episcopate indicated that these two bishops understood the need to negotiate a Catholic way in a staunchly Protestant world. Under them, both dioceses developed an identity that not only placed them on common ground with other religious organizations but also declared their staying power in American society. European roots had not prevented either of them from blending American and Catholic perspectives into organizational strength so that the church might find its deserved place within the spectrum of American denominations.

Hughes was to set an alternative style for the ongoing dialogue between Protestants and Catholics. Perhaps inspired by his ancestral roots and republican thinking, Hughes consistently pursued an aggressive path regarding Catholic institutional goals, sometimes anticipating the assaults of the Protestant press through strategically placed articles or timely public speeches. Once he even submitted a series of letters to a Protestant paper under the pseudonym Cramer in order to change the usual terms of the debate with Protestants, especially concerning their willingness to print undocumented libel against Catholics. If Hughes's direct style seemed a risky route to pursue, it nevertheless proved successful. He was prepared to take the consequences of his forthright approach. "If the American people can be induced to look that monster [of bigotry] in the face," he once wrote, "and observe his hideous features, they would turn from it in horror and disgust."[10]

Self-appointed to hold that kind of mirror up to Protestant New Yorkers, he was also quick to remind his fellow Irish immigrants of their need to adapt to new circumstances. During the Draft Riots of 1863, for example, he warned his fellow Irish-Americans that their claim of being loyal citizens would be jeopardized if they resisted the draft. To protect the faith of the children of immigrants, he encouraged the building of Catholic schools. He developed a model for the legal incorporation of church property, once again protecting Catholic rights through democratic means. His direct and honest style won him respect among the political elite and gathered friends in other high places. Presidents Polk and Buchanan both consulted him, and Lincoln's appointee William Seward was a particular friend. Hughes even became Lincoln's unofficial emissary in presenting the Union cause abroad. The overall strategy that Hughes developed to present the American Catholic church as a worthy part of American society helped to bring about improved attitudes toward Catholics that characterized the postbellum world.

As bishop of Philadelphia, John Nepomucene Neumann pursued a far less sanguine approach than Hughes's to the building of the Catholic church in the decade preceding the Civil War. Yet, even within the heightened climate of Know-Nothingism, Neumann found a sure means of convincing his contemporaries that the Catholic church, though increasingly of immigrant membership, had the capacity to contribute to the quality of American life. His was not, however, the more dramatic style of political gamesmanship at which Hughes excelled. Rather, Neumann aimed at presenting the best possible Catholic appearance. For sheer breadth of vision and courage to take risks, Neumann's achievements were astounding. They certainly must have amazed Philadelphia's business elite. During the eight controversial years that he headed the church in the City of Brotherly Love, he became the builder par excellence. Not only did he encourage the foundation of almost one hundred grammar schools and fifty churches, but he was also responsible for the establishment, consolidation, and administration of orphanages, hospitals, and other health-care facilities. To staff his schools, parishes, and institutions, Neumann either helped confirm or newly introduced a host of religious communities, almost all originally organized in Europe. Among them were the Christian Brothers (Ireland), the Sisters of Saint Joseph

(France), and the congregations of Notre Dame de Namur (Belgium) and Notre Dame of Munich. Little, besides style, differentiated his emphasis upon building from Hughes's concerns. Practical, concrete results—measured in numbers of institutions, quality of resources, and improved patterns of interaction with American circumstances—were the evidence of his response. What better way, Neumann might have argued, was there for immigrant Catholics to prove their appreciation for, and adaptability to, American standards than to seek to establish themselves within the solid framework of American religious, educational, or social services?

Two other outstanding immigrant bishops who understood the role that they were being called to play in the antebellum American environment were Charleston's John England (1786–1842) and Pittsburgh's Michael O'Connor (1810–1872). As the first bishops of their dioceses, both utilized American political and cultural concepts as they sought to organize institutionally. O'Connor's desire to adapt to the American environment, especially through recruiting personnel who were equally willing to readjust to American ways, even proved controversial. Throughout his seventeen years as bishop, he reminded the clergy and religious whom he had recruited of the importance of adaptation to present circumstances, but his overtures in this regard were not always understood. At the same time, he was always anxious that the needs of the foreign-born be properly attended to.

Even before his ordination as bishop, O'Connor had made the recruitment of personnel to serve the largely immigrant population of his diocese an important priority. Abroad when he received his appointment, he immediately visited the mission offices in Lyons and Vienna, corresponded with religious congregations, and made a general appeal to European and Irish archbishops and bishops for collaboration in the effort. He particularly sought out the Sisters of Mercy, a newly founded Irish congregation with whose rule he was familiar, because he knew that their ministerial approach would be particularly suitable to the Pittsburgh church. Because of his persuasive efforts, seven members of the congregation, headed by Francis Xavier Warde, accompanied him from Carlow to Pittsburgh in 1843. Establishment of a seminary to encourage native vocations was another important aim. Joining him on his trip back from episcopal ordination was a future professor of the seminary he envisioned.

Once in Pittsburgh, O'Connor immediately developed plans to reach out more efficiently to the 25,000 Catholics who lived throughout his sprawling diocese of 21,000 square miles in western Pennsylvania. Though he encouraged native vocations and worked to advance American perspectives, he also understood the importance of locating German-speaking priests to serve the vast German population of his diocese. Thus, on the one hand, he supported the establishment of a diocesan newspaper, whose purpose, he stated in a first edition, was to "enlighten ignorance, to unravel sophistry, to probe to the bottom the charges made against our holy faith, and to show to men the vile calumnies and unfounded misrepresentations by which they are excited to hate us."[11] On the other, he sought to defuse the anti-immigrant bigotry that had already resulted in a series of riots in Philadelphia by providing evidence of the Catholic corporate adaptation to the American environment. Calling for a synod of clergy similar to that initiated earlier by Charleston's John England, developing plans for the construction of a cathedral and an episcopal residence and seminary that could impress Americans, otherwise helping to found educational and health-care institutions—these were his calculated means to achieve the twin goals. All the while he kept up his search for personnel. Although anxious to obtain European clergy and religious to assist in his educational and pastoral work, O'Connor consistently sought out or accepted only those congregations willing to adapt to American ways. For this reason, his personnel search occasionally brought him into bad light, especially among German Catholics. Funds from the Ludwig Mission-verein were actually cut off more than once because of allegations that he had not shown sufficient interest in the proper care of his German-American flock. In fact, Mother Teresa Gerhardinger, founder of the Austrian-based School Sisters of Notre Dame, was one of many convinced that O'Connor did not care for the Germans. At one point, she wrote that he had "even said publicly that the German schools here in Pittsburgh had better close, since ultimately the Germans would have to unite with the English."[12] Such criticisms O'Connor seemed willing to endure to secure the proper result. Despite misjudgments, he continued his recruiting trips, seeking religious congregations especially from Germany, Ireland, and Italy. Over the years, he continued to encounter difficulties with this strategy: the departure of the Emmitsburg Sisters of Charity, seemingly dislodged because of his preference for the Irish Sisters of Mercy; a similar discouragement experienced by Mother Gerhardinger and her companions, the School Sisters of Notre Dame; and, finally, the disbanding of the Brothers of the Presentation. Because of his efforts, an impressive number of congregations began their American apostolates. Two German congregations of men became firmly established: the Benedictines, under Boniface Wimmer, who formally instituted the Rule of St. Benedict in his diocese in 1845, and the Redemptorists, who were encouraged to continue their parish and retreat work and educational projects. At the same time, two communities of German sisters and the Italian-based Congregation of the Passion were invited to engage in the fields of education and charity and to establish American provinces. Other communities, including the Franciscans, were recruited and initially subsidized so that they could minister within the diocese.

Even though an immigrant himself, O'Connor's record indicates that he projected an Americanist perspective. Recognizing the recent European roots of most of his Catholic population, he had no problem encouraging missionaries from Germany and Ireland, in particular, to join him in his American tasks. Yet he consistently reminded his membership that opportunities were to be made available to all Americans, native-born or immigrant, especially within the American urban context. He showed an openness to economic progress as well as to democratic rights. What he asked in return was a willingness among recent immigrants to move gradually in the direction of adaptation. His disappointment over the departure of the Americanizer Isaac Hecker from the Redemptorists was inspired by this concern. In 1857, he wrote to the Benedictine Bernard Smith at the Urban College in Rome:

> I was very sorry to hear of Father Hecker's withdrawal from the Redemptorists. . . . As to his alleged Native Americanism, I do not believe that he had it to any improper extent nor more than is proper for anyone to have for his native country. I do not think, indeed, that it would be well for the Redemptorists to establish an American House as such. The whole community should in small matters adapt itself more to the usages of the country than it does. I think they are too tenacious of their German habits, etc. But I think also that the whole order should move together in any contemplated change. Gradually, this would be as complete as would be desirable, and as all persons and things in this country Americanize themselves sooner or later it is a question of time when they will do it also. There may be some evils in its happening too soon, but there are others in its being deferred too long. . . . This I believe is the sentiment of most people. Dr. Kenrick made the same statement.[13]

More subdued in his arguments about Americanizing than some of his contemporaries, O'Connor was nevertheless prompt in arguing for the right to express Catholic truths in the public arena. Through apologetical treatises, sermons, lectures, and editorials and through ardent appeals for justice he chose to point out the rich Catholic heritage that had brought about the civil liberties that Americans were presently enjoying. As bishop of western Pennsylvania, Michael O'Connor remained until his resignation in 1860 a recognized spokesman of both American and Catholic values.

Just as O'Connor had used his intellectual skill, administrative talents, and Irish penchant for oratorical discourse to legitimate one Catholic diocese within the American context, so too, an earlier Irish immigrant, John England, who had assumed charge of the diocese of Charleston, South Carolina, manifested similar dispositions and aims. England had, moreover, managed to produce the more impressive results. His success had been largely due to his Irish intellectual background, which enabled him to develop a clear appreciation for American republican traditions. Despite its alleged attachment to foreign powers, the church he championed in the United States was to appear as revolutionary as the nation he adopted. From the start, his diocese developed a radically different governmental structure. In the words of one Charleston trustee, it was a "National American Church," one with "liberties consonant to the spirit of the Government, under which they lived; yet, in due obedience in essentials to the Pontifical Hierarchy, and which will add a new and dignified column to the Vatican."[14]

To historians, England stands as one of the nineteenth-century exemplars of Catholic adaptation to American republicanism. An intellectual giant, he was to create a Catholic blueprint fully consonant with republican traditions. Unfortunately, all that remains of England's legacy in this regard are the documents prescribing local church governance, which were never fully implemented and which were, in many ways, at least a century ahead of their time. Yet, even his peers grudgingly came to realize that England "had successfully witnessed to the capacity of the Catholic Church to become both acceptable and respectable within the American context."[15] Protestants were equally amazed by England; his oratorical largesse impressed many. As one appreciative Protestant observer commented, England resembled a fiery Irish patriot, as he threw himself "from side to side of the pulpit" or darted his "hands and head with pugilistic violence," the blood rushing into his face as if it would gush and his passions in an "uncontrollable tempest."[16] These skills earned him a wider audience of admirers. In 1826, England had the distinction of addressing the United States Congress; the president, John Quincy Adams, and congressmen expressed awe over his oratorical abilities and range of thought.

Although conversant on many topics, England was particularly anxious to offer his views on republicanism. With somewhat mixed results, he brought his persuasive skills to the task of convincing both Americans and American Catholics of the intimate ways in which constitutional practice and Catholic theory had been combined in the American setting. In difficult times, however, his rhetorical talents could be used for other aims. Sometimes bolstering Catholic spirits in the face of nativist attacks, his resort to dramatic overtures could serve the important purpose of encouraging Catholic self-pride. England was a master writer as well. To promote a climate conducive to the understanding of Catholic truths, he founded a newspaper in 1822.

Entitled the *United States Catholic Miscellany*, it served as a prism for his Catholic and republican views. Through this and other literary works, England was able to provide an immigrant community with a radically new system of religious meaning that helped explain the world of republicanism in which Catholics lived and allowed them to accept the trials of nativism under which they often suffered. Through his writings and prepared speeches, he continually enunciated his belief that Catholicism was essentially compatible with the American tenets of religious liberty, the separation of church and state, and voluntarism—all of which he attempted to prove were not only supported by the constitution but were fundamentally rooted in Catholic doctrine.

Often, however, both the content and expression of England's views proved particularly controversial to other immigrant Catholic prelates. French-born episcopal colleagues, especially Maréchal, for example, voiced suspicion over his democratic and republican language. England was incredulous. At one point in 1835, he wrote disparagingly of what he considered their narrow attitudes:

> The French can never become American. Their language, manners, love of la belle France, their dress, air, carriage, notions, and mode of speaking of their religion, all, all are foreign. An American then says 'It might be very good, but 'tis a foreign aristocracy.' The French clergy are generally good men and love religion, but they make the Catholic religion thus appear to be exotic, and cannot understand why it should be made to appear assimilated to American principles.[17]

The immigrant England worried over the impression other immigrants were making. Wherever possible, he mitigated the French influence exerted by Sulpician seminary training. He withdrew his seminarians from their Baltimore facility. Even-handedly, he placed restrictions upon candidates for the priesthood who were recent immigrants by delaying their immediate acceptance by his diocese. And, to make sure that both immigrant and native vocations would be nourished along American lines, he established his own diocesan seminary. The same concern caused him to found a religious congregation of women, which he styled on the flexible model of the Sisters of Mercy. He did this in order to emphasize the necessity of apostolic adaptation. By a variety of actions, attitudes, and policies, he made clear his intention to project the image of an American church, and he fought, energetically and passionately, any attempt to categorize his Catholic people as foreign. He wanted his fellow Americans to realize that Catholics should be seen for what they aimed to be: as American as any of their contemporaries.

The governmental structures that England was to encourage and the constitution that he drew up for Charleston's Catholics were other outstanding examples of how England put his theories about republicanism to the test. During the time when Marechal was archbishop of Baltimore, for example, it was England who asked repeatedly for a provincial council of the nation's bishops in order to introduce uniform legislation for the church. The councils that were subsequently convened were testimonies to his persistence. England's hope that the councils would pass legislation that would acknowledge the rights and duties of every member of the church—bishops, priests, and laity—never materialized. Even during England's lifetime the signs were clear that his worst fears—that episcopal power would become all encompassing—might be realized.[18]

If hampered from developing national church policies, England was, of course, free to develop new structures of governance within his own diocese. Consequently, in 1833 he submitted a constitution for the governance of his diocese to the Propaganda offices in Rome. An unprecedented action, this move proved all the more remarkable when he was permitted to implement his constitution and when eventually it was adopted by all the Catholics of his diocese. In guiding the Catholics of Charleston in the actual living out of this constitution, furthermore, England adapted other American practices. As their bishop, he helped Catholics sense ownership over their church by promoting local church councils and boards of trustees, so that lay members would be encouraged to cooperate in the running of their parishes. He put forth detailed procedures that spelled out rights and duties and appropriate governance. Perhaps merely the recognition that they had been included in the mechanisms of governance was reason enough to recommend England's mode of governance to the laity. In 1832, for example, one dissident group wrote England, "Instead of being tossed as for many years we have been, upon a sea of uncertainty, the beacon you raised soon guided us to that rock whereon the great God hath built his universal church."[19]

England's plan for his diocese was lost sight of in subsequent years. Still it was an alternative to the prevailing authoritarian model and, though unorthodox and radical to many, stood as a unique reminder of the American aims of the early U.S. Catholic church, as well as of the ability of American Catholic leadership to adapt an immigrant church to the new republican realities. The Roman-educated England had brought an urban Catholic culture to this momentous—albeit temporary—opportunity. Because of him, one local church was able to prove that Catholicism and the American political system could have common elements, aims, and structures.

Although often theoretical, England's genius also expressed itself in the highly practical ways characteristic of other urban missionaries. A builder and organizer, he remained a shepherd of his flock, applying his skills as a preacher, teacher, and liturgist to his administrative tasks as rector of his diocesan seminary and member of the diocesan board of examiners. He would visit at the local hospital and was chaplain for the city prison and Magdalen asylum. The continuing demands of urban Catholicism met him at every turn. Beset by the daily concerns of a growing population and diminishing resources of money and personnel, he also had to face the complex details of institutional growth and the task of promoting cooperative interaction in an overwhelmingly Protestant world. Parishes, churches, schools, and hospitals were built; new personnel were located and trained; institutions were monitored; and new perspectives were explored and developed. A frontier-style missionary and a skilled administrator, England moved in a daily ritual of liturgical practice, pastoral work, administrative duties, and theological and social dialogue.

In many ways, then, John England can be considered the quintessential example of early-nineteenth-century immigrant Catholic leadership in an urban context. American ideals—political, social, and cultural—permeated his life and directed his course of action within Catholic circles. Pronouncing republican ideals in the secular sphere, he promoted their implementation in the religious sphere as well. Yet, in an era in which almost all of church's finest leaders were immigrants, John England might accurately be described as an early and exemplary Americanist. By his insistence on following American patterns, and by his belief that there was no system more favorable to the security of religious rights of churches than that of American constitutional law, he had given the lie to the idea that Catholicism and Americanism were incompatible or that Catholicism in the urban context could not benefit the larger society. England's American perspective can be seen as his most important contribution to the American Church. Because it came from the mind and heart of an immigrant, it gave confirmation to the argument that the Catholic church could take its place among American institutions.

England's leadership provided the clearest substantiation of the view that immigrants in this early period were determined to, and could, create an American Catholic church. He was the first among *immigrant* bishops to evaluate American political ideas in a systematic way and to suggest a democratic governmental structure for the church as a whole. But neither England nor the other European-born bishops or clergy would have been able to oversee the kind of dynamic growth the church experienced without the assistance and support of those they had come to serve. Mostly immigrants as well, the Catholic laity were like-minded collaborators in the church's development in its first one hundred years; they were the chief source of both inspiration and support to immigrant bishops and clergy in the mission they had undertaken. If James Parton could claim in an 1868 issue of the *Atlantic Monthly* that this "despised minority" of Catholics was "well on its way to complete acceptance in Protestant American Society," this was largely due to the fact that both membership and leadership, whether immigrant or native-born, had proven their capacity to become integral parts of American society.[20]

Diaries and records document the role of lay men and women in the growth of parishes and show how the faith of the laity gave inspiration to the leadership. One touching story of mutual enrichment comes from New England in 1834; it was reported in a memoir by Father James Fitton, who referred to himself simply as "the missionary." According to the priest, he was traveling by sleigh the forty miles between Hartford and New Haven one cold Christmas Eve to say midnight mass when his troubles began. More than half way into the trip, the snow gave out. Undaunted by the setback and unable to find any other kind of transportation, he continued on foot, with vestments and sacred vessels slung over his back. Exhausted by the time of his arrival, he barely managed to offer a much-delayed mass for the tiny congregation. But the faith and patience of the people so enlivened his spirits, he confided in his journal, that his strength returned and he managed to deliver the expected homily at the end of mass. Of a similar faith-inspiring incident in a more remote setting, a contemporary missionary, Joseph Machebeuf, would write another warm, though more amusing, tale. After cajoling a tavern keeper at one Ohio town's only place of lodging into providing him, in advance, with a room for the night, this young priest did his spiritual rounds, knowing that after his trek among scattered immigrant settlements he could at least anticipate a quiet place to rest. Instead, he discovered that his bedroom had been taken over and was actually being used to conduct official town business. Bone-tired, but still exhilarated by the response of those he served, Machebeuf simply pushed his way through the assemblage, displaced the three men who were sitting on his bed, and fell sound asleep.[21]

Other missionaries were quick to admit that the spread of the Catholic faith in both frontier and urban settlements was largely due to the faith and convictions of the people themselves. Whether it was southern black Catholics or the Benedicta Abenaki Indians of Maine who were the object of their Christianizing efforts, whether it was impoverished immigrants crowded in urban ghettos or working the virgin land, a committed people, whose belief provided renewed strength for another day of ministry, was there to encourage the missionaries to continue. Thus, the far-reaching apostolic trail came to involve all in the sharing of the faith. Priests and sisters may have answered the call, but it was the people who responded and sustained their efforts. Their needs changed the focus of the American apostolate. In particular, missionaries discovered that the task of organization was to be shared. This realization confirmed the uniqueness of the shared relationship between clergy and people, a relationship upon which the American church was to be built. Laypersons, in fact, provided the last and most substantial link in the early organization of the church in the United States. In their continued role of assistance and collaboration, and as a source of vocations to the ministries of priesthood and religious life, immigrant Catholic laity added a special dimension to the building of the American Catholic church. They were in effect the cocreators and organizers of the American Catholic church.

Almost always, the work of the laity involved the direct provision of money or labor resources. It was not long before certain lay leaders initiated more organized, institutional ways of developing coherent programs for needy Catholics. Among early efforts were the various chapters of the Saint Vincent de Paul Society. The initial American conference of this society (1845) had as its president Moses L. Linton, a prominent scientist-convert; its worldwide organization was founded by a New York layman, Thomas Mulry. Saint Louis Catholics were among the first to embark upon such programs of organized material assistance. Other laymen inaugurated mutual benefit societies aimed at attending to the immediate financial needs of particular ethnic groups of Catholics. In this regard, national and local German- and Irish-American associations led the way. Still other Catholic laity became involved in self-help projects, such as the temperance societies styled after the Father Theobald Mathew clubs, the societies formed around patriotic themes, the military training clubs, and the ethnic organizations, which often included drama and music societies. Finally, colonization societies became the particular concern of certain layman. By encouraging a sense of solidarity among members, these organizations helped to fuse religious, national, or ethnic identity among immigrants. Occasionally such lay initiatives did cause serious tension within parishes and dioceses. "Trustee" battles over the right to make decisions involving certain roles within the church—such as with regard to the ownership of property or the appointment of pastors—occurred on a regular enough basis in the early nineteenth century to suggest that the working out of clergy–lay cooperation was no easy task.

For the most part, the stories of Catholic laity have remained relegated to collective descriptions found in parochial and diocesan histories. Even in these accounts, the laity have usually remained anonymous or have been recorded in mere listings of Irish, German, or other immigrant benefactors. Yet what the laity achieved has endured in the structures they helped build and continued to finance, as well as in the spirit that continued to animate the parishes and organizations to which they contributed. To a great extent it was because of lay pioneers who offered their skills as bricklayers, stone workers, and artisans and who contributed their few pennies and dimes to defray the expenses of these first monuments to Catholic faith that the early church progressed so remarkably. It was also because of the response of laity that vocations to the church advanced rapidly. Finally, it was largely because of the faith of the laity that interest in Protestant conversion was sparked.

Even if some of the immigrants sometimes embarrassed church leaders or became the unwitting objects of scorn and reprobation, it was from their ranks that Catholics were able to offer the best proof of patriotic allegiance. At times of political crisis, it was the Irish dockworkers and construction workers, as well as the German farmers and factory hands, who were the first to have their loyalty and devotion to their adopted country tested. During the Civil War, for example, they were the ones who accepted the call to arms. Side by side with their fellow Americans—the chaplains who accompanied them and the sisters who nursed them—they proved by their lives that Catholics could also make good citizens. Such was the unique, if unwitting, vocation of immigrant laymen to American church and society.

Some laypersons have been remembered largely because of their persistence in leadership during the early decades of Catholic history in the United States. Their lives were representative of countless others who projected an activist, devotional, and loyal stance. One, whose shaping of the urban American Catholic church proved especially dramatic, was a black entrepreneur, Pierre Toussaint. Born a Haitian slave, Toussaint became one of the most saintly immigrant philanthropists of the fledgling church. Brought to New York City in 1787 by a master who would lose his life in a rebellion that broke out that same year, Toussaint found himself not only in charge of his master's family and property but a Catholic leader as well. Despite the fact that he would not be freed until the death of his owner's wife decades later, Toussaint assumed these responsibilities with remarkable grace. He cared for his owner's wife and relatives. At the same time he took on leadership roles in church affairs. And, as hairdresser to New York's wealthiest, he became widely acknowledged as an outstanding businessman, confidant, and advisor. Thus, through both his professional career and volunteer work among New York's needy, he became an important symbol of the capacity of lay Catholics to enter into the American mainstream.

Despite the fact that he was often the victim of prejudice, Toussaint found ways to serve his fellow Catholics. He single-handedly initiated ways to finance the needs of the poor, collecting for such causes as aid to destitute youth, the elderly, the orphaned, and the homeless. He personally nursed the victims of the city's epidemics. As a member of Saint Peter parish, he not only supported its projects wholeheartedly by contributing time and money, but he volunteered to help Catholics build other parishes as well. Because neighborhood French-speaking Catholics wanted to start their own church, for example, he helped to collect funds. He was also involved in the establishment of a school for "colored" children, was a benefactor to a religious congregation of women who were recruited to staff social services, and served as a faithful contributor and collector of funds to educate seminarians and missionaries. Still, the good he did was often scorned by the comments of those who expressed concern over "the increasing insolence of the blacks in this city" or who warned him not to overstep his "immutable and fixed" place in society.[22] When Toussaint died in 1853 at the age of eighty-six, Catholics and non-Catholics alike flocked to his funeral. Addressing the many who mourned, his pastor at Saint Peter extolled the simple life of this saintly man with succinct, but telling, comment: There were few left among the clergy superior to him in zeal and devotion to the Church and for the glory of God; among laymen not one."[23] With varying results, other lay men and women exhibited a willingness to contribute to the building of the American Catholic church. Regardless of personal disadvantage and suffering, clergy and laity alike believed the church belonged to everyone and consequently accepted the responsibility for its growth as an American institution. According to the gifts of such men and women the American Catholic church would be shaped.

Another exemplary layman of this early period was a young Irishman from County Wexford, Nicholaus Devereux, who began his American stay in the same city in which Toussaint offered the service of his life. Soon moving to the rural northern areas of New York State, Devereux began an important chapter in lay ministry by assisting Catholic communities in the famed "burned-over" region. Like Toussaint, he demonstrated an indefatigable persistence and vision that provided both witness and a sense of direction for other early immigrant Catholics. Also like Toussaint, he had been touched personally by the effects of political rebellion (his father and several brothers were the victims of Irish revolts), and thus he appreciated both the value and risk of taking stands for justice and religious rights. But he was equally prepared to assume a quieter role by taking on parochial responsibilities aimed at improving the church's place in American society. Like Toussaint, Devereux accepted his status as

Catholic. For the most part, he expressed little desire to combat prejudice or argue the Catholic cause in any direct fashion. Instead, he worked to build communities and institutions that would proclaim Catholic values within an unsympathetic Protestant environment.

By the time that Devereux had become involved in assisting New York's rural Catholic community, he had already become a successful businessman in Albany and Utica. And his marriage to an Episcopalian, Mary Dolbear Butler, had gained him some respectability among New York society's wealthiest. But neither advantage could deter his ambition to improve the lives of his fellow Catholics. At first he was simply a leader of prayer, an organizer on behalf of parish need. But he soon became involved in seeking added personnel and volunteers to develop a mission outpost at Saint John's, Utica; with his help, it became the first Catholic church established in western New York. He also participated in the initiation of other rural communities. During the 1830s, Devereux became the sponsor of a school for orphans and helped recruit the Emmitsburg Sisters of Charity to staff the institution. Even the first church in Hartford, Connecticut, was made possible by one of his generous "loans" (this one for $10,000), sought by a business colleague while Devereux was visiting the city in 1829.

When the Erie Railroad opened up western New York to new business ventures, Devereux's philanthropy expanded further. Because he had wisely invested in a 400,000-acre tract of property along a projected railroad route, he was in a particularly advantageous position to make creative use of his land holdings on behalf of the church. He envisioned a planned village based on a European Franciscan model, to be called Allegany City, that would serve as both a haven for immigrants and a university town dedicated to Catholic culture. Although his utopian dream became "The City That Never Was," many Irish immigrants settled in the area, making it possible for some of Devereux's communal ideas to be brought to fruition. In thanksgiving for his wife's conversion to Catholicism and with the belief that his university community was still a possibility, he traveled to Rome to ask the pope's permission to establish a Franciscan congregation on his New York property. In the agreement, dated 1855, with the Italian Franciscan community whom he persuaded to come to New York for this purpose, the statement regarding financial arrangements reveals the practical role he played:

> A wealthy and illustrious citizen of Utica, New York, Mr. Devereux, has promised to give 200 acres of land and $5,000, so that a house for the religious can be conveniently and properly erected, and the things necessary for this work [obtained].[24]

With the approval of the pope, the enterprise was duly incorporated. Faithful to the original purpose, the Franciscans established a "missionary, scientific, charitable and benevolent society . . . in the village of Allegany." There they began to provide missionary services and pursue their agreed-upon aim to "aid the poor and orphans, instruct the ignorant by teaching divine and human knowledge."[25]

Only six months after the arrival of the Franciscans and the beginning of this lofty enterprise, which would culminate in the establishment of Saint Bonaventure University, Nicholas Devereux died. Like Toussaint, he was honored by both his fellow churchmen and the wider community he served. According to his widow, "Never has such a funeral been witnessed in Utica. Nearly 5000 persons assembled. Protestant and Catholic, old and young, rich and poor, all mourned together the loss of a common friend."[26]

There were many Irish, German, and other immigrant Catholics who proved, as Devereux and Toussaint had done, the power of the spirit in transforming an immigrant church into a respected American religious institution. Some did this through their business contacts or professional careers as lecturers, reformers, educators, editors, or journalists. Philadelphia's Matthew Carey and the itinerant Thomas D'Arcy McGee are examples of men who used their personal charm and literary skills to impress both society's intellectual elite and their Catholic constituents of the capacity of Americans and Catholics to improve their lives. Early efforts to develop colonies of Catholic settlement are another example of an effort by immigrant laity to improve the lives of Catholics within the American environment. One of the first attempts, organized by both laity and clergy, to colonize immigrants occurred in 1817, when the Irish Emigrant Society of New York was founded. Other communitarian efforts resulted in settlements of Germans at Saint Mary City, or Silver Lake, Pennsylvania, and New Westphalia, Missouri, as well as in projects begun at Pompey, New York, and in Stallotown, Ohio. Some colonizing efforts reflected sophisticated, joint planning between clergy and laity; most exceptional among these was the utopian experiment begun by Father Ambrose Oschwald at Saint Nazianz, Wisconsin, which was one of the most extensive attempts to build a free, cooperative physical and social Catholic environment in the United States. No plans, however were as renowned or significant as those engendered by Thomas D'Arcy McGee's Irish Colonization Convention, which first met in Buffalo in 1852.

Each of these colonization plans, whether loosely structured or part of a complex utopian scheme, reflected the general mid-nineteenth-century American trend toward communitarian living. Each indicated the strong desire on the part of both immigrant clergy and laity to help settle the West. For some, colonization became a means by which immigrant Catholic laity could advance under the aegis of the church, according to a pattern considered acceptable to Americans in general. Yet most projects were short-term phenomena. A future bishop of Saint Paul and a strong advocate of the colonization movement, John Ireland (1838–1918), embodied many aspects of the movement. The same year he attended a newly opened Catholic school in Saint Paul, an immigrant priest, Father Franz Pierz, of Austria, had been recruited to the diocese in order to assist in the developing of German colonies. A dozen years later, when Ireland returned to Saint Paul as a veteran chaplain of the Union Army, he had the advantage of remodeling Pierz's earlier ideas. Appointed president of the Minnesota Irish Emigration Society in 1864, Ireland later became well-known in wider American circles as a Catholic leader who wished to move his people along paths compatible to American sentiments. But, like other large-scale colony plans, Ireland's ideas for Irish Catholic colonization did not seem to fit the overall aims of Catholics in organizing their church in the United States.

When one surveys the lives of so many Catholic clergy, religious, and laity who were able to break through the confining cultural atmosphere of early-nineteenth-century America to develop various styles of Catholic settlement or colonization, one can conclude that being a Catholic immigrant during this period did not always mean encountering deprivation, prejudice, or frustration. Often, in fact, Catholics were caught up in the excitement and energy that emanated from their ability to share in the missionary work of the church. Their enthusiasm had effects upon Americans in general. For many antebellum immigrants, Catholicism proved less of a social handicap than it would later become. Despite isolated examples of prejudice, expressed in vicious sentiments and violent conduct, there were some surprisingly favorable encounters with the Protestant world. Especially before the 1840s, in fact, interest on the part of Protestants in the Catholic church sometimes proved so astounding that missionaries deliberately cautioned their peers not to accept new converts without sufficient explanation of the faith. Thus, there was the widowed Elizabeth Ann Bayley Seton, who became a member of Saint Peter's congregation in 1805; the conversion of an exceptional Episcopalian family, the Barbers of Claremont, New Hampshire, in 1816; the conversion of future priests, like Thomas S. Preston and Isaac Hecker; and the odyssey of the controversial Pierce Connelly and his wife, Cornelia, who proved the more committed Catholic convert. There were the stirrings of the "Oxford Movement," which resulted in the addition of the Episcopal bishop of North Carolina, Levi Silliman Ives, as well as the journalists John R. G. Hassard, Joseph Ripley

Chandler, James A. McMaster, and Jedediah V. Huntington. A harvest such as this, accomplished by clergy and laity who often still spoke with brogues or accents, could not be ignored.

Apart from what the cultural milieu often dictated, therefore, there were signs of a certain openness to Catholic growth during the first century of American Catholic development in the United States. Much of this was the result of the respect expressed by Catholics for the cultural and political structures within which their own work and worship was pursued. But what had also been required of all Catholics, clergy and lay, was the willingness to admit their faith publicly, the courage to stand up against any attacks by the Protestant church, and the initiative to defend their particular way of expressing both their devotion to the church and their allegiance to the country. Although Catholics continued to be perceived according to their cultural ways, their desire to become part of their new environment allowed them to meet the expectations of Americans in a straightforward way. Wherever openness to this adaptability existed, there transition was possible. In the process, an American Catholic church was built by the hands of immigrants. Without discarding old world religious styles and, in fact, often carefully preserving ethnic difference when it was deemed necessary, Catholics were able to forge ahead, often marching to the same beat as other Americans while they built their church. As a consequence, American democratic characteristics, such as collegiality and cooperation, tended to prevail over narrow, authoritarian vision; an apostolic zeal that included every nationality and race sometimes won out over provincial concerns; and enthusiastic loyalty for American institutions often overpowered the tendency toward parochial or ethnic squabbling.

In this bustling antebellum world, the American Catholic church had been established. Through the untiring efforts of clergy, religious, and laity, it had grown strong, especially in certain urban areas of the nation. Through mutual cooperation, a church that had once been the object of derision and scorn had begun to hold its own among other American institutions. From his western missionary outpost, the bishop of Colorado, Joseph Machebeuf, reflected the observations of many of the early-nineteenth-century bishops; on the choice of his successor, he wrote: "The clergy is mostly European, yet we are all in America and in time must all be Americanized, and a very special man is required at the head of the Church here."[27] Those who should lead the American church, the bishops argued, needed to identify themselves as Americans yet also understand the needs of immigrants. In 1850, Bishop Alemany, a Spaniard, had been chosen to head the church of California for this reason. His ethnicity was important, it was argued, but what was more important was that he provided a

linkage between the old and the new: he was held in veneration by
the Mexican people and yet was seen as an American because he was
"in full sympathy with American ideas and principles and enjoyed
the unqualified respect of the American people."[28] Whether immigrant
or native-born, America's bishops conveyed an American allegiance.
From bishop, to clergy, religious, and laity, an interest in furthering
democratic American aims prevailed. In this first stage of church development, immigrant Catholics wanted to project an American image
as they built their American Catholic church.

PART TWO

The Second Stage of the Immigrant Church, 1860–1950

United States Catholic church leaders during the period 1790–1860 had fulfilled a unique mission. With energy and an overall sense of cooperation they had worked together to develop from feeble beginnings an ecclesiastical institution that would both satisfactorily embrace its rapidly growing, ethnically diverse membership and more importantly, be perceived as fully American. They did this in a pervasively Protestant environment that was itself undergoing dramatic change and was coming to terms with the consequences of its decreasing numerical dominance. Eager for the challenge and well aware of the precedents they would set, Catholic leaders managed to create a structure that was, at least on the surface, both Catholic and American.

From a decentralized institution, one sometimes mesmerized by American republican notions and fragmented by ethnic and class differences, Catholic leaders continued to work toward institutional unity. To describe how the church worked to maintain a welcoming posture toward immigrants—regardless of numbers or national origin—is the task of Part II. This section will concentrate on the second stage of the creation of the U.S. Catholic church, the stage in which the desire to strive for unity through the Americanization of the church met with sometimes strident opposition and during which a cultural Catholicism, molded primarily by ethnicity and characterized by the parallel structures it developed, became the American accommodation to the new membership of immigrants. Finally, this study will detail the diverse loyalties, based on differing European ecclesial and spiritual patrimonies, that emerged after the Civil War and that, by mutual agreement between bishops and people, created the pattern of development by which the U.S. Catholic church is still known. In a word, it will attempt to interpret the American phenomenon of ethnic Catholicism that emerged in the postbellum world and the "separate but equal" church that it occasioned.

CHAPTER
4
The Ethnic Church
Develops, 1860–1950

*I*n the decades before the Civil War, pioneer Catholics—mostly English, French, Irish, or German immigrants or their descendants—had created a vibrant, sprawling church. The major effort toward unity was on the episcopal level; on several occasions the nation's bishops met in provincial councils to establish a common basis for discipline, planning, and action. Although they sensed some unity, American Catholics generally experienced themselves as outside the dominant religious culture and locally isolated from other Catholics. Especially during the 1840s and 1850s, as the first waves of immigration from Germany and Ireland produced economic and cultural tensions between natives and immigrants, Catholics concentrated on overseeing the needs of their own members. At this point, too, the Catholic church had reached numerical predominance: by 1850, it had become the largest religious denomination in the United States and accounted for 40 percent of the nation's church membership. Perhaps because of this, cruel episodes of violence, causing destruction of property, injury, and even death, dogged the attempts of Catholics to become integrated into American society. Prejudice against "papists" was a recurrent reality in the nineteenth century. On one level, Catholics worked to present a plain, undemonstrative, and unassuming image, one that could prove compatible with American values and goals. On another, they wrestled with the Protestant establishment, which presented a cultural threat. On still another, they sought to integrate their diverse membership into a unified body of believers. In this

59

complicated setting, the need to situate themselves within the American environment yet safeguard their traditions remained the essential motivating force for Catholics.

The cataclysmic Civil War—when tens of thousands of Catholic men and women on both sides marched off either to fight or to care for the wounded—marked a transition, a time of changing attitudes in which Catholics and non-Catholics would rethink earlier attitudes toward the place of the Catholic church in United States society. Catholic participation in the war successfully undercut the worst aspects of anti-Catholicism, granting the American Catholic church a grudging, but enduring, acceptance in Protestant America. Montgomery Guards of the First Virginia Infantry confronted New York's Irish Catholic Sixty-Ninth Regiment, or Alabama's Emerald Guards and Louisiana's French Catholics fought against fellow Catholics who defended the Union. Six hundred religious sisters from more than twenty religious communities nursed both the Yankee and the Rebel. Regardless of the side chosen, the heroism and patriotism which American Catholics demonstrated made positive impressions upon their compatriots. At the war's end, Catholics rightly sensed the first fruits of recognition. In a reunified nation, they could, for the first time, champion their own sense of belonging and cohesiveness.

As the second century of American Catholicism began in the reconstruction years, a more self-assured and unified Catholic church began to emerge. This was particularly obvious on the episcopal level, where Irish-Americans were the more numerous and the most vocal. Meeting together in plenary session in 1866, the nation's bishops presented an impressive front. Their opening session at Baltimore's classically styled cathedral featured a procession of forty-five archbishops and bishops, two abbots, and dozens of clerical advisers and assistants; it was resplendent with liturgical pomp and highlighted by classical oratory and the strains of Mozart. The "American" Martin J. Spalding presided. Sermon after lengthy sermon reminded Catholics of "the beauty of the Catholic church in the United States which knows 'no nationality' . . . or . . . 'no color or caste.' " In Spalding's words, "the land of Washington, affording a common nationality to the children of every clime, has become the home of men of many different nations." Respecting this and "struck with . . . single-minded devotion," the bishops stressed their need to develop a greater uniformity of discipline and a greater sense of oneness within the church. The closing session of the council was attended by Andrew Johnson and his daughter. Through religious and secular newspaper coverage from coast to coast, four million Catholics amid some thirty million Americans learned of the new direction that their church had set.[1]

Yet, just as quickly as Catholic leaders came to realize the new possibilities open to them, unity proved more elusive than ever. In the rapidly urbanizing and industrialing postwar world, the one problem that undermined cohesiveness was the constantly growing immigrant population. The new membership was even more heterogeneous ethnically than in the prewar era. The multitextured appearance of the Catholic population would, in fact, become the next stumbling block for American Catholics, once again undercutting identification of the church as American. The plain undemonstrative approach of leaders in search of American acceptance of their church would become lost as the ethnic backgrounds of the nation's Catholics grew still more diverse and as dispersion of ethnic Catholics throughout the United States resulted in differing views of the Catholic people. The factor of ethnicity would now impose a more explicit and divisive separateness.

Another related phenomenon became increasingly clear in the postbellum Catholic world: one ethnic group within the church had begun to take precedence over the others. Despite the fact that Irish and German immigrants had together spearheaded the church's mushrooming growth—a growth that swelled the Catholic population to approximately twelve million by the turn of the twentieth century—the Irish-Americans had been the ones who gained the dominant edge among Catholics. A number of factors led to the Gaelic victory. One involved the Irish advantage over other recent Catholic immigrants. Not only were the Irish fluent in English, but many Irish-Americans had improved their social and economic status through the years, and this aspect of the Irish heritage was appreciated by Americans in general. More than perhaps any other immigrant group, the Irish realized the value of integrating with American society. Convinced of the hopelessness of the political and economic situation in Ireland and as sure that they would never be able to return home, most immigrants from Ireland thought they had no recourse but to make of the United States their blessed haven. While mourning their status and bemoaning their "exile," they settled where their fellow Irish countrymen had developed communities, determined to make the best of things; this ability to blend into the American scene would influence every aspect of Irish response to life in the United States.

If better adjusted to American society than other immigrants, the Irish soon came to realize that they had a special advantage within the American church. Not only had they helped to organize most of the first parishes or other institutions in the urban Catholic clusters, but their sons and daughters had turned to the church to fulfill the vocational meaning of their lives.

In remarkable numbers, the second generation of Irish immigrants joined the priesthood and the religious life. Their role models were

the scores of Irish missionaries—constituting one-third of the clergy—
who had immigrated even before the Civil War to serve the church:
All Hallows, Drumcondra, Dublin, had been a major source of priestly
vocations for the American mission. Second-generation Irish-Americans found an inspiration in the idea of full-time commitment to the
church equal that of their forebears. The number of entrants into
American seminaries and novitiates was phenomenal. Thus, as Irish-
Americans became more visible among clergy or religious and more
numerous among Catholics, their importance was further enhanced.

By the 1880s, Irish newspapers were beginning to boast of the special attributes and dominating presence of the Irish. Articles in diocesan papers, for example, announced that not only was the Irish
population three times larger than the German, but that the clergy
was now dominated by the Irish. According to the *Connecticut Catholic*, listings of the nation's clergy revealed that four hundred of the
clergy shared just nineteen Irish names. Irish names also recurred,
sometimes consecutively in the pages of the annual Catholic direc-
tories. By 1900, when approximately 11,000 priests served the church,
just the names beginning with *Mc* or *O'* accounted for almost one
thousand of the total names listed. By then, too, the diocese of St.
Paul claimed 45 percent of its clergy to be Irish, and Boston's Irish-
American Catholic leaders purposely diverted attention from their
diocese's Irish distinctiveness wherever possible.[2]

Throughout the United States, moreover, young Irish-American
women had chosen ministry in the church as their vocational goal.
After 1843, when the first Sisters of Mercy arrived from Carlow, Ireland, to assist Pittsburgh's bishop Michael O'Connor, scores of women
eagerly joined their ranks. New communities were started from Connecticut to California. Within one generation, for example, the Hartford community of Sisters of Mercy increased from an original group
of four pioneers to almost one hundred fifty sisters. Although many
Irish women were attracted to this congregation, other Irish women
entered native-American communities founded in America—even
some whose roots were other than Irish—transforming sisterhoods
like the French-based Sisters of Saint Joseph of Carondelet or the
Belgian Notre Dame de Namur sisters into communities generally
assumed to be Irish-American.

Still more significant to the Irish advance in the American Catholic
church, however, was a related development. By late in the century,
the advantage of numbers in clergy and religious life had clearly
translated itself into predominance among the nation's bishops as
well. In 1900, not only were two-thirds of the nation's bishops either
Irish or Irish-American, but both the staff of chancery offices and
members of diocesan boards tended to be overwhelmingly Irish as

well. In multiethnic New England, Irish-Americans claimed regional hegemony; three-fourths of the episcopal sees were headed by Irishmen. Some midwestern areas were not too far behind. Across the nation, Irish-American clergy held important positions. Moreover, their future seemed particularly secure. Irish-Americans could, for example, continue to expect preferential treatment with regard to diocesan leadership. From appointment to key pastoral assignments and chancery posts to the opportunity to formulate diocesan policy, they were the ones who had the power to mold the church decisively and set the direction for American Catholics. The result was unfortunate for other immigrants, especially the German-Americans, who managed to hold on to a few leadership positions, especially in the Midwest.

The kind of interaction that occurred because of the predominance of Irish-Americans over other ethnic Catholics was perhaps the most distinct feature of the American Catholic Church in its second century. This new situation influenced attitudes concerning the role that American Catholics should assume in the United States as well as within the Roman Catholic Church. It became the reference point by which Protestant Americans viewed the prospects of Catholicism within the United States. Because Irish-Americans particularly nourished the American characteristics of the church, moreover, Catholic policy and practice would be along American lines. The earlier provincial and plenary councils had already demonstrated the impact of Irish leadership in this as well as other matters. The first of the provincial councils (1829) would not even have met have it not been for the immigrant bishop John England; his insistence upon developing an American church along democratic principles has already been noted. At the 1866 plenary council, it was Irish-Americans who led the debates concerning the direction the church should take in the postbellum world; the same was true when the question of papal infallibility arose during the First Vatican Council, held in Rome between 1869–1870. Two prominent Irish-Americans, Saint Louis's Peter R. Kenrick (1806–1896) and Little Rock's Edward Fitzgerald (1833–1907) were among the American bishops who opposed the concept; Fitzgerald was one of only two bishops present at the worldwide council to vote against the proposal. By 1884, Irish-American hegemony among U.S. Catholics was secure. When Rochester's Bishop Bernard John McQuaid (1823–1909) reviewed the history of the Catholic church in the United States at the Vatican Council, these words seemed only natural: "Of all the peoples of Europe they (the Irish) were the best fitted to open the way for religion in a new country."[3]

Despite their ability to dominate, however, Irish-Americans could not always control church affairs without precipitating a struggle. In particular, their announced desire to adapt to American ways produced tensions within the multiethnic church at the turn of the century. Abetted by certain German-American and French-Canadian prelates and clergy, Roman officials sought clarification of American views supposedly championed by a number of leading Irish-Americans. Both for theological reasons and because of complaints received from ethnic-minority Catholics, an apostolic delegate was dispatched from Rome to investigate so-called modernist tendencies and allegations of disregard for the newest members of the church. Both of these charges had been directed especially against certain Irish-American church leaders, including John Ireland and John J. Keane. By 1899, Leo XIII added his voice of concern through a papal document, *Testem Benevolentiae*. From that moment on, when Americanism began to be treated as a phantom heresy, American bishops began to concentrate on their policies with respect to European immigrant minorities. Despite the public humiliation the investigation and subsequent papal letter occasioned, however, Irish-American hegemony within the American church did not seem in any way weakened by Rome's correction. Those who emphasized the importance of developing the church along American lines simply retreated to safer and more solid ground, demonstrating greater restraint in expressing publicly views that could be designated theologically suspect.

Irish-Americans continued to have critics among Americans as well. Their growing power and presence in the workplace and in both national and local political arenas rankled many Protestants. The unavoidable fact of Irish ethnicity and its ever-growing presence became—apart from its implications with regard to other minority Catholics—a greater source of animosity, especially after the 1880s, prompting nativist employers and politicians alike once again to lash out against the church. In 1884, for example, the Democratic party as the haven of Catholics was nationally harangued as the party of "rum, Romanism, and rebellion." This, in turn, inspired another upsurge of anti-Catholicism, formally organized in 1887 as the American Protective Association (APA) and directed against "Irishmen and Catholics."[4] Generally antiforeign in sentiment, members of the APA in Massachusetts, New York, and many areas of the Midwest and West directed most of their animus at Irish-American voters, workers, and officeholders. Appropriately, Irish-Catholic newspapers throughout the nation responded as if the Irish alone were the Catholics under attack. Fortunately this surge of anti-Catholicism gradually subsided, as reasonable discourse prevailed, economic conditions improved, and political concerns shifted to international events.

For a variety of reasons, then, Irish-American church leaders were in an extremely vulnerable position as the twentieth century approached. But no situation was to prove more problematic, in the long run, than the internal challenge to their leadership that inevitably resulted from the rapid demographic changes in the membership and the growing disillusionment and frustration of "other Catholics" concerning their future and status within the church. The Americanism that the Irish leadership had espoused was to be sorely tested during this crisis. In effect, as Catholic immigration shifted, with immigrants increasingly coming from southern and eastern Europe (by 1907, 80.7 percent of newcomers derived from these areas), Irish-American leaders had to avoid two pitfalls: they somehow had to convey sufficient respect for American traditions to assuage non-Catholic Americans, yet not alarm Rome, while at the same time they had to incorporate the massive immigration of new Catholics. At this point, however, all too often embarrassment over the image that immigrants were projecting, compounded by the real difficulties of dealing with newcomers, overwhelmed Irish-Americans. How they would incorporate the million or more Catholics who immigrated in each decade between the years 1880 and 1920 became, ultimately, the most important test of their leadership. No longer could they resolve the problem of immigration in the manner they had in the pre–Civil War era.

Mostly from the impoverished farms and ghettos of Italy or the lands controlled by Russia and Austria-Hungary, the newest Catholic exodus was to prove the greatest dilemma to Irish-American Catholic leaders in the new century. Although Catholicism was predominant as an American church because of the sheer numbers of new members, Irish-Catholics felt required to search for suitable ways to surmount the disruption caused by the massive onslaught of poor, often illiterate, alien membership. In their attempt to solve this crisis of multinational European immigration, Irish-Americans finally had to forsake any desire to reinforce identification of the church as American. Relying on a variety of strategies, they first stressed the need to uphold the principle of accommodation. This form of adaptation to American ways was to point the church in the direction fostering separate, but equal, churches—territorial and national parishes. It was a decision that clearly resulted in a kind of Balkanization of the church; as it encouraged ethnic differentiation, it also created a whole panoply of new problems.

As the Catholic church expanded in the early twentieth century, particularly in the Northeast and Midwest, the urban landscape took on a drastically different appearance. The original Catholic parishes stood within the heart of the city; these were still staffed primarily by Irish-American priests who continued to care for all Catholics of a given area. But by 1900, second, third, and fourth generation territorial parishes had also been established; so too different national, ethnic churches had been organized, often only blocks apart from each other. Within these highly concentrated areas, clergy of various ethnic backgrounds provided spiritual care according to the special needs of Catholics. An array of buildings and organizations, including churches, rectories, schools, and social clubs, gave testimony to the variety of peoples and services. Side by side, the different aims and needs of all Catholic groups were pursued and addressed. Although this multiplication of parishes tended to confuse observers, it legitimized the concept of ethnic distinctiveness and enhanced the role that various minority Catholics played within the church.

A second consequence of the policy of accommodation was the competitive struggles among priests or between priests and their people or their bishops. The public face of the Catholic church betrayed a divisiveness in this exposure of its vulnerability. Because these changes were occurring at a time when Catholic leaders still battled with Protestants in defense of their faith, dissension could center around institutions deliberately established to protect the Catholic faith, namely, schools, orphanages, or hospitals; thus, a Catholic separatism developed during this period. Any sense of unity or Americanness that had characterized early Catholic development in the United States became blurred. Controversies over public versus parochial schools or over questions of loyalty to the nation in times of crises, even with regard to church doctrine, took on ethnic overtones and affected Catholic unity itself. Further, the internal discord whet nativist appetites, prompting a resurgence of anti-Catholicism.

The second century of American Catholicism witnessed the steady move toward this kind of separatist, ethnic Catholicism. Especially in the decades at the turn of the century, the U.S. Catholic church became clearly identified as an immigrant church, an ethnically layered institution. If ethnicity had in the past occasioned local or diocesan disputes—one group sometimes bristling about their treatment at the hands of either pastor or bishop—now a pattern of actions and reactions between minority Catholics and their bishop could produce more lasting and more widespread consequences. Aware of the potential for discord and scandal, secular newspapers, in particular, became attuned to rumors and published reports of the conflicts that arose among Catholics. In these confused times, such disputes might long remain unresolved; episodes hung on for years, until either bishop or sympathetic priest managed a breakthrough. To the end, neither bishop nor the leaders of an ethnic minority knew whether their attempts to resolve issues would achieve harmony. Sometimes staged battles occurred. These could erupt within a parish or between parishioners and their bishop. In the background, rival clergy might foment trouble, but seldom took the blame. Almost always, bishop and church were the final scapegoat. One can, for example, hear the frustration experienced by Milwaukee's Archbishop Frederick X. Katzer (1844–1903) when, relatively early in a series of confrontations, he wrote to one of his troublesome priests: "Every individual makes mistakes, even a bishop. But I made a very large mistake when I accepted you into the diocese." But one can also understand the emotions of Wenceslaus Kruszka, the clergyman whom the bishop addressed. In bitter words, this embattled Polish immigrant priest later complained to Katzer: "It is the twelfth year that I am oppressed [by being left in a stifling pastoral assignment]. . . . Don't wonder then, I have a bitter feeling of 'no confidence' in you. . . . Every oppressor is guilty not only of the wrong he does but of the evil to which he inclines the heart of the oppressed."[5]

In the "separate but equal" world of the territorial and national parishes, the Catholic church continued its growth as an American institution. In the south, the segregated parish for blacks became the obvious parallel. Regardless of the degree to which they were able to adapt to the American environment, ethnically diverse Catholics progressed within isolated worlds in which more than one set of loyalties could prevail. In the civic arena, also, they interacted in diverse ways: they voted, but not as a bloc; they volunteered for military service in times of war; some headed labor unions or struck for just wages. In the privacy of their church and home, they worked to improve the quality of their cultural and spiritual lives, especially regarding the education of their children. If they were allowed some say in the development of their church, they responded by raising money for the needs of the parish, offering their labor generously, and collecting for a wide variety of designated missionary funds. They donated funds for the Indian and Negro missions; for victims of earthquake, fire, or financial disaster; even to aid in the development of a center for higher education at the Catholic University of America. However, ethno-cultural projects always carried the day. In ethnically specific institutions Catholics were assured special adaptations with regard to the conferring of the sacraments or the celebration of liturgical ceremonies; they could enjoy their own festivals and social activities; or they could devise curricula for their schools. Sometimes virtually nothing differentiated their Catholic activities. Total acceptance of the doctrines and practices of the American church, as verbalized through the bishops of the diocese, provided the unifying element of their Catholic membership.

While national organizations and societies provided a larger frame of reference for ethnic groups, parishes remained the center of social life for American Catholics. With close-knit communities, ethnic Catholics, regardless of their relative numbers, functioned within these citadels of worship, devotion, and culture. With Irish-Americans formulating decisions on the diocesan level and managing the more prestigious territorial parishes and ethnic-minority pastors energetically committing themselves to maintain the religious culture within their own parish institutions, the church offered a rich diversity of traditions to American religious culture. It presented an interacting system, capable of coordination, yet just as able to function separately, especially with regard to charities, educational plans, and even evangelizing. By being allowed to maintain religious loyalties through different cultural traditions, Catholics were assured twin securities within the church: acceptance and separateness. Immigrants and those of succeeding generations who wished to maintain the same degree of separateness were free to choose this way of relating to the American Catholic church. But they bore the responsibility for translating their ethnic loyalties into a united stance and for weaving their communal fabric into that of the larger church. It was also up to the bishops of the dioceses to assist Catholics along this path. Unity and uniqueness remained hallmarks of the church.

Judging from the overall record of Catholic achievement in the United States, the efforts of both Irish-American leaders and ethnic minorities were successful in the second century of Catholic development in the United States. As cultural differences multiplied, the realization grew that it was possible for differing perspectives to cohere on behalf of unified Catholic ventures and in essential matters of faith and practice. Since Catholics shared similar attitudes, especially with regard to sin and sanctity, they had little trouble expressing the same message, each according to his own ethnic perspective. Whenever some breach loomed over administrative matters, one could appeal for unity in these terms. This is certainly one reason why both episcopal and clerical leadership gathered strength during these years and a hierarchical model of the church (one in which the authority of church leaders was emphasized) gained greater acceptability. Such a model found ready support among both Irish and minority leaders, albeit for different reasons. In the long run, sensitivity to parochial needs may have been the chief reason for allowing the development of "separate but equal" worlds, but these choices were as much motivated by the desire to strengthen the church by not allowing unity to be eroded. Bishops and clergy required Catholics to remember their obligations to overcome any separateness that would undercut that sense of oneness.

Both Irish-American and minority leaders found that fostering the common elements of Catholic faith and practice was an excellent solution to the problems that cultural diversity could raise. They encouraged every Catholic practice that enhanced the sense of unity. Thus, for example, they became enthusiastic about the value of conducting parish missions. Adopted in many parishes throughout the nation, missions could provide, among other things, common models of behavior and devotion for the laity. A common theme taken up in missions in both territorial and national parishes and discussed in mission prayer books was the importance of the priest and the authority invested in the clergy. That this concept was valued by immigrant Catholic clergy and was found acceptable by their congregations can be inferred from the support given missions among Irish-American and especially German and Polish Catholics. The following assessment of the nature of authority within the church, by the Resurrectionist preacher Vincent Barzynski, would have rung true in almost every early-twentieth-century American Catholic parish:

> If you desire to work in the name of God, pay heed to the words of Christ. . . ; if you labor for Christ, then listen to Peter; . . . if you want to work in Peter's name, obey the Pope; . . . if you wish to work in the Pope's name, obey the bishop. . . ; if you wish to obey the bishop, then, you must obey your pastor, for the bishop gave you only one pastor.[6]

These words are echoed in a directive from a handbook for parishioners that was issued by the heavily German archdiocese of Milwaukee in 1907:

> The Church is not a republic or democracy, but a monarchy. . . . All her authority is from above and rests in her hierarchy. . . . While the faithful of the laity have divinely given rights to receive all the blessed ministrations of the Church, they have absolutely no right whatsoever to rule and govern.[7]

The spelling out of rules and regulations to docile parishioners was, furthermore, a widely accepted pattern among American Catholic clergy. Not only was this approach adopted from diocese to diocese, but pastors within both territorial and ethnic parishes followed similar patterns, freely directing the etiquette of their members or even deciding upon the criterion for parish membership. Much of this was accomplished through clubs, confraternities, and parish associations organized as convenient vehicles to reinforce parish discipline. Groups such as the Children of Mary or the Sodality provided excellent ways to bring parishioners together. Young women and men joined these or other societies in large numbers, attended instructions, received the sacraments often as a group, and supported numerous Catholic projects. The core of most of these organizations was attention to ceremonial detail. In the case of young women, for example, much importance was placed upon such externals as the wearing of white dresses, veils, and the medals of the association; for young men, honors were conveyed by the privilege of close association with the priest, such as that had while serving at mass, leading processions, or participating in novenas or other ceremonies.

In the ethnic parish, solidarity was further enhanced through elaborate ceremonies or by systems that regulated parish behavior and support. For the Polish, for example, the practice of paying dues was carefully monitored and combined with the recording of attendance at the sacraments. But colorful processions, magnificent displays, or grandly staged festivals were equally essential to the cultivation of a sense of belonging. At times of special religious observance, the Polish community often tendered invitations to all Catholics within traveling distance. Sometimes, mammoth celebrations were even organized around a single event, such as the baptism of an adult. In New Britain, Connecticut, for example, the ebullient pastor of Sacred Heart Church, Lucyan Bojnowski, outdid himself on one occasion—an event that did not escape the attention of his Irish bishop. We have this account from Bojnowski's biographer:

> The Knights of Boleslaus the Brave, an honorary guard similar to the Knights of Columbus, founded by Father Bojnowski in 1895, joined the Society of Saint Stanislaus and its choir in Meriden, Connecticut, and together they marched before the churches, . . . along the way being joined in comradeship by the Lithuanian Society of Saint Joseph and its choir, and the German Society of St. Peter. All of these Societies and choirs then marched to the New Britain passenger terminal where they were in turn joined by the Polish of Union City, Connecticut. Upon the arrival at the terminal of Bishop Michael Tierney and his retinue . . . the entire throng then marched to Saint Mary's Church on Myrtle Street. . . . The high point of the mass was the newly baptized Mary Ann Gegendora's approach to the communion rail, and the sermon delivered by Bishop Tierney.[8]

For Lithuanian parishes, art, music, and literature were key elements of ethnic identification. But integration into the American fabric was also pursued. To achieve this, much attention was paid to the value of the spoken and written word. On the parish level, paternalistic sermons became an especially important means of forging a sense of American Catholic community, while the establishment of printing presses and the publishing of both local and national papers became another means of educating the Lithuanian immigrant community. From parish to parish among Lithuanians, pastors assumed they had the right to dictate norms of conduct and behavior; they gave sermons, which often became harangues, or dispensed advice through columns in newspapers, addressing impressionable immigrants on such personal aspects of life as how to dress modestly, of what good citizenship consisted, or the evils of drink. Acceptable behavior, it was felt, was one way in which the Lithuanian-American could impress American leaders and become more united to the Catholic community in general.

Finally, there were concerted efforts on the part of a number of the Irish-American clergy or minority pastors to develop some sense of integration among Catholics through spiritual or devotional events or ceremonies. This was best accomplished at the highpoints of seasonal devotion. During Holy Week, for example, many Catholics were encouraged to visit at least seven churches, several of which would likely represent a distinct ethnicity, as a sign of shared grief and repentance. Corpus Christi processions were another expression of faith that were carried out commonly or in parallel parish ceremonies, thus demonstrating universality of belief. Furthermore, although each ethnic group seemed to favor certain heavenly advocates for their intercessory power, there were saints, like Jude or Ann, that every ethnic group readily claimed. With the passage of time, one expression of devotion might tend to lose popularity over another, especially among second- and third-generation congregations. But as long as the new waves of immigrants continued, a normative piety based on European models showed that some consensus of faith prevailed among Catholics of different ethnic background. For the most part, Marian devotions, special commemorations during the seasons of Lent and Eastertide, the cult of such highly venerated saints as Saint Joseph, the veneration of relics, and certain processions and pilgrimages remained symbolically unitive. Although expressed in a form or style particular to each ethnic group, these appeals could transcend separate congregations to convey a feeling of Catholic unity.

The Knights of Columbus provided a different model for moving beyond the particularized expression of Catholic unity. Founded in 1882 by an Irish-American priest, Michael J. McGivney, it produced a strategy and a ceremonial that attracted Catholic men regardless of ethnicity. Its rapid rise as the national Catholic men's association resulted from a variety of commonsense practices and the practical wisdom of its early founders. Because they wanted their organizational ideas to appeal to Catholic immigrants in general, they chose not to emphasize the Irish roots of the association. That Catholics of other nationalities did respond to the program of mutual financial aid and brotherly assistance, as well as to its unique ceremonials, seems to indicate that the need to express Catholic, rather than ethnic, solidarity was deeply felt. Significantly, the Knights retained their "Columbian" theme; the ethnic diversity of its membership continued as a priority.

Thus, it often became the burden of Irish-Americans to bring together their divergent aims as well as those of their multiethnic membership. For the most part, Irish-Americans accomplished this well, varying or even shifting emphases if other postures better suited them. Certain of the tactics resorted to in order to accomplish this sometimes seemed contradictory. For example, Irish-American bishops occasionally imitated the strategy of dissidents by taking their cases to Rome, appealing for protection from ethnic complaints— just as they had themselves been the objects of disapproval by immigrants. In other areas of interaction, they sometimes expressed discomfort concerning the ceremony or public display of certain ethnic groups during festivals, but this did not stop them from often attending such or, more, freely adopting those parts of the ceremonies or events that best suited their needs.

At times, furthermore, the strategies used by Irish-Americans to accommodate or integrate immigrants could prove extremely alienating. This was especially the case when rhetoric did not seem to match reality. For example, Irish-Americans often spoke of the need to protect Catholic minorities and of the minorities' rights to maintain their religious traditions. Yet, as often, they would also refuse to accommodate those whose traditions impinged upon their own views of church discipline. What befell Eastern-rite Catholics at the hand of Saint Paul's archbishop, John Ireland (1838–1918), is a case at point. Ireland refused to accept the widowed Eastern-rite priest Alexis Toth into his diocese, apparently because of his disapproval of the Oriental rite's acceptance of a married clergy. The archbishop also ignored the visit of a Holy See representative sent to examine this matter, as well as the spiritual condition of Ruthenian immigrants. All this despite Ireland's insistence that "the Church in America must be, of course, as Catholic as even in Jerusalem or Rome."[9]

In the encouragement of the development of separate styles or in their appeal to internationalism, therefore, the dominant Irish-Americans were in a stronger position to champion diversity or distinctiveness. But they were also in a stronger position to choose those situations that suited their needs and that they could best understand. Depending upon the issue under discussion, then, the Irish-American leadership could either praise ethnic differences, be enriched by them, ignore their implications, or inhibit their expression.

Irish-Americans could also influence the way in which Catholics perceived American society in general. As the dominant group within the church, they had the advantage of imposing their preferences with regard to how Catholics were viewed. Thus, for example, even the development of the nineteenth-century version of liberalism among U.S. Catholics, and its short-lived hegemony as Americanism, can correctly be seen as influenced both by the American religious environment that encouraged the Social Gospel and by the biases of the dominant Irish leadership, whose "exile" mentality often led them to find in liberalism a congenial political and religious posture. Not surprisingly, the holistic approach to social justice issues as espoused by certain German-American spokesmen was overlooked. Instead, through the rhetorical brilliance of such renowned Irish-American liberals as New York's folk-hero priest Edward McGlynn, or because of prestigious prelates such as John Ireland or John Keane, the Irish perspective prevailed. To this day, in fact, the liberal-conservative split among Catholics continues to manifest itself along lines set by the Irish-American intellectual elite of the late nineteenth century and only reluctantly supported by other ethnics in the church.

In the same way, other factors influencing the direction of U.S. Catholic ideology in the twentieth century were filtered through the dominant Irish-American expression. Chief among these was the continuing influence of individualism over community-building in a nation whose focus was becoming more and more national in scope and content. Thus, the principle of the separation of church and state, the overriding importance of political democracy with regard to church policies and strategies, as well as the creation of new roles for members (manifested by the growing power of religious congregations of women or of the laity) were all viewed according to the perspective of the Irish-American majority, which outlined the American Catholic church's distinct response. Despite the emphasis on personal individualism, however, an interest in developing national, as opposed to regional, Catholic identity was advanced.

In a wide variety of ways, therefore, Catholic perspectives became increasingly influenced by Irish-Americans. Just as labor issues had earlier engaged the pen of John T. Roddan, mid-nineteenth-century editor of *The Pilot*, so too would the Boston paper's subsequent editor, John Boyle O'Reilly, hammer away on the theme of the injustices of capitalism and racism. From other writings and lectures by churchmen such as Baltimore's Cardinal James Gibbons (1834–1921) and Catholic University's scholar and social strategist Monsignor John A. Ryan (1869–1945) came guidance on social reconstruction. Well into the twentieth century this pattern of leadership would continue. The difficulty of Catholics in choosing between Germany or Great Britain after the outbreak of the European war in 1914, for example, was complicated by the ancient Irish antipathy for the English. The wholehearted response of Catholics to their subsequent entrance on the side of the Allies reflected Irish-American willingness to change sides out of loyalty to their adopted land—a position collectively immortalized by Father Francis P. Duffy and the "Fighting Sixty-Ninth." The increased Catholic involvement in national politics in the postwar years can also be seen in terms of Irish-Catholic leadership. From popular political figures like New York's Alfred E. Smith to the more controversial figures like Michigan priest Reverend Charles E. Coughlin, Catholic leadership gave clear acknowledgment that Catholic laity and clergy wanted full participation in the nation's political life.

In church affairs, the case was as clear. Heading the nation's most important dioceses were Irish-American prelates who understood how to make American institutions work for them. These include such impressive personalities as Cardinal William O'Connell of Boston (1859–1944), who cultivated an almost princely splendor as he worked to upgrade the Catholic image, and Patrick J. Hayes of New York (1867–1938), who, as "Cardinal of Charities," also commanded influence from his chancery. And it produced as well the demanding archbishop of Philadelphia Denis J. Dougherty (1865–1951), whose nickname "God's bricklayer" emphasized his capacity to develop a diocese. Under Dougherty, Philadelphia achieved an amazingly complex institutional framework that included ninety-two parishes, eighty-nine parish schools, a number of diocesan high schools, academies, orphanages, schools for the disabled, and institutions of higher learning.

Not that the only major voices of authority and prestige in the American Catholic church were of Irish extraction. Chicago's Cardinal George W. Mundelein (1872–1939) heads the list of important exceptions. But the predominance of Irish-Americans in episcopal and clerical leadership positions produced a self-perpetuating system. At center stage, they exercised their leadership in a style that reflected the cultural values of their Irish forbears and emphasized their Americanizing preference. Whether they galvanized Catholics to support a Boy's Town, impressed them with football's "Fighting Irish," or made them aware of neighborhood problems in a "Bells of St. Mary's" world, Irish-Americans led Catholics—or so it was perceived—in confronting every issue. In fact, even for those Catholics who did not identify as ethnic Catholics or as members of national parishes, there were consequences resulting from Irish influence. Being raised in a neighborhood, territorial parish and attending its schools often conferred an implicit Irish mentality, a kind of "hibernization," upon Catholics regardless of nationality.

Perhaps it was because of this overarching Irish-American influence regarding both Catholic and American values that well into the twentieth century contemporaries tended to mistake the American Catholic church for a monolithic institution. Perhaps it is for this same reason that recent observers of the church have dismissed the degree to which insufficient attention to the implications of ethnicity produced negative consequences. Some have, in fact, applauded the achievement of the American Catholic church—and its Irish-American leadership—in handling the implications of ethnic difference so efficiently and gracefully. They have suggested that the pluralism of the American Catholic church today is a gift of Irish-American genius that was instinctive, pragmatic, unself-conscious, and unreflective. They have argued that, despite the church's occasional errors of insensitivity to minority groups—even its occasional antiethnic stands—Catholic pluralism in the United States was a success. But others do not see ethnic Catholicism as such a "breathtaking achievement."[10] In fact, to the ethnic historian, it still seems too soon to evaluate the overall process of the integration of the past century's European immigrants. Moreover, it seems much too early to assume that this pluralism was successful. As most students of American Catholicism admit, one must recognize that there are still some rather negative vestiges of ethnic pluralism within the church.

Much about the ethnic factor in the development of American Catholicism remains unclear. Have, in fact, the right questions really been raised about the manner in which European Catholics were accommodated within the American church? Do we yet know enough about what really happened from diocese to diocese, parish to parish, ethnic group to ethnic group? Can we really suggest a direction for the future? There are some points of agreement, to be sure. By the end of the massive waves of European newcomers in the 1920s, the American Catholic Church had already become ethnically diverse. Since the 1950s, the newest refugees and migrants have merely added to the highly complex ethnic culture of the church. Thus, the Catholic church in the United States remains today a church that can still be readily identified as ethnic.

Furthermore, the millions of turn-of-the-century immigrants still form the core of present Catholic membership. They account for the church's ethnic base as 20 percent Italian; 16 percent Irish, 16 percent German, 16 percent Hispanic, and 12 percent Slavic, with the remaining 20 percent representing current influxes of European, American, African, and Asian minorities. Now the present membership of the church comprises the children and grandchildren of immigrants who had to grapple with the problems of providing institutions and organizations to supply its members according to their needs. Now the challenge for those who have inherited the diverse devotional and spiritual aspects of Catholic culture is to search for new ways of accommodating the latest newcomers; now church officials are called upon to learn the lessons of history so that these new waves of immigrants can be guided toward developing an even more vibrant church than the one their forebears created.

CHAPTER
5
The Irish Take Charge

*E*ven John Carroll would probably have been much dismayed to discover that, by the later decades of the nineteenth century, the Irish immigrant had come to play such a key role in shaping the American Catholic church. The first impressions that the Irish made in the pre–Civil War period upon American society in general and upon the American Catholic leaders could hardly be described as auspicious. To Americans, they were readily perceived as drunken, boisterous threats to stability and civility and feared as henchmen of a foreign power. To American and French émigré clergy they tended to stand as constant symbols of embarassment. Even, at mid-century, these "exiles" from Ireland still worried American Catholic leaders. Many were recent immigrants, willing to take on the heaviest of workloads as wood haulers, canal diggers, railroaders, miners, and stevedores. Their situations were often so desperate that death stalked them from the "coffin ships" to the tenement houses, where childhood mortality rates ran shockingly high. Andrew Greeley has written that their passage, arrival, and early ghetto homes were often horrible scenes of human misery. Increasing in numbers almost daily, they could not go unnoticed by the natives, who saw them as a "slovenly, crude people" who "seemed satisfied to live in crowded, dark, dank basements."[1] As late as 1862, a New England bishop, himself a second-generation Irish-American, described them as "generally attached to their faith . . . attentive . . . although often rude and ignorant . . . poor and generally laborers. They suffer much from the prejudice of Protestants."[2]

Had this image endured beyond the Civil War, the history of American Catholicism would probably have been extremely different.

But respectability was one of the postbellum legacies which happily befell more and more of the American Irish. Prejudice, of course, endured; but it was usually local and often trifling. Even when the Molly Maguires became involved in a series of violent labor disputes that rocked the Pennsylvania mining communities during the 1870s, for example, the general reputation of the Irish was not sullied. There were other felicitous circumstances that positively affected the Irish role in American society and in the American Catholic church. For example, by the 1860s enough Irish-Americans had risen to prominent positions in business and politics in the major urban areas of the nation to have altered the original universally negative image. New York City had already become well acquainted with such reputable lawyers and professionals at Charles O'Conor and Cornelius Heeney; Philadelphia enjoyed the presence of the textile manufacturer Dennis Kelly and the coal shipper Thomas Cahill. Working wherever the invitation presented itself, another Irish immigrant, architect Patrick Keely, had begun to provide designs for cathedrals and churches that gained him a reputation beyond Catholic circles in both the United States and Canada. Even San Francisco's Nob Hill elite were anxious to welcome the upwardly mobile Irish, and Chicago's Irish-Americans were beginning their move to more congenial neighborhoods, first to the city's South Side and then beyond in a process accelerated by the Great Fire. While a frontier church continued to struggle in the far western and southern regions of the nation under the inspiration of pioneers like Machebeuf, Mazzuchelli, and Segale, Irish-Americans continued another kind of struggle, striving to gain prestige for themselves and for their church, especially in the nation's cities.

In the postbellum world, a new sense of Irish self-importance and strong faith was apparent from coast to coast. Newspapers, sermons, and lectures were constant reminders to Catholics and non-Catholics alike of Irish aims and expectations. A June 1863 issue of the *Boston Pilot* concluded that not only were the Puritans in fast decline in New England, but the Irish were on the rise, because of their "great health, vigor, strength and purity." New Englanders, its editor suggested, "are marked by abortionism in every stage of uterine growth" but "the Catholicizing and Hibernicizing of the land and the disappearance of the Puritan are proceeding with swiftness." Three thousand miles away, San Francisco's *Monitor* would echo similar words in 1869. "Irishmen," the editor wrote, "have made themselves a position here fully equal to that of any other nationality. . . . Catholicity has struck as firm a root in California as in any part of the United States not including Maryland or Louisiana, and, as probably over a third, if not a full half, of the State belong to her fold, Catholics need not fear." The editor's words were borne out by reality: Irishman Frank

McCoppin had been elected mayor in 1867; during the same decade, several Irish immigrants had taken seats in the United States Senate; and within the next decade, the city's schools, hospitals, and social services had already become highly influenced by Irish initiation and continued effort.[3]

In many other burgeoning areas of the nation, church spokesmen easily attributed much of the growth of the Catholic Church to the Irish. In 1875, New York's Cardinal John McCloskey (1810–1885) commented on the "glorious" Saint Patrick's Cathedral: "Even now, the noblest ecclesiastical building ever erected in this City, or in the United States, is slowly going up on Fifth Avenue, and where does the money for it come from? Largely out of the pockets of poor Irish servants, some of whom we have known to give as much as five or eight dollars a month out of their wages to this one special project." The same double-edged compliment would be repeated time and time again as the donations of Irish-Americans helped build magnificent cathedrals from coast to coast.[4]

Many even saw the Irish immigrant's role in the United States as a divinely sent "spiritual errand into the wilderness," one that was specially ordained for the Irish alone. Rochester's Bishop Bernard J. McQuaid (1823–1909) dwelt on this in a speech he delivered during the 1884 sessions of the Third Plenary Council:

> The first immigrants coming in large numbers were from Ireland. Of all the people of Europe they were the best fitted to open the way for religion in a new country. Brave by nature, inured to poverty and hardship, just released from a struggle unto death for the faith, accustomed to the practice of religion in its simplest forms, cherishing dearly their priests whom they had learned to support directly, actively engaged in building humble chapels on the sites of ruined churches and in replacing altars, they were not appalled by the wretchedness of religious equipments and surroundings in their new homes on this side of the Atlantic.[5]

And while admitting that German-Americans had always been important contributors to the building of the church, McQuaid reserved his highest accolades for his Irish ancestors: "All the other nationalities of Europe can kneel at their feet," he pronounced, in reference to both the Irish and the Germans, "and imbibe salutary and profitable lessons."[6]

Yet, perhaps no other prelate sang the praises of the Irish to the extent that Peoria's Bishop John Lancaster Spalding (1840–1916) did in his book *The Religious Mission of the Irish People*, published in 1880. He argued in his introduction:

> The general truth is that the Irish Catholics are the most important element in the Church of this country. . . . Were it not for Ireland Catholicism

would today be feeble and non-progressive in England, America, , and Australia. . . . The Irish have made the work . . . possible and effective . . . have given . . . a vigor and cohesiveness which enables it to assimilate the most heterogeneous elements, and without which it is not at all certain that the vast majority of Catholics emigrating hither from other lands would not have been lost to the Church. . . . No other people . . . could have done for the Catholic faith in the United States what the Irish people have done. . . . No other people had received the same providential training for this work; of no other people had God required such proofs of love.[7]

According to other contemporaries, the "generous Celt" had indeed accomplished much since his first impoverished days on American soil. If they were not quite as willing as McQuaid or Spalding to suggest that the greatest credit for building the American Catholic church should be given to the Irish, they were aware of the strong advance of the church under Irish leadership. They were also conscious of the qualities in the Irish personality that had fostered Catholic achievement in the United States. To their minds, the "exile" status which the Irish immigrant continually bemoaned in letters home had not really interfered with his advancement in America. For all practical purposes it appeared that the Irish immigrant had made himself acceptable in the United States and that it was his engaging qualities of personality that had allowed him to make the transition. His upward mobility was an indication of his ability to succeed in the most competitive business enterprises. Gregariousness, love of adventure, an even greater love of learning—especially in the fields of language and culture—an aggressive devotion to faith: all these had served the Irish immigrant well, whether he was involved in the work of the church or making his way among the working classes.

The more established Irish immigrants had, for the most part, successfully met the major challenges involving acceptance within American society. With enthusiasm, the laity had helped build and financially support their churches; in secular society they had adapted easily, assuming the economic and political values that characterized the American creed to a greater degree than any of the other Catholic immigrants. A sense of respectability that derived from self-reliance and adherence to the work ethic became as much a part of their world as it was for native-born Americans. Irish women, who had come to the United States in proportionately greater numbers than those of any other immigrant group, responded to the challenges of the new world in ways that were uniquely Irish yet uniquely American. Careers in secular and religious spheres allowed thousands of Irish women to enter into a new world of social and economic opportunity which would have subtle, long-lasting effects on generations to follow.

Wherever vocation, employment, or leisure brought them, twentieth-century Irish-Americans continued to prove their worth and find their proper place in church and society. Even if engaged in the secular sphere, however, seldom did they lose sight of their Catholic heritage. Across the nation, their ambition brought them much favorable attention. Chicago's Irish Catholics were but one example of the trend. By the 1890s, they had not only built up an impressive Catholic environment, but they had also gained political importance. They had come to dominate the central committee of Chicago's Democratic party; where the pragmatic "boodle and patronage" creed prevailed, they had become politically influential. An Irish middle class had developed; it was composed of those who had succeeded in such diverse fields as construction, brewing and distilling, undertaking, meatpacking, importing, the theater, and sports. By purchasing property in areas that had previously been Protestant strongholds, Chicago's Irish began their geographic climb to social importance as well. In these improved circumstances, they openly and enthusiastically celebrated the establishment of parishes with lavish parades featuring marching groups of military and Clan-na-Gael guards or platoons of Irish policemen. Along the same political, social, and economic lines, Irish Catholics had also found similar acceptance in the urban areas of the northeast and midwest United States.[8]

The very progress of social and economic achievement which second- or third-generation Irish-Americans began to experience, however, sometimes put them into both embarassing and conflictual situations, even with other Irish-Americans. As a result, in some cases, a divisiveness engendered by class differences began to characterize the Irish posture. Even before the turn of the twentieth century, for example, upwardly mobile Irish-Americans in Worcester, Massachusetts, had begun to question the social worth of elaborate celebrations that encouraged heavy drinking, especially the parades on Saint Patrick's Day. To improve their image, many endorsed temperance, organized new societies, and campaigned to increase their membership. Wherever possible, they cooperated with their fellow Yankees in both civic and charitable ventures. Boston's Irish were in much the same position. The more affluent dominated the church and gained a certain political respectability which often made them adopt an aloof posture toward the more recent Irish immigrants. As Donna Merwick has suggested in her study of Boston's priests, "The official Roman Catholic policy towards the ill-suited Irish immigrants in the last half of the nineteenth century was that they be slipped into Boston society like a soiled handkerchief into the back pocket." Two levels of Irish-American culture developed. Both staunchly Catholic, one was a decidedly elite, "permissive" kind of Catholic culture that later became more "Romanized" under the influence of Cardinal William O'Connell; the other remained identified as a "pre-packaged," blue-collar Catholic culture.[9]

In Philadelphia still another pattern emerged among Irish-Americans. There, some managed very early to become incorporated into the upper realms of Philadelphia's four-tiered status system. Other Irish-Americans, still closely associated with middle- or lower-class Irish, found it preferable to retain their sense of community with one another provided all were willing to acknowledge the same work ethic and goal of respectability. Two of the largest ethnic institutions that they chose to sponsor during this period were, in fact, the Irish Catholic Benevolent Union and the Catholic Total Abstinence Union. Though Catholic in name, American values were stressed: members were barraged with exhortations to work diligently, be thrifty, submit to authority, live orderly lives, and strive for personal success. By accepting these norms and standards of Protestant American culture, many of Philadelphia's Irish found a means of achieving ethnic solidarity across class lines. By the turn of the century, many of the Irish working class supported the doctrines of respectability and self-help as vigorously as did the native elite. A sense of success, rather than oppression, and of achievement, rather than exclusion, bonded the Philadelphia Irish Catholic community together.

If the Irish had seized upon the many opportunities made available to immigrants to the United States by making their mark in political, economic, and cultural spheres, their involvement in the continued development of the American Catholic church itself was especially remarkable. After 1880, Irish-Catholics were the most numerous Catholic churchgoers. Moreover, Irish-Americans accounted for more than 60 percent of the nation's episcopal leadership (even the few American cardinals, appointed before 1924, were of Irish descent). By 1900 they held all the seats of ecclesiastical power, including those of New York, Baltimore, Boston, Philadelphia, Detroit, Saint Paul, and San Francisco. Even in Saint Louis, where the German clergy outnumbered the Irish, all but one of the dozen priests raised to the episcopal ranks between 1854 and 1922 were Irish. Further, the majority of the Catholic clergy was of Irish descent; in fact, the number of Irish clergy within certain dioceses sometimes reached preponderant levels. For example, almost 90 percent of the candidates to the priesthood in several New England dioceses claimed Irish ancestry. Irish women responded even more quickly to the explicit call of the church to serve. A number of women's congregations that had originated in continental Europe filled their ranks to overflowing with Irish-American aspirants, and Irish based communities burgeoned.

Whether with regard to church or politics, the Irish were the first to congratulate themselves on their achievements. Especially where the church was concerned, their enthusiasm seemed to know no bounds. Their exuberance, even if tempered by pessimism and guilt, could be easily channeled into displays of eloquence before mesmerized Catholic congregations or in rebuttal against the Protestant challenge. Their fierce loyalty, deep faith, and dogged trust could lead others to commit themselves unstintingly to the development of the rapidly growing church. With a charm which engaged others, a great gift of humor, and an innate sense of the dramatic, they could negotiate the best arrangements not only with Protestants but among other Catholics as well. Their resourcefulness, moreover, could easily support their intellectual gifts. In a highly innovative and often confusing American environment, they seemed the right people at the right time to tackle the job of organizing the American Catholic church.

In many ways, the Irish saw the challenge of building the church as one especially close to their own hearts. As victims of political and religious oppression in their homeland, they had long before come to emphasize their Catholicism over their Irish identity. No wonder, then, that they seemed to attach themselves so wholeheartedly to a church that was in need of cohesiveness and direction. As they became clearly dominant numerically, both in personnel and membership, a multitude of Irish clergy and laypeople utilized their special status in the church to influence it according to their own vision. Like a network of successful brokers, Irish-American "business bishops" and enterprising pastors nationwide efficiently administered the institutions of the church. Outside of the few traditionally German dioceses in the Midwest, they gained power and influence among American Catholics. If the antebellum Catholic church had achieved a certain balance among ethnic groups, following the war it would operate instead from this Irish-influenced perspective for one hundred years. Their important place secured by that time, Irish leaders assumed the roles of mediators between the church and American society, proclaimers of policy and practice for their church, innovators of programs, personnel recruiters, decision makers, and official spokespersons for the church.

Several major consequences resulted from the pervasive presence of Irish-Americans in church affairs. One was their effect upon the institutional development of the church. From the time of their initial involvement, Irish-Americans manifested a paternalistic, even controlling, attitude toward the development of the local church. Their first concerns for Catholics were simple enough: members of gathered Catholic communities should be provided with a pastor and a place of worship. Almost as soon as a Catholic congregation, whether specifically ethnic or not, could be defined, negotiations for these were commenced. Under an authorized priest, church property was purchased and a church erected. Continued financial solvency was monitored as a sign of the healthy development of the parish. The successful parish also reflected Irish preferences with regard to community cohesiveness, relationship with the pastor or other priests, and artistic and liturgical tastes; it served as well to symbolize Catholic presence in an area. Only if the church could be established firmly within a community did the Irish-American leadership encourage other institutions, such as schools, orphanages, or other social or health agencies. When ethnic minorities insisted upon developing their own institutions, Irish-American church leaders could adapt to these new parish constellations provided the same measures were taken to guarantee the continuity of spiritual care and financial well-being. Especially by accepting ethnic diversity within the pattern they set, the predominantly Irish-American hierarchy accommodated immigrants. In their promotion of this concept through the establishment of separate national parishes with their satellite institutions, they safeguarded the faith of immigrants and insured their cultural cohesiveness in general even as they preserved for themselves the appropriate symbols of authority.

By validating their own preferences regarding the centrality of the parish, the role of the pastor as the delegate of the bishop, and the division of labor within parishes and dioceses, Irish-Americans set a lasting pattern of American Catholic development. In their eyes, final decision making belonged to the bishop and to his authorized appointee, the pastor of the local parish. According to a widely accepted description offered in 1884 by Bishop McQuaid and shared especially by Irish-Americans, the pastor was the sole resource of his parish: he was liturgical leader, confessor, teacher, counselor, social worker, administrator, youth and recreational director, and more. The degree to which both parish and diocese would be further developed depended upon the personal talents of pastor and bishop and their continued ability to lead their people toward expansion. In this regard, the Irish-American clergy seemed particularly well prepared. Early they mastered an ability to take charge of their overwhelmingly Irish congregations. Through a greater show of willpower, they gained the respect of their parishioners. Setting their dramatic, oratorical style to good use, they presented their congregations with a commanding presence that tempered intense loyalty to the faith with an iron determination to pursue their American goals.[11]

The authority of Irish-American priests was further confirmed by the status bestowed upon them by those whose work became integral to the development of both parish and church. Wherever possible, for example, the pastor recruited coworkers—especially dedicated corps of religious women—who would not threaten his primacy. These became for him his alter-ego; they worked in areas of education and health care that were considered essential to the development of a resourceful Catholic population. It was always clear to those who worked with the pastor, however, that their task was one of assistance or collaboration in the priest's ministry; it did not encompass any sharing of his authority. John Ireland's words at the time of the fiftieth anniversary of the Congregation of Sisters of Saint Joseph confirm that this attitude was characteristic of Irish-American clerical thinking. Perhaps not fully conscious of the implications of his words of praise, Ireland reminded the very congregation of which his sister had been major superior:

> The Catholic Church understands woman's soul, and draws all her energies into its service. . . . This, on the part of the Church, is supreme wisdom. . . . To its sisterhoods, the church commits a very large part of its work; and so effectively do they perform their task that they take rank among the Church's choicest and most valuable agencies.[10]

Within this energetic circle of Irish-American Catholic activity, priest, sisters, brothers, and laity collaborated—with the pastor always retaining the voice of authority. Sisters performed the yeoman's task; they were unrivaled "agencies" for good. Regularly, their corporate praise was sung. Lay associations assured financial and spiritual support; they too could expect both approval and nurturance. But it was to the bishop and the priest, and to continued vocations to the priesthood and religious life—a call to which Irish-Americans seemed particularly drawn—that Catholics knew they must turn for reassurance about the future of their church.

As twentieth-century church personnel became more conscious of business techniques and practices, the network of parochial and diocesan arrangements developed into even more tight-knit, complex, efficient institutions. The priorities these received and the degree to which each was fostered also depended upon Irish-American perspectives. Thus, the building of schools was important to Irish-Americans, but their reasons for establishing them were different from the singleminded explanations presented by other ethnic minorities, namely that schools were necessary in order to nourish the faith within a particular culture. For Irish-Americans, the concern for schools was predicated on the degree to which public schools had been overly influenced by Protestant or secular values. Moreover, it was only when Catholic education could not be obtained within the family setting (preferably at the mother's knee) that the concept of schools was strongly advanced. In fact, alternatives to schools, including parish educational services, cultural and reading groups, newspapers, or lecture series were often advanced as equally appropriate Catholic strategies. Fearing that the faith of their young people might be threatened, some Irish leaders, such as Archbishop John Purcell of Cincinnati or John Hughes of New York, pastors like Thomas Scully of Cambridge, Massachusetts, or religious women like Mary Frances Clarke, founder of the Sisters of Charity of the Blessed Virgin Mary, did gain reputations as Catholic leaders committed to the fight for parochial schools. At the same time, there were other Irish-American clergymen, including Saint Paul's John Ireland or New York's Edward McGlynn and Richard L. Burtsell, who found it just as agreeable to downplay the need for parochial schools or to develop cooperative plans with public school systems. Once assured that their children would, in some way, receive sufficient religious education, the Irish seemed more easily able to divert their concern for schools toward other social issues than the German-Americans or other ethnic minorities, who remained totally committed to the establishment of parochial schools.

When it came to the inauguration of schools of higher learning, however, Irish enthusiasm tended to run high. The early nineteenth century had set its own style with the establishment of such colleges as New York state's Fordham and Saint Bonaventure's and the Midwest's universities at Saint Louis or Notre Dame. Colleges would expand and proliferate in the twentieth century; a network of twenty-six Jesuit colleges alone began to stretch across the United States. Endowments often bore the names of Irish millionaires, and the student bodies were overwhelmingly Irish. For the first time, too, several colleges were organized for the education of Catholic women; Trinity College in Washington, D.C., founded at the turn of the century, was the first in this line of colleges designated to issue degrees to women and strongly backed by Irish-American funding. Some of its support had come from John Lancaster Spalding, who had earlier been responsible for the founding, in 1889, of Catholic University, a pontifical university in Washington, D.C., begun in 1889. The early funding of Catholic University was substantially Irish-American; from the start, it received its strongest support from prominent Irish-American churchmen and laypersons. During the early years of most of these institutions, their faculties and student bodies were overwhelmingly middle-class Irish-American.

Other Catholic institutions also became more structured under Irish-American leadership. The founding of Catholic hospitals, together with specialized health-care facilities such as orphanages and homes for the elderly, accelerated at the turn of the century. By then, Sisters and Daughters of Charity, Sisters of Saint Joseph, and Sisters of Mercy had already begun to staff many of these hospitals; as three of the largest congregations of women, they contributed substantially to the development of health-care facilities nationally. Furthermore, by this period all three had become, for all practical purposes, Irish-American communities. Much of the large-scale planning and organization had received the approval of the nation's Irish-American hierarchy. Under several administrative geniuses who headed key dioceses, health and social services multiplied. The actual work was brought speedily forward largely with the financial assistance of Catholic millionaires, such as Philadelphia's Martin Maloney, the papal countess Genevieve Garvan Brady, or San Francisco's James D. Phelan. This is not to say that ethnic-minority congregations were not integral parts of the development of health-care systems as well. The Sisters of Charity of Saint Augustine, Franciscan, Benedictine, and Dominican Sisters, the Sisters of Saint Mary, the Sisters of Saint Casimir, and the Missionaries of the Sacred Heart represent only a partial list of the religious women who initiated and developed infirmaries and hospitals. Mother Cabrini's Columbus Hospital, founded in 1892 in New York, and subsequent orphanages and hospitals that she established in Chicago, Denver, New Orleans, San Francisco, and Seattle were outstanding examples of the kinds of projects to which every immigrant group devoted its energies. So, too, in the West, were the accomplishments of Mother Joseph of the Sisters of Providence, who saw to the establishment of fifteen hospitals. Still, like the bishops who received the accolades of the communities served by these facilities, it was the rising middle-class or wealthy Catholic laity, largely Irish or German, whose generous donations made these endeavors financially possible and who were the first to congratulate themselves for the overall Catholic accomplishments. Because of these committed Catholics, the institutional church was well on its way to its most heralded decades in the middle of the twentieth century. Through the joint efforts of clergy, religious, and laity, a maze of diocesan and national organizations had been made to fit smoothly into the American fabric, guaranteeing institutional scope and social importance to the Catholic church.

A second consequence of Irish-American dominance in the American Catholic church was the sense of preferred status it implicitly bestowed. This preference, in effect, encouraged Irish-Americans to view themselves as the official commentators on Catholic affairs and the spokespersons for the church. As a result, an Irish perspective tended to inform every vital religious, social, or political issue of the day. Not only did an Irish mentality dictate certain viewpoints and choices, but it became the source of Catholic truth whether addressed from the pulpits of the most prominent parishes or through the national Catholic or secular media. This advantage could, of course, also have its drawbacks. For example, the alignment of the sides of a philosophical or theological debate within the church might become influenced, or even distorted, by ethnic bias. In the case of the highly publicized Americanist controversy, the liberal majority just happened to be composed, for the most part, of leading Irish-American prelates who had done much to initiate an Americanist rhetoric. Not coincidentally these liberals found that some of their most vocal dissenters were German-American conservatives who were especially fearful that the cultural dimensions of the argument would sabotage their efforts to safeguard the faith of immigrants. One could not argue that the sides of the Americanist controversy were clearly drawn on ethnic grounds. Still, it is impossible to ignore the impressive roster of Irish-American leaders on one side and the German-American challengers to this so-called American heresy on the other.

Similarly the American Catholic approach to the prevailing Social Gospel rhetoric of American religious leaders was also influenced by strongly Irish sentiments concerning economic oppression and the search, by Irish-Americans for practical, often immediate, solutions to economic crises. From the nineteenth century, the cause of labor had been a particular Irish preoccupation. As early as the 1860s, Irish factory workers had aligned themselves with the Knights of Saint Crispin in Lynn, Massachusetts, and with the strikers in the coalmines of Pennsylvania; during the late 1870s, the Irish had backed Denis Kearney and the San Francisco Working Men's Party. By the 1880s, the moderate philosophy of Cardinal James Gibbons was judiciously applied to certain more radical approaches in order to insure continued church support and general American Catholic approval. Throughout every decade, there were activist priests as well as lay men and women like Terence Powderly, who headed the Knights of Labor, or Elizabeth Rogers, Leonora Barry, or Mary Kenney O'Sullivan, who were organizers and heads of local, state, or national chapters of labor unions.

Pragmatic rather than ideological about the labor issue, the Irish-American leadership tended to echo the positions enunciated by Leo XIII in his encyclical *Rerum Novarum*. Original thinkers or not, they were quick to champion the cause of labor in both word and action. Earlier espousals of social reform were given voice through the eloquent sermons of Irish-American clergy or the pen of gifted writers and editors. John Boyle O'Reilly of the *Boston Pilot* heads the list of Irish-Americans early committed to social justice causes. Twentieth-century academics such as the sociologist Father William Kerby, who became an architect of both Catholic Charities and social theory, or Monsignor John A. Ryan, whose informed programs of social reconstruction began a national trend, provided other examples of encouragement that gave structure to Irish aims. Furthermore, progressive Irish-American bishops, including Cincinnati's John T. McNicholas, O. P. (1877–1950), Detroit's Cardinal Edward F. Mooney (1882–1958), Chicago's Bernard J. Sheil (1888–1969), and San Antonio's Robert E. Lucey (1891–1977), provided continued leadership to sustain the cause of social justice throughout the century. Their defense of the worker encouraged the efforts of the clergy of their respective dioceses in organizing labor institutes and otherwise providing solidarity for the cause.

But particularly impressive were the many Irish-American priests whose careers revealed a commitment to social justice issues and whose influence spanned decades. Because of them, generations of Catholic laymen became involved in local and national labor movements as members and organizers. Just as the nineteenth century produced nationally prominent social-activist priests like New York's Sylvester Malone and Missouri's Cornelius O'Leary, the twentieth century had its counterparts in activist clergy: the Pennsylvanian John J. Curran, who was called the "miner's friends" because of his enthusiastic support of the United Mine Workers; Thomas H. Malone of Denver, who was a strong advocate of trade unionism; and Peter C. Yorke, who became known even before his death in 1925 as the father of the organized labor movement of San Francisco. When issues expanded to include national programs to alleviate the social and economic crises of the 1930s, other prominent Irish-Americans could still be counted on to provide leadership. The most celebrated of these was the controversial clergyman Charles E. Coughlin of Royal Oak, Michigan, whose series of weekly radio broadcasts and lectures was heard without fail by millions of Catholics. Less well known were the many priests and bishops who would develop labor schools within their dioceses during the 1930s and 1940s or otherwise encourage social justice plans. Among these were Joseph Donnelly, a priest and later auxiliary bishop of the archdiocese of Hartford, Connecticut, whose assistance to the migrant farm-workers and to their charismatic leader, Cesar Chavez, was acknowledged as crucial in gaining nationwide sympathy for their cause. There can be little doubt that it was the priestly education and training received in universities such as Catholic University or Fordham that had, in large measure, given these strong-principled and often charismatic clergy support and encouragement enough to address a broader American audience.

Still another consequence of Irish predominance was the opportunity it provided Irish-Americans to influence Catholic modes of behavior, including devotional styles and attitudes. Thus, both liturgical worship and prayer reflected the Irish preference for a somewhat plain ceremonial style—but one which, nevertheless, always made room for oratorical display. (Fulton J. Sheen was, perhaps, the most well known for his Irish-American verbal skills; his ability to command the attention of an audience wider than just members of the Catholic faith makes for a legendary chapter in the history of American radio and television.) Typical, however, of the simple liturgical style were the examples set in the Irish-dominated dioceses in the Northeast, where the congregation remained silent, and the sermon often droned on. Especially in parishes where Irish-American clergy and laity dominated, such an atmosphere could cast a spell that demoralized other ethnic Catholics. In fact, if it were not for the German-American predominance in the Midwest and the tenacious retention of ethnic ceremony among southern and eastern Europeans throughout the United States, the same plainness of style might have become standard in the United States, casting the same monotonous spell upon Catholic life everywhere. Paulist Father Walter Elliott's earlier comment that "catacombical public worship" suited Saint Paul's John Ireland because he "was a Celtic American through and through" described a stance that persisted well beyond Ireland's episcopate.[11] Even para-liturgical services, such as novenas, benediction, or the celebration of feast days which were held in Irish-American parishes reflected the same overly formal, repetitive pattern. These, too, lacked the spontaneity, beauty, and charm upon which the devotional life among other ethnic groups could easily depend.

Furthermore, Irish-American influence could and did exert a tremendous impact even upon general Catholic attitudes toward morality. Thus, the Irish penchant for certain rigid Jansenistic interpretations of morality influenced Catholics—this was often a consequence of the massive parochial education directed by religious teachers of Irish background. Both in the classroom and from the pulpit, generations of Catholics learned about sin and guilt or, for example, how salvation was all too easily lost because of sins of the flesh. The Legion of Decency in the 1930s and 1940s which protected Catholics from "morally objectionable" films was but one twentieth-century manifestation of this mentality. The movement was guided by Irish-Americans, such as Martin J. Quigley, a Catholic trade publisher, and Daniel A. Lord, S.J. Moreover, the redoubtable Cardinal Dougherty was one of the most stalwart defenders of this form of social control. In 1934, he personally called for a boycott of all movies by Philadelphia Catholics.

Through their role as most-available builders of the institutional church and as both spokespersons and trend-setters in Catholic thought and action, Irish-American Catholics tended to hold sway, often determining the larger matters, from planning to prayer and from education to social action. Through their eyes, American observers came to know and understand the American Catholic church. As one surveys the record of American Catholic development, especially during the period of its greatest organization, one must evaluate the successes and failures of the American Catholic church on the basis of Irish influence. It was they who guided the church toward identification with the American dream and worked to gain acceptance and respectability among Americans. For the sake of their own image, they downplayed separatism, championing the unity of the church and its participation in the Roman Catholic church. Indeed, they sought to emphasize the unified institution by which the American Catholic church came to be identified.

Certain aspects of the Irish approach to the church as institution and as equal community of believers would have negative effects. For example, their overemphasis upon organization often seemed too great a preoccupation, especially in the later decades of the twentieth century as the march toward order and efficiency prevented the more humanistic building of the community. The fact that many American bishops actually struggled to gain a reputation based on the same "brick-and-mortar" approach to church development as had impressed earlier generations of Catholics indicates a certain loss of ministerial focus which did invade the immediate pre–Vatican II experience. If one were to evaluate the impact of Irish-Americans upon the development of the American Catholic church with respect to community cohesiveness, moreover, one would also discover some problematic results. Andrew Greeley made a rather facile conclusion that no other ethnic group could have performed better in the leadership role than the Irish had done; yet he seems to have overlooked at least some of the consequences of such leadership, especially those involving the sharing of leadership and authority within the American church. The major result of this leadership was that ethnic minority leaders were sometimes prevented from developing talents which would have benefited the church on a national level and from being utilized on the higher ranks of church administration—a fact consistently testified to, first by the Germans, and then by other minority Catholics.

Undoubtedly the most damaging aspect of Irish-American leadership within the American Catholic church during this period of the institutionalization of the church was the monopoly of ecclesiastic power. Whether intended to separate Catholics vertically on the basis of ethnicity or not, the effect was precisely that. The American Catholic world became a "We Over Them" reality, influenced by a "separate but equal" frame of mind. So pervasive was this ethnic imbalance by the mid-twentieth century that even the Irish could not deny that, all too often, they were inevitably the first in line to receive greater privilege and preference than any other group. History is replete with incidents that indicate that this imbalance did at times create serious problems; it was occasionally extremely hurtful to "other Catholics." Worst of all, it undid the sense of equality that had characterized the antebellum American Catholic church. In vain could the Irish later argue that the status shifts that occurred in the last decades of the nineteenth century had become essential because of the demands of the newcomers, or that equality was preserved through the establishment of parishes that protected the Catholic rights of other immigrants. Even when they were particularly well treated, the latecomers recognized they were indeed a separate cultural part of the American Catholic church and that they were dealt with in this way, so that many of the characteristics of their separateness would endure. All too often, invisible walls divided ethnic Catholic parishioners each from the other, with still another wall dividing minorities from the Irish majority. The failure of the Irish leadership to consider ways to break down these walls cannot be overlooked.

For the most part, however, the Irish had built an extraordinarily vital church, as can be seen by even a superficial scanning of the institutions that the church either owned and operated. Irish-Americans had successfully addressed and proposed solutions for some of the most difficult social problems facing American society, and they had presented the nation with a faith whose beauty of expression and soundness of principle gave fitting testimony to its historic grandeur. Most important, they had found creative ways to accommodate one of the most complex phenomenon facing the United States: the rapid increase of its population through immigration. The Irish had succeeded in building a church that was united by its enlightened leadership in understanding the need to incorporate all Catholics, yet divided because this unity was achieved through the benevolence of one group of Catholics toward "other Catholics." Little wonder, then, that this imbalance would become perhaps the source of the greatest conflict, even of public scandal, by which the church would be known. It was not until the mid-1950s that Irish and other ethnic Catholics began finally to appreciate the implications of the separateness that typified the American Catholic church and to realize that the approach had not really led to the desired effect of unifying the American Catholic church. Ironically, by that time, ethnic Catholicism had begun to develop a respectable name.

CHAPTER
6
The Germans Make the "National" Difference

❧❧❧

*I*n the years immediately preceding the Civil War, German-American Catholics began to play as influential a role in the creation of the American Catholic community as had Irish-Americans. Like the Irish-Americans, they had been early immigrant arrivals to the new republic; well beyond the middle of the nineteenth century they continued their pattern of rapid growth and dispersion. Like the Irish-Americans, they were, at first, among the nation's poorest; priests who could care for their spiritual welfare were especially scarce. Sometimes, as one Baltimore account of the 1850s put it, their daily lot meant nothing more than selling scraps of rags, bones, or coal, salvaging, even stealing; it would lead them—or worse, their children—into lives of crime and destitution. Although well acquainted with such desperate thoughts as well as anxieties over the fear of desertion or abuse, however, the German immigrants were able to reverse the trend, learning how to eke out from their initial poverty honest and productive lives. At first, imitating "American ways" typified their response; with characteristic stubbornness, they gradually found adequate employment and moved upward into more important positions in business and industry. Since many had come as skilled artisans and laborers, some were able to become entrepreneurs or builders, ascending even more quickly into the ranks of middle class Americans. In this respect, they often did better than their Irish-American peers.

But as members of the Catholic church, German-Americans

seemed to remain at a disadvantage. Although often participating in mixed ethnic congregations, they feared the loss of the special ethnic qualities of their own expression of the faith. In a few dioceses, they were able to achieve special consideration without tension; appreciated by their bishops, they exhibited remarkable initiative in building communal faith communities. Soon after Irish-born John Baptist Purcell (1800–1883) was appointed bishop of Cincinnati in 1833, for example, he began a unique relationship with the Germans of his diocese that was to last his entire administration. Within a year, he had established Holy Trinity, the first German national parish in the western frontier; in its first year it served over five thousand parishioners. A generation later, Cincinnati was to claim twelve German national parishes, each with schools, social organizations, and mutual-aid societies; a newspaper, orphanage, cemetery, and hospital were some of the other institutions organized. In Philadelphia, German Catholics also attained an impressive record of church-related endeavors, again because of the support provided by their bishops. Although the German population in that city had peaked during the 1840s, twelve German national parishes were established between the years 1842 and 1900. Each was a display of lay Catholic ability and loyalty. In Philadelphia, too, every parish had a school; spiritual confraternities and mutual benefit societies were common, and an orphanage and hospital had been established for German immigrants. In fact, one of Bishop Neumann's first acts when he became head of the diocese in 1852 was to insist that an orphanage be started "for our German children," as the "best and only means of wresting them from the grasp of error, of infidelity, and even godlessness."[1]

Nevertheless, the complaints that were sent during this period to the Ludwig Missionsverein, a powerful German sponsor of the American missions, pointed to the tendency on the part of some American Catholic leaders to use even missionary donations from German sources without regard to the needs or ethnic minorities in the United States. Overlooking their concerns bothered the Germans, since they realized that the Germans who had preceded them had been as important to the early church as any other immigrant group. Besides, they knew that present conditions warranted continued support, since their numbers had continued to escalate, especially after the European revolutions of 1848. During the 1850s, approximately 245,000 German Catholics arrived, another 200,000 came during each of the next two decades, and in the next twenty years, following the *Kulturkampf*, another 400,000 Catholic Germans came to the United States. Numbering almost one-fourth of the U.S. Catholic population by 1870—or approximately one million Catholics—they would be double this figure by 1890.

Yet, even as their increasing numbers which made them the largest non-English-speaking Catholic group, German-Americans still knew that their place in the American church was being jeopardized by the growing influence of Irish-Americans. Feeling naturally defensive among Protestant Germans, who were equally numerous as immigrants, they began to be almost more troubled by what they perceived to be the disapproval of English-speaking Irish-American Catholics. In particular, they found Irish immigrants much too willing to adapt to American ways. Deriving identity more from their religion than nationality, German-Americans determined to make their presence, as Germans, felt within the American Catholic church.

As the Irish gained more influence within the church, the friction between German and Irish Catholics mounted, especially with respect to their different views on parochial schools. By the 1880s, German antagonism toward Irish-American episcopal biases and priorities took the form of written complaints and memoranda, often directly addressed to Roman officials. Not only did German-Americans become more insistent that Catholic schools, in which their own customs and language could be taught, be provided in order to protect their children's faith, but they began to argue for proper representation of their German clergy among the episcopate. Only in the twentieth century would these issues diminish, as both German- and Irish-American Catholics strove for a greater mutual respect and greater openness to accommodation.

Since they had early voiced the need to protect their rights as equal members of the American Catholic church, German-American Catholics gained the distinction of being the first of the Catholic foreign-language-speaking groups to question episcopal policy with regard to Catholic immigrants. They had, for example, been the first to ask for a parish in which their language and culture would be given special consideration. Holy Trinity parish, begun in Philadelphia in 1788 as a result of these demands, was the first American parish formed to provide for Catholics whose language and culture differed from the American norm. By this move alone, German-Catholics pointed the way to further alternative planning for ethnic groups within the context of American Catholicism. Convinced that European immigrants needed to express their religion according to their own language and culture (their motto was "Language Saves the Faith"), German-American bishops, clergy, and parishioners persisted in encouraging the national parish alternative to Catholic parochial development. As the decades passed, they grew more and more convinced of the importance of this approach, perhaps in reaction to their frustration over losing influence in those dioceses where Irish-American clergy had begun to dominate. With the help of their priests (by 1860, there were already approximately 1,200 German clergy in the United States), they worked to pass the faith of their German ancestors on to the next generation. Because of their logical minds, strong convictions, and persistence, as well as their massive numbers, they were able to offer a model of Catholicism that was different from the one presented in Irish-American parishes. Furthermore, it was the Germans who would emphasize the need to maintain—indeed, to build—strong protective barriers between the hostile Protestant environment and Catholics; it was the Germans who would offer alternative liturgical styles and devotional practices; and it was the Germans who would provide a multiplicity of social and spiritual organizational frameworks for developing close bonds between the parishioners and their church.

Yet, even in those parts of the country where they were not numerous enough to speak with one voice concerning their place within the church, German-Americans played an important role in establishing Catholicism in the United States. Thus, German names were often among those who either led or helped form Catholic communities in both rural and urban areas—wherever a handful of the faithful expressed a need for priest or church. Even Connecticut's first churches in Hartford and New Haven were partially financed and supported by German immigrants; so too were the early immigrant Catholic communities in New York City, Brooklyn, and Newark, New Jersey. Several Texan Catholic communities, such as those in San Antonio or Galveston, were guided by talented German immigrant clergy and received similar support from the Germans in their congregations; the founders' lists of the some of the first churches in Wisconsin, Minnesota, and Nebraska reveal a preponderance of Germans among the early membership. In fact, German-Americans were an important segment of the rapidly growing Catholic membership throughout the country. Their move into the middle class in the last quarter of the nineteenth century and consequent new social status further strengthened their desire for full incorporation into the American Catholic church. Spreading out from the port cities where they had first established themselves, they either gave loyal support to parishes organized to preserve their language and culture or joined other Catholics in the formation of mixed ethnic parishes. From Milwaukee, Saint Louis, and Cincinnati, which formed a loosely structured ethnic triangle reaching south and west, the Germans continued to expand their influence. American Catholicism today bears the marks of German distinctiveness that resulted from both patterns of development. Especially in the Midwest and in certain rural communities of Pennsylvania, Ohio, Wisconsin, and Minnesota, German-American Catholics still draw attention to their special religious contributions and their close-knit communities, which paved the way for the development of the multiethnic American community.

In the consistent manner of a people strong in the faith, both German-American clergy and laity strove to "preserve incorrupt the sacred treasures of religion" within their "ethnic fortresses."[2] By 1870, more than 700 churches had been built as solid statements in stone, baroque or Romanesque design. These they furnished with beautifully crafted interiors that drew the attention of aesthetic sensibilities through delicately carved statues and elaborate high altars. Guided by religious congregations of men and women such as the Redemptorists, Jesuits, Christian Brothers, and School Sisters of Notre Dame, German-Americans found peace and continuity in these settings. Sermons in their own language could be heard and appropriate instructions given; devotions and liturgy could be celebrated. In parish centers often organized by the laity, German-Americans had ample opportunity to strengthen their communal ties to their parish through dialogue, debate, and programs aimed at developing their intellectual abilities and creative talents. Schools became the key to the future, the training ground for the next generation; 95 percent of German parishes saw to their establishment. As a statement of religious conviction, German-American Catholics amply reinforced their Catholic, rather than their American, identity, vocation, and significance within the parish environment; in that milieu, they were comforted by the thought that their own salvation was now possible within the American setting.

To be sure, not every attempt to develop German-American communities succeeded according to this plan, especially in the earlier decades of immigration. But even in these cases, progress was usually apparent. One short-lived experiment at Saint Mary City in Pennsylvania, begun in the 1840s, led instead to more important developments elsewhere. Encouraged to bring members of her religious community to that experimental German city so that her community would serve the American church, Mother Theresa Gerhardinger and the School Sisters of Notre Dame soon moved on, expanding beyond that ill-planned community so that they might educate German-Americans in many states. Sometimes, too, what appeared to be opposed aims for the advance of religion in America gradually found resolution within the American setting. Thus, the immigrant Benedictine monk Boniface Wimmer, O.S.B., who had a singular vision concerning setting up monasteries and forming German communities there, had to modify somewhat his idealistic approach if he was to be accepted in the Pittsburgh diocese. Comprehending the needs of American Catholics as well as the proposals of the Bishop Michael O'Connor (1810–1872), who sponsored him, Wimmer came to realize that he could not expect to serve only fellow Germans in either the schools he would found or the parishes his monks would be asked to direct. As early as 1846, when documents established life according to the Rule of Saint Benedict in the United States, this reconstructed notion of American monasticism was spelled out. If they were willing to conduct parishes irrespective of nationality, then O'Connor promised to allow "other monasteries in the diocese, where they will be able to undertake the work of monastic life either of educating youth to the lay or clerical state or of pastoral care." Understanding the need for Benedictines to adapt to an American church, and as founder of American monasticism, Wimmer would simultaneously take up duties as the first pastor of the ethnically mixed church of Saint Vincent and as prior of the Latrobe monastery.[3]

Wherever they developed parishes, however, German-Americans generally proceeded in a manner faithful to their Central European traditions. A communal spirit predominated; the clergy were in charge but they never domineered. Often, the very idea of initiating a parish began among the laity. Thus, lay leaders were the ones who gathered their community together with the aim of founding a church, purchased land jointly, raised funds, and even began building the church—all this before they asked the bishop to send them a pastor. Even in the later decades, when episcopal directives made it clear that the forming of a parish was primarily an episcopal prerogative, the pattern of German community involvement in parish-building remained marked by cooperative planning between laity and church leaders. In particular, the lay trustee system, which had been characteristic of Cincinnati and Chicago, continued to influence the structure of the German parish. In some localities, the balance of decision-making power remained more implicit. In either case, German-Americans retained a more democratic, communal concept of parish life than was true of neighboring parishes where the Irish were in the majority.

Missions, retreats, liturgical celebrations, artistic display, and musical performance were the chief means of nurturing the *Gemeinschaft* of the German parish. This was true in Chicago, where Redemptorists and Franciscans developed *Deutschtum* in some of the thirty-five parishes that had been established by 1916 and where School Sisters of Notre Dame and German branches of Franciscans, Benedictines, and Holy Cross Sisters staffed schools. It was equally true of German communities farther west. In San Francisco, Franciscan ideals animated the members of Saint Boniface Church, over which they took charge in 1887. There, music became the focal point. For thirty years, a forty-member choir performed Latin, English, and German music on a regular basis and occasionally gave concerts that had a wide secular and ecumenical following. In these settings, German-Americans routinely organized parish *Vereine* and published theological or spiritual materials while their parish *Pfarrbote*, written in German, reported on German news and products. Parish anniversaries became the focal points of celebrations in which singing fests or dramatic productions created a heightened *Gemütlichkeit*. Through ceremonies and satellite organizations, the German parish retained its centrality for Germans; it served as a living organism where every member of the family could celebrate the important passages in life. It represented the fullest expression of German Catholic faith.[4]

It was only in the closing decades of the nineteenth century that German-American Catholics felt required to defend their reasons for maintaining this alternative cultural style within the Catholic setting. During this period the need to safeguard their specialness became more pressing, and the importance of providing a counterbalance to Irish-American preferences seemed clear. While some of their leaders presented the neglect of recent immigrants by certain Irish Catholic leaders in national and international forums, within their own parishes German-American Catholics tended to become more introversive. Aware that their insistence upon special rights might threaten and even provide a bad example for other immigrants, German-Americans still persisted in pursuing these aims. To them, it was essential that Catholics be free to develop the spirituality and ecclesiology that reflected traditionally cherished values. Some outside observers suggested that in adopting this view the Germans were neglecting their duties toward other Catholics and shutting themselves up within their own closed circles. For the most part, German-Americans ignored these opinions; they needed to maintain their stand because of the hostile forces of Protestantism and because, at times, they felt misunderstood within their own church.

Well into the twentieth century, the continued emphasis upon the establishment of schools reflected this dual concern of German-Americans. It was so essential to stress the preservation of the faith through education that, on occasion, plans for building schools took precedence over those for the construction of churches. The school, in fact, was the basis of the so-called ethnic fortress; it was to be the bulwark for the defense against Protestantism, "Godless" secularism, even the loss of ethnic identity within the church. In these critical years of the immigrant church, therefore, there seemed to be almost no limit to the value that German-Americans put upon the importance of the school. As the editor of a German weekly, Detroit's *Die Stimmen der Wahrheit*, put it in 1884, the Germans were convinced that the church was "only a passing thing" but that, without a school, their children would become "totally ignorant, or what is worse, unbelievers, Godless, and immoral."[5] At the turn of the century, another

German-American bishop, Cleveland's Ignatius F. Horstmann (1840–1908) stated the importance of beginning a school even more strongly: "A parish without a parochial school is not a Catholic parish. The parochial school is a rock foundation. Without it all else is valueless—a priest's work without a parochial school can only be half done and is very discouraging."[6] At one point during the 1890s, in fact, every German national parish reported having its own school; in the twentieth century, the figure would be only slightly reduced. A study of Irish and German patterns of founding schools underscores this preference of the Germans. It points out that, while 27 percent of the new Irish immigrant parishes studied began schools within two years, two-thirds of the new German parishes had done so within the same period; further, over a ten year period, 46 percent of the new Irish parishes had become involved in school-building, as contrasted with 86 percent for the Germans. Moreover, the Germans' ultimate goal for school-building was total, or 100 percent, commitment—an ambition that rankled some Irish-Americans and proved divisive when school campaigns were mounted in a number of dioceses in the West.

Reflection upon the progress of the School Sisters of Notre Dame and their successful involvement in American Catholic parochial education underscores the extent to which the German bias would ultimately influence American Catholicism in general. Even before the 1850s, the School Sisters, under Mother Theresa Gerhardinger, had accepted schools in the dioceses of Baltimore, Philadelphia, Pittsburgh, Buffalo, and Milwaukee; by the Civil War, they were teaching in thirty-eight foundations from the eastern coast to the Mississippi. Ironically, it was the Bavarian roots of the School Sisters that gave them an advantage as American educators. Because the elementary schools they started were modeled on the Bavarian *Volksschule*, adapted from Pestalozzian ideas, their teaching methods were often praised as being years ahead of those of many of their United States contemporaries. Their interest in the education of young women would also put the School Sisters in the forefront of progressive educational thinking. In 1873, the congregation established the College of Notre Dame of Maryland in Baltimore as the first Catholic higher educational facility with the authority to accept women through the doctoral level. Perhaps it was the success of the School Sisters in teaching at every academic level that was primarily responsible for the growth of their membership: by 1900, the order comprised 2,752 women, making it the largest American community of women at that time. Their reputation for excellence had by then involved them in work far beyond their ethnic boundaries; they had assisted other ethnic minorities, especially Slavic groups, by providing a model for developing their own schools. To this day, the record of the educational achievement of the School Sisters of Notre Dame continues to indicate their foresight, adaptability, and educational ability.[7]

The German-Americans' total commitment to education tended, unfortunately, to narrow the focus of German leadership and perhaps led toward what would be the most serious debate between German- and Irish-American leaders in the last decades of the nineteenth century. This commitment was, for example, a major aspect of the contention that divided Catholics in the diocese of Milwaukee during the administration of Bishop Michael Heiss (1818–1890), as English-speaking Catholics balked at his attempts to establish parochial schools in every parish. During the public discussions of these differing ethnic points of view, the implications of separatist Catholic practice were made especially clear.

For most German-Americans, the perpetuation of German language and culture through the structures of parish and school had always been viewed in terms of the important goal of preserving the Catholic faith in the American setting. In itself this perspective did not contradict any views held by many of the Irish-American bishops, for example, New York's John Hughes and Rochester's Bernard McQuaid, both of whom articulated their concerns about the threat that Protestant culture posed. Provincial and plenary councils had certainly made the topic of Catholic education an important one since 1852. By 1884, education had become such a key issue that about one-fourth of the legislation of the council held that year involved the obligation of pastors to provide Catholic schools. At that meeting, moreover, not only were the majority of the bishops who addressed this issue Irish-American, but almost all of the major addresses were delivered by them. It was, however, the Germans who held their ground with respect to requiring parochial education. During the meeting, Milwaukee's Heiss argued for "commanding" the establishment and maintenance of schools; chief collaborators with him were two other German-American prelates, Joseph Dwenger (1837–1893) of Fort Wayne, Indiana, and Kilian C. Flasch (1831–1891) of LaCrosse, Wisconsin.

By the 1890s, however, the education debate included such issues as the right of the state to educate and whether compromises could be reached with public authorities to ease the burden of supporting public schools. On these points in particular, Irish- and German-Americans tended to hold opposing views. The major spokesmen for alternative educational proposals, especially those who argued for adapting to the public school system, were Irish-Americans. When German-Americans became aware of the growing tendency to argue that education was an essential means of Americanizing Catholic immigrants, they viewed the combined attack on their own perceptions of Catholic education as particularly alarming.

The overarching debate that engaged these two dominant ethnic Catholic groups after the 1880s concerned the meaning of Americanization within the American Catholic church. The very term had always signaled danger for most German-American Catholics. It was not that they did not value being Americans; at first they even imitated their Irish-American co-religionists in attempting to appear American. Many even preferred membership in territorial parishes in order to indicate their independence from old-world traditions. Moreover, their leaders consistently argued that it had never been their intention to "Germanize" their adopted land. By fully exploring their right to establish schools side by side with public schools, they rather intended to indicate their adaptation to the American system. But their worry that their culture would be lost and their anxiety over the possible erosion of the faith of their children prevented them from any full-scale endorsement of Americanism. Furthermore, in the debates of 1893 that included the apostolic delegate Francesco Satolli, there had been a solid bloc of German-Americans who voiced their added fear of the consequences of Americanization within the context of the Irish-dominated church. What they suggested in their discussions was that, in reality, the move to Americanize was nothing other than the move to Hibernicize the church through a takeover by Irish-American bishops. With their identity as Germans recently heightened by the unification of their homeland, they were hardly willing to lose their new ethnic solidarity because of an imposed Irish interpretation of what it meant to be American.

Concerns over their identity as German-American Catholics did not, however, cause problems in every instance. In those dioceses where their influence had been traditionally strong, German-American leaders were able to maintain the proven course. There, both German- or Irish-American bishops continued to be attentive to their special needs. Cincinnati was a shining example of the accord that could develop between German- and Irish-American Catholic leaders. Because of a unique relationship that Germans had enjoyed with the episcopate since Archbishop Purcell's tenure, Cincinnati's German Catholics had been able to develop a network of churches, schools, and affiliated societies. Moreover, they had been provided with a vicar who could arbitrate problems. Even the German pattern of lay involvement seemed to meet with official approval; it was affirmed in regulations issued in 1851 and 1865 and reaffirmed by Purcell's successors after 1880. Similar developments in Chicago indicated that it was possible for Germans to maintain prestige in other dioceses as well. This was partly because episcopal decisions made previously by Irish-American bishops in the archdiocese had virtually encouraged accommodation; because of this attitude, every aspect of Catholic life had, in fact, become subdivided along ethnic lines, to the satisfaction of all sides. It was especially true under Patrick A. Feehan (1829–1902). As archbishop of Chicago after 1880, he gave the Germans a voice in archdiocesan administration through a consultor and a school committee, allowed the controversial Deutsch-Amerikanischer Priester-Verein to hold its first meeting there in 1887, and endorsed the work of the Saint Raphael Society. In the eyes of the Germans, the Cincinnati and Chicago experiments proved that there were successful ways of integrating Irish, Germans, and other minorities. To upset such arrangements was to risk losing the rich patrimony of Catholic traditions · before adequate measures to integrate them into American culture were assured.

But the German-Americans were also aware that some of their requests had not received proper attention in other areas of the nation; moreover, they realized that those who favored Americanization questioned the extension of special treatment. Because of sensitivity to ethnic demands, for example, quota systems had insured some semblance of equal representation for Germans on the leadership level. Still, every German-American priest was fully aware that only 11 percent of the nation's bishops in 1870 were of German background and that this rose to merely 14 percent by 1900—despite the fact that one-fourth of all Catholics were of German background. Worse, German-American Catholics felt compelled to complain to Rome that there were indications that the Irish intended to gain control even of the dioceses traditionally held by Germans. What would happen, they wondered, if the church became even more enthusiastic about Americanization? Both the Milwaukee and the Cleveland dioceses were cited as beleaguered German-American strongholds. By the 1880s, nine of the seventeen bishops in the two provinces to which these dioceses belonged were still ethnic German; only one was of Irish descent. Obviously, by the appointment of an Irish-American, a change in the balance of power would occur. Thus, when Michael Heiss's successor was being selected in Milwaukee in 1890, it is not surprising that John Ireland observed that he looked upon the choosing of the next candidate as the most important issue then facing the American church. The German-Americans were even more concerned than Ireland. They received a reprieve when another German, Frederick X. Katzer (1844–1903), was chosen. Since Katzer was a noted proponent of the German efforts to preserve their language and customs, the German-Americans were temporarily put at ease.

Meanwhile, in Cleveland, there was what German-Americans con-

sidered a catastropic development. Irish-German infighting had been
rife there since the early 1870s. The situation worsened, both in 1891
and 1908, when the appointment of a new bishop was pending. While
the Germans had, to that point, seemed successful in holding on to
a certain dominance within the diocese, the fact that Irish-American
membership in Cleveland was increasing resulted in a stronger case
against the retention of German-American hegemony than had been
possible in Milwaukee. As one Irish-American priest complained in
1870, "It makes me disgusted to see Americans become Germans
without necessity."[8] The choice of a compromise candidate, Richard
Gilmour (1824–1891), delayed the resolution of the problem. When
it became apparent that Gilmour, a Scotch-Presbyterian convert, did
not intend to side with the Irish-American clergy, the Germans even
seemed temporarily to have regained an upper hand. But after another
respite under Ignatius Horstmann (1840–1908), whose Americanism
rested "on a very thick German foundation," but whose abilities as
peacemaker did ease tensions, the German-American preference came
to an end.[9] For the first time they found themselves at the mercy of
an allegedly unsympathetic but efficient administrator, John P. Far-
relly, during whose tenure from 1909 to 1921 German power was almost completely obliterated. According to German-Americans, the
threat posed by Irish-American clergy had manifested itself in Cleveland.

Would Chicago's way of integrating immigrant Catholics be a more
acceptable means of Americanizing the German population? There,
three "major leagues," as some irreverently chose to term them, had
developed by 1910. Ninety-three territorial parishes predominated;
but there were also thirty-five German, thirty-four Polish, and scores
of other national parishes that competed for their proper place within
the church. Similar accommodations, organized explicitly to avoid
power struggles, were made in other dioceses during these critical
years. Conflicts sometimes developed regardless of precautionary
measures. Wherever they did, the rhetoric of Americanization was
used to justify appointments or decisions concerning the development
of parishes. For the most part, however, the struggles revolved around
questions of sharing leadership and opportunities for advancement
in the diocese. When conflicts occurred, words were used as smoke
screens to cover the ambitious motives of the clergy. The result, all
too often, was that statements like "a foreigner who loses his nationality is in danger of losing his faith and character" actually referred
to a "demoralization" that primarily affected ethnic leaders.[10]

In a number of dioceses, this sense of second-class standing also
took its toll upon the German-American clergy and laity. German-
Americans in Saint Louis often experienced problems over what they

considered unfair treatment, which they had experienced since 1842, when German national parishes were made dependent upon territorial parishes. When they presented their case to Rome in the 1880s, the Irish-Americans voiced little sympathy, describing the German reluctance to withdraw their demands for equal treatment as a "canker eating away the life of the church." As in the Milwaukee situation, they criticized the Germans for violating the "Unity and Catholicity of the Church to perpetuate the curse of Babel in Language." But to the Germans, what was happening was more the result of Irish-American Catholics' foisting their kind of Catholicism upon them. To them, it simply meant a sustained state of confusion over the degree to which they might share full membership in the American Catholic church.[11]

Twice toward the end of the century, all the frustrations of the German-American Catholics were joined under one banner and brought to worldwide attention. The spokesman for the first of these causes was Peter Paul Cahensly, a Center party deputy in the German Reichstag and secretary of the Saint Raphael's international immigrant aid society. His argument, put forward in the mid-1880s, amounted to a demand that German-Americans have equal rights within the Catholic church. In reality, his claim was for independence from the Irish-dominated hierarchy. Because of Cahensly's work for the aid society, his demands received an extremely wide hearing. The second advocate was Peter M. Abbelen, a priest of the diocese of Milwaukee, who in 1886 brought to Rome a detailed list of complaints that alleged neglect of German-American Catholics by American church leaders. At Lucerne in 1890 a memorial was drawn up based on these charges. It recommended the continuance of national parishes and schools, broader representation of the nationalities among American bishops, and papal support to train European missionaries for work in the United States. In effect, in both cases of advocacy, there was a call for a restructuring of the church along ethnic lines. Most importantly, these cases underscored the claims of Germans that the best way to incorporate them into the American church was by ensuring the representation of German clergy in the ranks of the hierarchy.

German-American complaints before international audiences only reinforced their separatist position. Whether justified or not, they had widened the breach between themselves and the Irish-Americans and they had set a precedent for other American Catholics to follow. Richmond's John J. Keane (1839–1918) was so affected by the implications of this German strategy that in 1887 he wrote to England's Cardinal Manning, "The social question and the German or nationalist questions are the two wedges with which the devil is trying to destroy the unity of the Church in this country."[12] And Bernard McQuaid, who had sided with German-Americans over some aspects of the school issue in 1884 wrote: "The power now at work will never rest until it has got complete control of the Church in the Mississippi Valley and all other parts of the country worth having. . . . it would be a dangerous precedent to set, to let nationalities legislate through Rome, in an underhanded way, without the knowledge of the other bishops of the country." Later he referred to the Abbelen forces as schemers who had perpetrated a "dirty, mean, underhanded business."[12]

In the end, the crusading Germans lost both the battle and the war. Rome did not back their proposals for separate jurisdictions or satisfy their demands for greater representation in the hierarchy. Few among Catholic leaders, in fact, sympathized with their particular predicament. Even during the period of episcopal squabbling, some German-American leaders themselves expressed concern over the adamant posture of their more vocal fellow Germans and tried to soften the attacks. Four issues of Saint Louis's *Pastoral Blatt* in 1883 were devoted to easing tensions. "Let us . . . allow things quietly to take their course and to develop themselves in a natural manner," the editor wrote, "We should live together peaceably, like true Catholics."[13] Father Abbelen himself tried to use tempered language in dealings with Cardinal Gibbons. From the diocese of Providence, furthermore, came a pamphlet by a progressive German-American priest, William Stang, who would later be named bishop of Fall River. Entitled *Germany's Debt to Ireland*, it argued that "Germans, who are by nature grateful, have always acknowledged their religious and literary indebtedness to Ireland. . . . A thousand years of strange and sad changes have not cooled the warmth of gratitude in German hearts toward Ireland."[14] And in 1892 Cincinnati pastor and author Anton Walburg publicly supported Americanists. In a letter to Ireland, he summed up feelings that were shared by other Germans: "Cahenslyism is not wanted here either in the church or the country. . . . The Church wants to be American and must accept American institutions and do the best she can."[15]

There was, however, much about the German Americans' desire for inclusion within the episcopal structure of the Catholic church that was worthy of consideration. From the start, a number of bishops and clergy had sympathized with the German-Americans. Unfortunately, both the timing and form of the German-American offensive did not work to their advantage. In particular, their actions threatened unity just at a time when the most enlightened Americans were being shaken by rising xenophobia. If Irish-Americans were hurt in their socially upward move in American society by this new turn of events, German-American Catholics were to feel the impact in both church and secular worlds. The German emphasis upon nationality only served to draw the attention of critics both within and without the church. Further, it seemed to remind Americans that the U.S. Catholic church was, as they had always argued, a "foreign" institution bene-fitting from immigration. In this milieu, the German drive for special status was doubly damaging. Twentieth-century German-Americans came to realize that their campaign for inclusion had been misguided. By then, moreover, a more complex situation had developed within the church, as the floodtide of new Italian, Slavic, and other southern and eastern European immigrants began to settle in the United States. At this juncture, a different situation confronted German-Americans as they discovered that, instead of being concerned about their own status, they were now forced to decide whether to back the protests of the latest immigrant Catholics or to array themselves with the Irish-American majority.

For their part, Irish-Americans had also changed some of their views about how the church and American society should run. By the turn of the century, they too had been forced to clarify their under-standing of Americanism and Americanization. Earlier, John Ireland had been among the first to express concern over the exclusiveness of some German and other ethnic clergy. In 1888, Ireland spoke of Americanization explicitly as "the harmonizing of ourselves with our surroundings, so that we will be as to the manner born, and not as strangers in a strange land, caring apparently but slightly for it, and entitled to receive from it but meager favors." He was the one who would insist that Americanization was "the knowing of the language of the land and failing in nothing to prove our attachment to our laws, and our willingness to adopt, as dutiful citizens, all that is good and laudable in its social life and civilization." But by 1900, he too began to emphasize the universal claim of the international church and its influence upon American Catholics and thus added greater nuance to his motto, "All in all."[16] His shift in rhetoric was duly noted. As did other German-American members of the hierarchy, Sebastian G. Messmer (1847–1930) began to sympathize with Ireland and his encouragement of Americanization. When rumors hinted that Ireland might be named a cardinal in 1911, for example, Messmer com-mented: "I am only happy to state that the sentiment [of the past] has changed very much of late. There is more than one reason for that. I have spoken with a number of German-American priests and laymen who were unanimous in expressing their disappointment that the red hat had not landed in Saint Paul."[17]

As the twentieth century advanced, many second-generation Ger-man-American Catholics began to rethink previous separatist policies. For one thing, with massive immigration at an end, their identification as American—rather than as German-American—Catholics became more important. For another, some of their clergymen and journalists had begun to emphasize the important role that German-Americans could play in critiquing the weaknesses of American social practice and political policy. Thus, the German spokesman and editor of *The Review*, Arthur Preuss, argued for a united front among all Catholics, so that the "weak-kneed" and "servile among American Catholics would cease "wasting energy and accomplishing little" and produce a "consequent regeneration of Catholic life."[18] Another sign of change was the shift away from the use of German-language newspapers as a major means of disseminating news. By 1900, twenty-six of sixty-four such papers had already closed; only three new ones were started. There was also a drop in the number of German-language parishes. From a peak of 705 registered German parishes in American dioceses in 1870, the number was reduced to 500 by 1906; by 1916, only 206 parishes claimed that status. Within dioceses themselves, there were genuine Americanizing overtures. In Green Bay, Wisconsin, Messmer pressured German-Americans to take their place as leaders among U.S. Catholics, particularly by developing programs aimed at reforming American society. In nearby Marquette, Michigan, another bishop, Frederick Eis (1843–1924), issued instructions in 1900 that were aimed at widening German parochial horizons. Soon imitated by other dioceses, his plan was to have English sermons preached at least once in the Sunday masses held in his diocese. When some resistant Germans, as well as some more strident French-Canadian and Polish-American nationalists, fiercely criticized these moves toward integration the Germans simply clarified their motivation. As Preuss put it, the French-Canadians should heed the danger of making "Americanization" such a condemning term that they blind themselves to the real needs of the times. He also warned them that they would gain nothing from a policy of "rancorous isolation" and added that the Germans had learned "almost too late" that the only way to "save" many of their city parishes was to make room for English.[19]

Gradually, German-American bishops began to view their role in the American Catholic church in far broader terms than had their nineteenth-century predecessors. Not only were many of them convinced that demands for equal representation only seemed to work against their best interests, but some grew anxious to become more integrally involved in shaping American Catholic thought and action. Messmer and several other German-American members of the hierarchy took a leading role in the formation of the American Federation of Catholic Societies in 1901. According to Messmer, there was a great need for a core group of American Catholics—irrespective of ethnic background—who could mobilize the church along social, religious, and even political grounds. Thus, he envisioned a massive multiethnic pressure group, under the leadership of ecclesiastical superiors, that could influence Americans on behalf of truth and justice. "Away with all un-Catholic and pernicious national self-conceit!" he said on several occasions as leaders of the federation attempted to organize on the national level, "In this battle we are neither Germans nor Yankees, nor Irish, neither French, nor Polish, nor Bohemian, only Catholics, keeping our eye on one thing only, religion and church."[20] In the same spirit and with a corresponding fervor, many clerical and lay German-American Catholics would echo Messmer.

There had also been a concerted effort to reinvigorate the Central Verein, a nationwide organization that had served as the major institution through which German-Americans had organized for social action since the 1850s. At Golden Jubilee proceedings held in 1901 to assess the direction the Verein should take, the question of reshaping the organization along ideological lines of social reform, with less emphasis given to the preservation of ethnic perspectives, was discussed at length. Gradually, under the leadership of Monsignor Francis Goller, a veteran of the Priester Verein, and with the guidance of Nicholas Gonner, a creative strategy for Catholic action began to emerge. Then, under Frederick P. Kenkel who assumed the leadership of the reorganized Central Verein in 1908, a holistic philosophy for the German mission was more clearly and cogently presented. Under Kenkel and other like-minded theorists, the new Verein began to call for a fundamental restructuring of society and for a reordering of attitudes and values so that human life could again be lived within an integrated Christian community such as the one that prevailed during the Middle Ages. Another Verein member, Anton Heiter, who was editor of the Buffalo Catholic paper, had earlier touched upon the same theme at a national meeting held in Bridgeport, Connecticut, in 1901. Disturbed because one Americanist bishop, John Keane, had suggested that the United States had no real social problems, Heiter declared that it was time to address the sickness that was inflicting American society, the symptoms of which were gigantic labor strikes and the accumulation of trusts and monopolies.

While Kenkel and other visionaries worked to spread the Verein vision of reform, moreover, a priest of the diocese of Cleveland, Peter E. Dietz, was focusing on more practical matters, especially those involving the rights of labor and the role of labor unions in solving social problems. In his capacity as advisor to the American Federation of Catholic Societies, Dietz not only led the organization's commitment in this regard but also was responsible, especially during the 1910s, for forging significant ties between it and established unions, such as the heavily Catholic American Federation of Labor. The convictions that German-American leaders held concerning the role of

American Catholics in advancing social justice were to have broad ramifications for the church's ethnic minorities. As it drew more and more Germans into the mainstream of the American debate, it also gave them a greater sense of belonging as Americans. Moreover, it provided American Catholics, irrespective of ethnic group, with an alternative way of planning for improved social conditions. By approaching Americanization from a sociological point of view, in particular, German-Americans had contributed to the debate over the economic problems of the day, motivating many to consider the root causes of the social, political, and economic problems that confronted Americans daily. In the process they had led fellow Catholics into lively debate proving that they had, indeed, much to offer the Catholic church.

That American attitudes had also changed was even more clearly evident after 1910. At that time, Peter Cahensly, whose name had been associated with ethnic protest and disillusionment as well as with bitter ecclesial disputes, was able to return to the United States for the first time in twenty-seven years. On what turned out to be a triumphal tour, he was warmly received by German-American bishops such as Cleveland's Joseph Schrembs (1866–1939) and Grand Rapids's Henry J. Richter (1838–1916). But more important, he was extremely well received by Irish-Americans, including the rector of the Catholic University of America, the bishops in such key dioceses as Baltimore, Philadelphia, and New York, and by other Irish-American bishops and clergy. New York's John Farley (1842–1918) even asked Cahensly to write the archdiocesan report on immigrants—a report in which Cahensly would comment favorably on advances among Catholics.

The sympathetic reception given Cahensly was not influenced by his well-known connections with Popes Leo XIII and Pius X, both of whom had publicly expressed gratitude to Cahensly (and to the Saint Raphael Society) for his excellent work on behalf of immigrants. Rather, the reception represented a climate of appreciation for past endeavors that had begun to typify the church's attitude toward immigrants. Could American Catholics lightly ignore the statistics that were testimony to the Saint Raphael Society's work: over 21 million emigrants from Germany, the Austro-Hungarian Empire, and Italy had been provided aid since the Society's inception. Like the German missionary efforts of the previous century, assistance spoke eloquently of German intentions. Little wonder that in 1911 the editor of the *Central Blatt* was able to offer an assessment not only of Cahensly's reputation, but implicitly of the general efforts of Germans to address the immigration crisis. In a 1911 issue, Preuss wrote of the necessity of reexamining old prejudices that had obscured the German record: "Cahensly's name will live in history, but it should not be held in reprobation, but in honor, because its possessor was an exceptionally enlightened and zealous Catholic."[21] Risking the same kind of misunderstanding and criticism that had met Cahensly, German Catholics were ready to assume his burden.

If German-Americans had already begun to move away from any deliberate emphasis upon special ethnic needs before the First World War, their unfortunate position as objects of suspicion after 1917 hastened their retreat from separatism. Never again would German-Americans insist upon their difference from other Americans. Instead, both laity and clergy stressed the ways in which they could attend to the social ills of postwar American society, pressing forward in pursuit of social reform, especially through their national organizations and publications. Reconstruction of the social order became, in fact, their official crusade. Through the Verein, they continued to distribute the *Central Blatt and Social Justice*, the expanded German-English language newspaper of the Verein, as well as pamphlets, newsletters, and other literary materials. In addition, they offered lecture series that included such prominent Americans as David Goldstein, the Jewish convert and evangelist; Peter W. Collins, a prominent leader of the International Brotherhood of Electrical Workers; and John A. Ryan and William Kerby, leading social theorists and professors at Catholic University in Washington, D.C.

During the 1930s, primarily through the journal of the Central Verein (renamed *The Social Justice Review*), other writings, and lectures, German-Americans continued to address social justice issues. In particular, they expounded a theory of "solidarism" that had been developed by the German Jesuit Heinrich Pesch. They identified three fundamental stages of social life that they hoped Americans would advance, namely, self-help, voluntary social assistance, and energetic assistance from the state. They argued that these should be counterpoised against the New Deal strategy of increasing federal intervention. On a more practical level, they spent their energies supporting certain forms of unionism, creating workmen's societies, organizing educational and social welfare projects, and directing lobbying efforts for protective legislation. As the Second World War approached, they again became involved in relief programs and gave patriotic allegiance to the allied cause. While backing the war effort, they offered their critique of the economic crisis spawned by depression and wartime inflation. Although the strength of the Central Verein began to wane after this period, German-Americans would continue to emphasize their dedication to the causes of social justice. In the person of such a remarkable priest as Francis J. Haas they had a German-American who was bishop, social activist, and spokesman for justice at the national level. A man of action and an influential government official,

Haas gave German-Americans reasons for national pride. As one of the New Deal's most successful labor mediators he helped arbitrate hundreds of disputes during the 1930s and 1940s. His practical talents helped to restore industrial peace and protect workers' rights to an adequate wage, reasonable hours, unionization, and steady employment. He provided German-Americans with prestige by association.

In the long run, then, although German-Americans had been the first to emphasize the differences of nationality among American Catholics, they also became the first to shed the implications of those differences when they could no longer substantiate their value. For several decades, they had stood up to Irish-Americans, and thereby they provided a pattern for other ethnic minorities in the church to follow. Yet their own desire to enter more fully into mainstream American life, their interest in providing a sociological alternative to American perspectives on politics and economics, and especially their retreat from any position that might be characterized as un-American—all these moved them away from separatist patterns of Catholic identification in the twentieth century. In their changing world, German- and Irish-Americans began to downplay the implications of earlier rhetoric and to find ways of defining Americanization that would be suitable to both groups. Slowly, Irish-Americans retreated from their negative views of the German ethnic demands, sometimes termed "Cahenslyism," or a "fungus" that inspired "alienism." Gibbons and Ireland had long before expressed their regrets that so much misunderstanding had occurred. In his retrospect of fifty years of Catholic history, Gibbons refused to even mention either Cahenslyism or Americanism. To a great extent, discussions concerning Americanization were universally downplayed. Church leaders would almost always suggest that the rapid move to Americanize, as urged by some earlier churchmen, had been a mistake. Instead, when Catholics now addressed the issue, they spoke of the need for a more natural, gradual transformation. It would occur, they seemed to agree, not so much because of the immigrants' adjustment to their new setting, but rather because their children would be formed according to American ways. In other words, they had come to understand what the German Anton Walburg had suggested decades before: "We must hold a tight reign; check the impatience to Americanize, and though there may be some wrangling among conflicting nationalities, if we move slowly we will finally land in the American nationality with the Catholic body under full control and faithful to the Church."[22]

German-Americans had proven both desire and their ability to integrate through their national efforts for social progress. Between federated societies, Central Verein organizations, and other multi-ethnic Catholic societies, they found forums to address every American issue openly. Their numbers strengthened national Catholic organizations. They joined the Knights of Columbus, the major national Catholic laymen's organization, which deliberately cultivated a spirit of openness to all nationalities. In this organization they began to achieve leadership roles, as state deputees or in other elected positions, especially in the Midwest. Another sign of their equal standing was their cooperation in the establishment in 1910 of the Catholic Colonization Society of the Church Extension Society, whose aim was to reach beyond the city and the "churched" Americans to aid both immigrants and migrants.

Finally, German-American Catholics had begun to perceive themselves—and to be perceived—in the same light as were Irish-Americans. For the most part, they had developed beyond narrow national lines by using the very structures of their parishes and ethnic communities to widen their focus toward Americanization. Their local societies reached out to work in conjunction with other immigrant groups so as to lead them beyond the limits of their own closed worlds. Their schools fostered the American way. But the Germans had also been able to present a dual image of ethnic solidarity and respect for pluralism. On the one hand, they could stand united, as they did at the 1926 International Eucharistic Congress, held in Chicago, where they alone were represented by a dozen cardinals, sixty four archbishops, over three hundred bishops, and eight thousand priests. In that setting, they could take the major responsibility in hosting "nationality" meetings, reminding American Catholics of their support of the U.S. Catholic church as well as their special obligations to represent ethnic particularity. They could present a corporate German-American presence, made strong by numbers of personnel and parochial strength: at least 11 percent of all parishes were still German; some seventy thousand German sisters and four thousand German brothers had offered their services to the spread of Catholicism. On the other hand, German-American Catholics had begun to represent a second image quite as readily. That the German-American archbishop of Chicago, Cardinal George W. Mundelein (1872–1939), was a recognized and outspoken Americanizer was well known. In him, German-American Catholics both acknowledged and witnessed to a natural development that had occurred within their ethnic ranks.

By mid-century, upward mobility, the spread of mass culture, declining isolation, and a residue of anti-German sentiment had caused many changes, leading more and more German Americans to abandon patterns of introversion and follow closely in the footsteps of Irish-American Catholics. For them, ethnicity had become a cultural rather than a national influence; for this reason, they joined Irish-Americans in attempting to present the image of a fully integrated American

Catholic people. Especially with regard to immigrant incorporation into the American church, their original stance would continue to force constructive solutions—at least in certain dioceses. Their influence could be equally profound with respect to social analysis. Most notably, their understanding of the need for systemic change led them to advance theories of social justice and action that were at times utilized within wider political circles.

Because of the Germans, moreover, the sacramental and devotional life of the church was constantly given new expression, and the quality of liturgy, art, music, and architecture was enriched. Furthermore, the Catholic church benefited by the Germans' concept of parish life. German-American Catholics were not only among the first to recognize that the parish must provide a social as well as religious center for its members, they were also consistently ready to uphold the system of parochial education that could prepare their children for the challenge of secular society. In the more controversial days of Protestant–Catholic difference, it was the German-American Catholics who, as a solid bloc, sustained and accelerated the call to social justice and the need for education within the faith. Significantly, in this regard they were supported by some of the more outstanding non-German prelates. Through their belief in the capacity of local institutions to strengthen the church as a whole, German-American Catholics provided constructive leadership that deserves both attention and evaluation. There were, of course, some particularly negative aspects of the German-American influence upon American Catholicism. At times, a stubborn clinging to certain sociological and cultural positions could and did antagonize. They were, after all, as capable of shortsightedness and ethnocentrism as they criticized their Irish-American colleagues of being. These tendencies, in fact, seemed to cloud the reputation for achievement and influence that they more justly deserved. Unlike the Irish-Americans, who seemed to be the right people at the right time, German-Americans were destined to be always in a secondary position. Nevertheless, what they achieved on behalf of the American Catholic church remains an impressive tribute that should be neither forgotten nor undervalued.

CHAPTER
7
"The Polish Kind of Faith"

*I*f the Germans were sometimes relegated to secondary importance among American Catholics, one may argue that the "new" immigrants—those who migrated in massive numbers in the last decades of nineteenth century—had a still less enviable position among Catholics, because of their large numbers and their foreignness. Since they were among the most numerous of the latter-day immigrants and because, as Catholics, they immediately looked to the church for spiritual assistance, the Poles were perhaps the most affected by the consequences of the inferior place to which they were consigned within the church. While aware that their basic needs were being attended to within the territorial Catholic parishes and that attempts were being made, at least in some dioceses, to organize national parishes for them, Polish immigrants were more conscious that their "foreign appearance" was often an embarrassment to the more established Catholics and an obstacle to their advance within American society. And another reality became clear to Polish-Americans after the turn of the century: their clergy were almost entirely excluded from the inner circles of prestige and influence among the nation's hierarchy.

Because of the continuing immigration of the most poor and illiterate Polish, who sought the lowest paying employment, Polish-Americans continued to be perceived as a threat to American Catholics. All too often, they were treated by bishops and clergy more as a group in need of spiritual care or corporal assistance than as a group capable of leadership whose incorporation could enhance the general reputation of the Catholic church. Poles had but to look at the German experience to see what they could expect in the United States. Just as nineteenth-century German-Americans had gradually found themselves neglected or overlooked for promotion within the major dioceses or institutions of the American church, so too would the Poles find themselves not only segregated because of their need for special treatment but also blocked from incorporation or advancement within the church.

Cultural differences based upon language, custom, and tradition, as well as economic handicaps, contributed to the Polish-American experience of isolation. But there was another side to the unequal relationship between dominant Irish-American Catholics and Polish immigrants. From the start, there had been an implicit agreement between bishops and immigrant leaders concerning the establishment of parallel parishes and church institutions for the Poles. Both saw the advantages of developing separate parishes. Immigrants had found it particularly difficult to adapt to Irish-American Catholic practices and perspectives. For them, being a member of the church meant that their families would be blended with the community in an organic way that was lacking in American parishes. If allowed to establish their own churches, they knew that they would not have to fear a push toward rapid adaptation or assimilation into the American system. Thus, while often using the rhetoric of American republicanism in order to attain specific practical ends, Polish-Americans made it clear from the start that they preferred to reestablish Old World traditions. Above all, they needed their own clergy to help them maintain what they proudly referred to as their Polish kind of faith, namely, the devotional expression of Roman Catholicism in ways that totally reflected their homeland traditions. Only in that way, they believed, could they be assured the perpetuation of their communities and their families and the preservation of their faith.

From colonial times there had been Polish emigrants who had settled in America. But in 1854 the first of the large-scale settlements of Poles was founded. In that year, a group of about one hundred Silesian Poles, led by the Franciscan Leopold Moczygemba, arrived by way of Galveston, Texas. There they established the first Polish Catholic parish at Panna Maria. From the 1870s on, continual waves of immigration, first from lands held by Prussia and then later and more heavily from Russian and Austrian Poland, brought massive numbers of Polish immigrants to both rural and urban United States. By the end of the nineteenth century, rapid industrialization had determined the urban dimension of their dispersal. Handicapped by their foreign demeanor and lack of marketable skills, these newly established Polish-Americans struggled in the city environment. In an effort to safeguard their faith and culture, they claimed their right to worship in parishes specially designated for their purposes. They were not to be totally ignored by American church leaders. By 1870, seventy-four Polish parishes had already been established; by World War I, seven hundred Polish national parishes and five hundred schools served more than two million Polish immigrants and their children. American institutions were to be greatly altered by the Catholic world created by these "other" Catholics who worked unstintingly to maintain their own cultural traditions and, more important, to validate their way of being Catholic. The Polish immigrants and their clergy were to make a resounding impression upon the American Catholic church.

Although some Polish immigrants migrated to midwestern or New England farm communities, where they first worked as hired hands and then gradually became property owners involved in the political and civic developments of their localities, urban settlement remained the more typical Polish pattern. In the rapidly growing industrial cities where they labored in refineries, foundries, factories, or slaughterhouses, they settled in close proximity to one another and created Polonia in the midst of urban sprawl. By 1913, Chicago, known for more than a generation as the American Warsaw, claimed 250,000 Poles and twenty-three national parishes, thirteen of which were administered by the same religious community. Two of the city's Polish parishes alone claimed sixty-five thousand parishioners. Milwaukee and Buffalo ranked next in terms of numbers; almost seventy thousand Poles lived in each community, where they received special consideration from church officials. In Buffalo, one Polish priest, Father Jan Pitass, was assigned as vicar-general specifically to oversee the needs of Polish immigrants residing there. In other urban areas, such as New York City, Cleveland, Toledo, South Bend, Pittsburgh, Minneapolis, Omaha, Saint Louis, and Detroit, Polish ghettos emerged, clustering around churches and schools—the brick-and-mortar testimony to Polish Catholic development. By 1910, Connecticut ranked first among states in terms of the percentage of Poles in its total immigrant population (13 percent). By that date, the state had twelve Polish parishes, one for each of the concentrated urban areas, and 40 percent of the national parishes established in the diocese by that time had been founded for Polish immigrants.

By the 1920s, Polish-Americans had become even more numerous in every region where they were concentrated. By then, there were 400,000 Polish Catholics in Chicago alone, while New York and Pittsburgh had 200,000 each. Buffalo, Milwaukee, and Detroit numbered 100,000 each; Cleveland and Philadelphia each had 50,000. The overall region of Polish settlement continued to be bounded by the Great Lakes, the Mason-Dixon Line, and the Ohio and the Missouri rivers. This tendency among Poles to cluster geographically became an important factor in maintaining, even to the present time, a persistent

Polish Catholic culture. Despite competing traditions, which often divided the Poles on the basis of old- and new-world sentiments, there were several attitudes commonly held by the several million Polish immigrants living in the United States by 1920; these strengthened the common expression of their Catholicism, provided a unique meaning to the concept of loyalty and belonging within the Catholic church, and set them apart from other immigrant communities within the church.

More so even than the Germans, the Poles emphasized the importance of maintaining European religious traditions. They stressed the essential importance of the local parish to maintain their "Polish kind of faith." For them, the parish was the core of their religious identity, the place in which a special, corporate relationship to their authorized pastor would ensure both their earthly protection and their eternal salvation. In particular, they believed that their role as members of a congregation was to give primary allegiance to their pastor, who was the interpreter of religious meaning in the new environment. But by so doing they did not abdicate their place within the church or their belief in the significance of community rights, needs, and interests. According to their view, priest and laity had to operate from independent perspectives, even as they became Polish-American Catholics.

Although Polish-Americans viewed the pastor in patriarchal terms as the head of the parish—separate and distinct from any other clergy associated with the parish—they also believed that he held this cultural and religious leadership because of them. As they developed their faith in the United States, the relationship between pastor and congregation became a crucial means by which they maintained religious identity. In every respect, they expected proper conduct from their pastor; he became their model of virtue, obedience to the church, and competence. In return they gave him the right to observe and criticize their behavior. As for their own responsibilities, Polish-Americans believed they were obliged to respond cooperatively—though not necessarily as silent, obedient children—to every phase of the parish life that they created here. In their American setting, Polish immigrants saw themselves as equal, activist builders of the faith and members of the parish family, by whose freely given permission the pastor had the right to lead. Initiative on the part of the laity was, therefore, as much a right to be claimed by parishioners as it was a force to be exercised at the discretion of the pastor.

Although this understanding seems to reflect some aspects of the German conception of lay trusteeship as it was developed in the United States, there were several differences that made the Polish way of accommodating to the American church unique. For one thing, Polish-

Americans seemed more willing to submit to the far-reaching authority of the parish pastor than were the Germans, provided they retained the right to be selective about their response to pastoral demands. For another, the Poles sensed the corporate nature of their membership in the parish more than did the individualistic Germans. They particularly understood the parish's communal capacity to bring about salvation. To their minds, in fact, it was the collective strength of pastor and membership that supplied meaning to their lives, allowing them to survive in a hostile, new environment; it was the parish that affirmed their families' right to a sure spiritual destiny. In the words of one Polish pastor: "The Polish Catholic who does not belong to any parish is homeless—without any support, religious or national, he is a social bankrupt, a bandit on the open highway, and sooner or later he must perish because without support and help he will not be able to meet the test."[1] Furthermore, his warning that "the Lord God created you Polish men and women; therefore do not seek, as they say, foreign gods, but register and belong to a Polish parish" fell upon comprehending ears.[2] Group solidarity, based on loyalty to the pastor of their church, was fundamental to Polish thinking; it was absolutely necessary in order to give a sense of identity to a politically and religiously oppressed people.

Newly arrived Polish immigrants found this corporate view of parish life already in practice in immigrant communities by the 1870s. Churches, schools, and cooperative and self-help societies had been founded in every parish. Pastor and people worked within these tightly knit communities united by the one all-embracing sentiment that only in this setting could their salvation be assured. Each generation of Poles continued the trend, giving total loyalty and support to pastor and parish, and, if necessary, agitating for the establishment of additional national parishes. From the sixteen parishes that had been established by 1860, the number of Polish parishes climbed to some eight hundred by the 1930s. When the possibility of organizing new parishes was jeopardized by uncomprehending authorities, moreover, the Poles continued their complaints and protests—even beyond their own diocesan base if necessary. This fierce insistence upon their right to share in the decision-making concerning the establishment of churches and the appointment of pastors not only set them apart from most other Catholics but sometimes caused permanent separation from the church. Even when the German-American Catholics, whose confrontational attitudes the Poles sometimes emulated, began to deemphasize their need for special ethnic and cultural preference, Polish-Americans did not alter their course. In fact, they seemed to have increased the tempo of their complaints. In their criticism of church policy, they insisted upon maintaining a decision-making role in their own affairs and questioned why their clergy were not properly represented at higher levels of church governance. To the present day, the insistence upon maintaining these two rights has remained an important characteristic of Polish-American Catholics.

In the presence of such self-determined attitudes, even the most gifted of the early immigrant Polish clergy recognized the need to gain the cooperation of his parishioners. Regardless of the degree to which he was supported by his bishop, he realized that he had to prove himself able to lead the community to which he was assigned if he were to remain its pastor. In the early throes of any contest, moreover, priests often found their lives complicated by nearby Polish clergy willing to provide a rationale for parish dissent. From diocese to diocese in the decades at the turn of the century, episodes of intraparish rivalry bore testimony to this parochial phenomenon. If a new Polish pastor expected to achieve the cooperation of his parishioners, there were a number of important stages through which he had to pass. His first test almost always involved his spiritual leadership: his way of life had to assure his congregation of his moral rectitude. Moreover, his liturgical and ceremonial performance had to reflect the rich religious practices of the old world experience with which his parishioners identified. But to accomplish this, the pastor also had to be attuned to more practical, and more politically sensitive, details. He had, for example, to gain the support of the laymen who may have helped to found the church, recruited him, or raised the initial funds for parish expenses. To be guaranteed an extended pastorate, the Polish pastor had to balance the spiritual and practical aspects of parish life. Sacramental leadership, spiritual and educational assistance, and appropriate devotional expression of the faith had to be alternated with continued appeals for financial help to sustain the many social and pastoral ministries of the parish. If all this was achieved in the first several years of the parish's history, the undying loyalty of parishioners could be expected. Citadels of Polish accomplishment were built upon this model, each a testimony to the depths of Polish spiritual and physical persistence in the American setting.

Two examples of remarkable immigrant clergy who commanded gigantic community-parish systems were Vincent Barzynski, C.R. (1838–1899), and Lucyan Bojnowski (1870–1948). Barzynski was the guiding force behind the development of the Polish Catholic community in Chicago. A strong-willed, overpowering man who had been a member of a resistance group during the unsuccessful Polish uprising of 1863, Barzynski had gradually made his way to the United States as a member of the newly founded Congregation of the Resurrection. There he worked with Polish immigrants, first in Texas and then, with his appointment in 1874 as pastor of Saint Stanislaus

Kostka, in Chicago. He would be pastor of this parish until his death twenty-five years later. Despite episodes in which his authority was strongly challenged, he won the allegiance not only of his parishioners but of most of Chicago's Polish Catholic community. During his tenure, he founded an astounding range of Polish-American enterprises. He constructed a gigantic community system that included the largest Polish parochial school in the United States, the first Polish-American Catholic paper, *Gazeta Katolica*, and the first Polish daily in the United States, *Dziennik Chicagoski*, as well as a national fraternal organization, known as the Polish Roman Catholic Union, an orphanage, and a home for the aged.

Recognizing the importance of having a religious congregation to take charge of the schools he planned, Barzynski was also responsible for inviting the Congregation of the Sisters of the Holy Family of Nazareth, who arrived from Poland in 1885 to assist in his educational work at two of the Resurrectionist parishes. A model of personal moral integrity, Barzynski set the standard of excellence for all; because he was fiercely ambitious for the sake of his church and fearful that the faith of the Polish people would be jeopardized in the United States, he enjoined his clergy and sisters to provide the same kind of guidance and devote the same singlemindedness to every religious enterprise. Barzynski accomplished all of this in an old-world autocratic style that was buttressed by his favorite themes of authority, parish unity, and the need to build churches. In Barzynski's words, "We must and should do our utmost to protect and prolong the life of the Polish Catholic church. It is our life, our backbone; without it we are lost."[3] His oratorial skills did much to convince his parishioners of their need to be shepherded toward their heavenly goals. "We must cling together, even if despondent and in tears, and lift our hearts to God in heaven as brothers," he once pleaded. Who could refuse the next fervent request:

> Let us work together. Everyone! Everyone! Everyone who believes in the Triune God, in Jesus Christ's Redemption, in the Real Presence. Everyone, the young and the old, the married and the single, the rich and poor, everyone with the spirit of good will—Let us all mutually love each other.[4]

Despite defections that several times reached the stage of secession, his parishioners alone numbered more than 40,000 at the time of his death, and he had been responsible for the creation of at least thirteen of Chicago's Polish parishes. During his long tenure, Vincent Barzynski had been provincial of his religious congregation, had organized churches, encouraged new religious foundations, and had accomplished monumental achievements for the archdiocese of Chicago. At his funeral, five hundred carriages with ten thousand marchers alongside, hundreds of clergy, and thousands of the laity honored a powerful pastor and acknowledged that "dead is a patriot, who after his first love of God, always had his eyes fixed on the Fatherland."[5]

In Connecticut, another Polish-American pastor created a similar "surrogate diocese." From 1895 to 1948, Lucyan Bojnowski governed Sacred Heart parish in New Britain as if it were a medieval fiefdom. Like Barzynski, whenever he addressed his parishioners he expected to be obeyed. Civic officials anticipated this as well: they counted on him to keep the Polish people in line. Like Barzynski, not only had Bojnowski built a magnificent church and a first-rate school, but he also founded other institutions, including an orphanage and a home for the elderly. He, too, established a congregation of religious women, the Daughters of Mary of the Immaculate Conception, to serve the many apostolates that his parish sponsored. Like Barzynski, he accomplished many of these aims in the face of divisive episodes aimed against his authority, on several occasions only barely overcoming the wrath of dissenters among his own congregation. Yet by the 1920s Bojnowski had become a legendary figure to which both city and church officials could turn to interpret and to guide events concerning the Polish immigrant community. His energies and ambitions unbounded, Bojnowski even went beyond the needs of his own Connecticut flock, keeping Saint Joseph Immigrant Home in New York City from closing through financial assistance, establishing a home for girls in the same city, even spurring Polish-Americans on for the sake of the Allied cause during the two world wars.

Both Barzynski and Bojnowski achieved their aims because they had created a corporate system of Polish faith that met the needs of the Polish communities they served. Despite episodes of discord and threats to establish secessionist parishes, these two priests had been able to project values that motivated faithful Poles to follow. Their careers reflected those of other first-and second-generation Polish clergy, who had to confront similar circumstances and likewise meet with the approval of their congregations. These clergy also had to work within the shadow of dissent or internecine rivalry. Among the immigrant priests whose careers resembled those of Barzynski and Bojnowski were Joseph Dombrowski, who founded Saints Cyril and Methodius Seminary in Detroit for Polish-American candidates to the priesthood and who directed the development of a highly influential congregation of religious women, the Felician Sisters (the Congregation of Saint Felix of Cantalicio, Third Order of Saint Francis) and Jan Pitass, named dean and vicar-general for all the Poles in the diocese of Buffalo in 1892. Under Pitass, not only had Buffalo's Polonia been created (his parish comprised over 30,000 members) but so too were a number of Polish communities in western New York made possible. Under him as well, the "equality of rights" for Polish immigrant clergy was fostered.

Over time, the exact meaning of "a Polish kind of faith" and the implications of equal representation as voiced by Polish pastors began to assume shades of difference within Polish immigrant communities. In Barzynski's time, when American culture could only be painted in the darkest of hues by Polish-Americans, the idea strongly suggested that there was no possibility that religion and nationality could ever be divorced and that American clergy who served Polish communities must personify the unity of these two aspects of being Polish. For the next generations it would begin to mean a gradual melding of both Polish and American Catholic ways. But as the strong-willed, gifted Polish writer and priest Wenceslaus Kruszka would later suggest, adaptation to America could only occur naturally among Polish Catholics "as long as the inner feelings of Polish identity and a sense of obligation to Poland remained."[6] For him, representation on the episcopal level was the essential ingredient that would ensure the maintenance of the faith of every immigrant. In his view, his people must be served by "polyglot bishops for polyglot dioceses," so that, at least through the symbolism of language, it was made clear that the American church intended to be equally attentive to all its people. His feelings were, in fact, extremely vigorous on this point, as expressed in this controversial statement:

> I do affirm with certainty . . . that nowadays in the United States, whosoever [a candidate] dares to assume the duties of bishop in a polyglot diocese, without being a polyglot himself, takes duties upon himself which he knows he is unable to perform, and therefore commits a mortal sin. He should either learn "to speak with divers tongues" (for he cannot expect a miracle from God), or he should refuse to assume the responsible duties in such a diocese.[7]

Fortunately, Kruszka's argument was never developed. As time went on, the discussion over the degree to which "Polishness" should be protected revealed a certain mitigating tone. By the 1920s, Polish rhetoric suggested that one's ancestry should be enough to enrich the faith of Polish Catholics, regardless of specific national setting; that it was in American parishes of Polish ancestry that Polish faith could flourish; and that, while proper representation on the episcopal level remained an extremely important goal, the public parading of this grievance probably detracted from more important Polish aims, amounting, at times, to indefensible failures of diplomacy and etiquette.

Before this later, more enlightened, perspective reached maturity, however, the demand for special status remained among Polish-American Catholics in the decades at the turn of the century. Given the importance put upon parochial loyalties, Polish discontent was often focused on the parish—and often expressed before an audience of uncomprehending fellow Catholics. Although there were a variety of reasons why discord would flare up, each new episode undoubtedly testified to the same root cause of Polish dissension: namely, the Poles' inability to gain an appropriate hearing for their grievances, either because of lack of appreciation for their needs or lack of representation on the episcopal level. Well into the new century, the experience of having pastors and bishops unwilling to hear their requests, of discovering that their efforts were blocked by neighboring clergy whose jurisdictions were threatened, or, worse, of learning that some of their own people objected to their initiatives—these became the usual sources of Polish humiliation. The sense of rejection that such feelings produced was expressed through demonstrations and protests, usually directed against church authorities who, they argued, either neglected them or dealt with them unjustly. Only strong and consistent leadership by their own clergy could help them avoid such confrontations.

In almost every instance of lay protest, another discordant factor surfaced. Its presence revealed a unique factor that helped to shape the Polish-American way of adapting to American Catholicism. At the basis of much discord was an intense rivalry among Polish clergy themselves. No other immigrant group seemed so affected by competition between their clergy. When rivalry mounted, furthermore, the ambitions of disaffected parishioners and rival clergy were easily joined, strengthening intraparish rivalry, setting the stage for confrontation between the clergy involved, and subverting any notion that parishioners were in good faith with regard to the official church. The impact that these episodes, in particular, were to have upon the image of the Polish immigrant church and the American Catholic community generally was especially devastating. Regardless of the skill with which these protests were handled, the vulnerability of both Polish clergy and laity had been exposed. "Why is it," Bishop Horstmann of Cleveland complained when beset by Polish demands for a new pastor, "only the Poles cause trouble in this regard?"[8]

And Rochester's Bishop McQuaid, who had earlier confessed that he was not willing to believe the criticism directed against the Poles, wrote that because of one disastrous affair in his own diocese he could "no longer be patient with the misguided parishioners of Saint Stanislaus, who by their lawless and barbarous conduct of the past four months have become . . . a cause of blushing shame to every true Catholic in Rochester and in the country." Threatening excommunication and interdict at this point in the crisis, McQuaid ended by echoing the sentiments of other churchmen, suggesting that "there never was anything to compare with these Polish rows and conflicts."[9]

The discord that divided Polish communities had an intensity that often sealed any chances Polish-Americans had of demonstrating their ability to conduct their own affairs in other dioceses as well. Episodes in Michigan, Connecticut, New York, Pennsylvania, Ohio, and Illinois greatly disturbed the American hierarchy generally. In Detroit, for example, Saint Albertus parish became the scene of notorious outbreaks of violence beginning in the 1880s. During a twelve-year period in which a series of riots occurred, two parishioners were killed, many were injured, and much property was damaged. Scenes of jeering men and women pelting priests and police in rectories or in front of church property were matched by disturbing displays that took place within churches during solemn services. On one occasion, thirty police officers were required to stand in the aisles, with a half dozen more blocking the way to the altar, so that a substitute priest could say mass. Undaunted by this official show of force, the parishioners resorted to hissing, booing, and catcalling to drown out the words of the priest and effectively prevent him from continuing the ceremony. In a Connecticut parish, a beleaguered pastor wrote this disturbing note to his bishop, which he appended to the annual report: "Those conspirators against my spiritual authority, some sort of unduly americanized old Polish patriots, day and night in their Jewish-Polish saloons harassed the Polish people against me, telling them to expel the Priest and pay no heed to the Incorporation-act published solemnly at the church by the Reverend Rector."[10] And in Brooklyn, New York, the Reverend Leon Wyciecki suffered such a vicious round of *ad hominem* attacks instigated by fellow priests that he would soon return, defeated, to his homeland.

Such shocking incidents were reported in the secular press and became daily conversation in chanceries and rectories across the nation. Although both bishops and some of the Polish clergy attempted to defuse these episodes of discord, their efforts were usually delayed or seriously hampered by the rivalries that existed among Polish priests, rivalries that fueled lay discontent. Thus, in an incident in Chicago, Father Antoni Kozlowski became a leader of protests against two priests who were brothers; in Scranton, Father Francis Hodur took on hapless Reverend Richard Aust. Both eventually parleyed the support of disaffected parishioners in exchange for the expectation of acquiring leadership themselves, in the end precipitating a schism. The Catholic world looked on, sometimes in shock.

In some dioceses, the turmoil was defused by consistent policy developed by thoughtful leaders. Patrick J. Feehan of Chicago (1829–

1902) and Michael Tierney of Hartford (1839–1908) were two bishops who were able to develop a certain rapport with key Polish pastors; to these they often entrusted discretionary control over Polish affairs in their dioceses. When their plans succeeded, Polish communities retained self-respect. But tense situations and hard feelings between bishops and Polish-American clergy and congregations were far more typical, and "independentism" gained force by the 1890s. Despite Feehan's efforts in Chicago, for example, the dissident Antoni Kozlowski was able to gather 1,000 of 1,300 families from Father Barzynski's parish in 1885 to form an independent Polish Catholic church. In Wisconsin, where the first independent parish had been organized in 1873, a so-called Polish Church War gathered momentum under the fiery leadership of two outspoken brothers. Michael Kruszka, a layman whose newspaper presented the rhetoric of protest, and Wenceslaus, his brother, a priest who supplied much of the inspiration, laid out arguments stressing the need for equal treatment and for responsible administration on the part of America's bishops. Intensified by the editorializing competing newspapers, this Wisconsin crusade went on unabated until the second decade of the twentieth century. By that time, the first permanent schism to affect the American Catholic community had also occurred.

The creation of the Polish National Catholic Church, under the authority of bishops who were not in union with the Church of Rome, was the logical result of the Polish tendency to emphasize the special qualities of their Catholicism and their willingness to entertain independentism. In 1896, a "synod" of disaffected Poles met at Buffalo. At that assembly, a Polish-American pastor, Stephen Kaminski of Freeland, Pennsylvania, was elected bishop. Two years later Kaminski was consecrated bishop by a Wisconsin prelate who represented a schismatic, Old Catholic sect. The die had been cast. The same sense of solidarity and the unique understanding of the corporate nature of parish membership that had allowed Poles to resist solutions supplied by American Catholic bishops had now given way to the development of a church that was totally independent of Roman jurisdiction. A second breach occurred in Chicago under the direction of Feehan's adversary, Antoni Kozlowski. Accepting ordination as bishop from an unauthorized Swiss Old Catholic bishop in 1897, he too created a congregation independent of Roman authority. Kozlowski affiliated his church with dissident Polish communities in Indiana, Wisconsin, and the East. In Pennsylvania, after a series of bloody battles (tempered by sincere attempts to enlist papal support), Franciszek Hodur became the third major dissenter. With symbolic words of loyalty, Hodur's followers testified, as had the earlier groups, that they were willing to join him in taking the awesome step toward independence. In turn, Hodur accepted consecration as their bishop. Bolstered by the ordination of these three charismatic leaders, the varied groups of Polish-Americans eventually combined, and the largest schismatic church to develop within the American Catholic church became a reality. Until his death in 1953, Hodur was to be the driving force behind Polish-American independence from the Roman Catholic church. By 1960, the Polish National Catholic Church included more than 280,000 members, 151 priests, and 148 parishes and was located in many of the more traditional centers of Polish settlement in the United States.

Although its numbers declined subsequently, never reaching more than 5 percent of the entire Polish population and not extending far beyond the concentrated areas of Polish settlement, the existence of the Polish National Catholic Church was a warning to American Catholic leaders that it was possible that other ethnics might unite solidly in dissenting churches—even though these would be based more upon cultural or jurisdictional differences than on theological ones. What had encouraged separatism was the same characteristic that kept other Polish communities loyal to the church. Wherever the relationship between pastor and people was strong and there was support for an independent expression of their Polish kind of faith, dissatisfied Polish-American Catholics were able to be seduced into choosing their pastor over ties to the American Catholic church. Often it was a sense of betrayal, whether justified or not, that pushed them to this decision.

Despite the destructive consequences of these episodes, the sustained Polish discord and the eventual schism did have some long-term constructive effects for the Poles and for the church. It underscored the general reality of ethnic dissatisfaction within the American Catholic church and the fact that it could not be ignored. In particular, it forced Catholic leadership to consider the truth behind Polish dissension. Few could deny, for example, that little had ever been done to include Polish clergy in the ranks of the episcopate or to consider the language and cultural needs of Polish immigrants as a means of evangelization. Schism produced a consciousness-raising among church leaders and probably accounted for some minor breakthroughs for the Poles, if not for other groups. The Reverend Paul W. Rhode (1871–1945) was named auxiliary bishop in Chicago in 1908; seven years later he was appointed ordinary of the diocese of Green Bay, where 30 percent of the population was Polish. These appointments were considered milestones by Polish-American Catholics. In 1913, moreover, a second Polish-American priest, Edward Kozlowski of Bay City, Michigan, was named auxiliary bishop for Milwaukee. While considered important benchmarks in the developing relation between

Polish-American Catholics and the larger American church, it was clear to many that the naming of Polish bishops was but one, quite feeble step toward redressing the inadequacies of diocesan policies, especially with regard to promoting capable Polish clergy. Kozlowski tried to signal the more promising direction in his inaugural sermon. Reflecting first on previous difficulties, he told of the reason for his acceptance: "My decision and reflections were affected in no small way by the thought that it would be faint-hearted and cowardly to decline because the conditions among which I come to work in Milwaukee are unusually difficult."[11] And he attempted to set the future course with the words, "Yes, charity towards everyone, towards friends and enemies, towards Poles and others—love always and everywhere."[12]

But bitterness returned to afflict Polish-Americans by 1920. In that year, a memorial that the Polish clergy addressed to Rome, recapitulated the frustrations that continued to distress Polish-Americans who remained loyal to the church. Presented on behalf of Polish Catholics who were still working within the structures of the American Catholic Church, it enunciated their continued concerns about incorporation. The letter began:

> After more or less 30 years, the Polish Americans are beginning again, for the second time, persevering efforts to obtain from the Holy See the nomination of a Polish Bishop for America, who would have the mission to keep alive the faith among his countrymen, and also national feelings, which has always contributed so much in Poland to the conservation of the Catholic religion.[13]

The protest document contained a series of petitions. Yet, concern for the future of the all-embracing religious and social-service institutions of the Polish-American community somehow remained secondary to the episcopal concern. The authors of the memorial repeatedly returned to their theme, that "the best mediators between the Polish population and the American bishopric" were Polish-American bishops. In their discourse, they were willing to state that their people had assumed a "more or less separationist" character, which resulted in "almost a state within a state," but the petitioners defended their motivations, saying that this separatist tendency was based on "the most simple sentiment of justice" and that it "doesn't harm the church." The petition to have more bishops of Polish background appointed was, in fact, predicated upon their conviction that "the American Bishopric doesn't have, as always, a clear enough vision of the situation"; thus, they showed "little good will toward the Polish immigrants." By way of illustration, the authors referred to one American archbishop who publicly suggested not only that the Polish clergy had "become almost savages" but also that "no other Catholic element is so cordially hated as the Polish." Furthermore, they argued, even if such animosity could be avoided, there were other problems that arose from certain prejudices within the American church. Among these was "the apparent systematic and premeditated indifference . . . by most of the American Bishops" that made itself apparent, for example, in the kind of seminary preparation Polish-American candidates received and in the lack of opportunities afforded Polish seminarians to further their education in Rome.[14]

The statistics on Polish representation at higher church levels bear witness to the conviction of second-class status expressed in the memorial. In the 1920s, for example, only one of the nation's 119 members of the hierarchy was Polish; there were no vicars-general or chancellors of Polish background; among diocesan consultants only 15 of 595 were of Polish background. How then, the authors of the memorial wondered, could the proper needs of Polish-Americans be understood or attended to? According to the memorial, moreover, the recent efforts on the part of American bishops to develop a "new order of ecclesiastical operations" were particularly upsetting, especially because they might jeopardize the system of national parishes and, worse, encourage a move toward the consolidation of diocesan charities. "This reform dissolves almost completely," they argued, "the intimate tie between priest and the poor of the parish, takes away in a large way the paternal care of the priest, and introduces instead a bureaucracy of an official American committee, that limits . . . without being able to exert the moral control that the priests had over their parishioners."[15] In words reminiscent of the late-nineteenth-century German-American bishops, the authors concluded that only an episcopacy that made room for Polish-Americans in its ranks could ensure the protective environment needed to safeguard the Polish kind of faith. A vision of a church that valued pluralism and protected the religious traditions of every Catholic, especially through appropriate episcopal representation—this was the quintessential Polish-American dream.

Unfortunately, the tone of this statement was both scolding and critical. Because it also included a share of complaints about the Irish-American dominance of the church, it was particularly unwelcome among the American bishops. To their swift defense came the archbishop of Chicago, George Mundelein, who quickly registered his disapproval of the Polish memorial to Roman officials. The protest would eventually become much more of a source of embarassment to Polish-Americans than a means of redress. But it had accomplished some objectives. It had exposed the accumulated misgivings of one of the largest of the ethnic minorities within the American Catholic church, and it honestly named what was and would continue to be the most important expectation of minority Catholics within an Irish dominated church.

If one were, then, to name the most obvious way by which Polish-American Catholics contributed to the shaping of the American Catholic church, one would have to single out the Polish views on leadership and parochial structure as highly significant influences. These notions had not only largely determined how Polish-Americans strove to relate to the church but also influenced American Catholicism in general. They were, for example, what motivated Poles to work so zealously to build the kind of impressive parishes that inspired one journalist to write: "The immigrants Poland sends us edify us . . . by their attachment to the faith and by their marvelous self-sacrifice for the upholding of the material edification of religion."[16] They were the source of new vocations to the religious life and priesthood and of opportunities for leadership on the part of the laity. Through their parishes, moreover, Polish-American Catholics continued to strengthen their faith and their resolve to succeed within the American setting. Through collaboration on the parish level, they developed insights that helped them come to terms with their needs as both Catholics and Americans. In the American parochial environment, the spiritual functions of their old-world faith had been given new shape and direction—even if much had been accomplished through intense interaction with the larger church and the larger society. No other immigrant group seemed to comprehend so deeply the importance of retaining tradition in order to renew the faith.

The ecclesiology that enabled Polish-Americans to build an impressive network of institutions and to safeguard the thousand-year-old religious traditions of their homeland had both positive and negative ramifications. It had, for example, clearly strengthened them against the rhetoric of both church or civic leaders who argued for rapid Americanization. Their continued concern with preserving their religious and cultural heritage through their own community structures resulted in their repeated statement that American communities had the right to reflect the ethnic culture of their members. In this regard, they continued to remind the American Catholic church of its universality and American society of its need for diversity. But this same preoccupation with maintaining a separate culture would also lead them to their darkest moments. Their contentment over short-term successes with these strategies allowed them to ignore the long-term implications of their separatist stance. By emphasizing difference, they sometimes seemed to suggest that separatism in itself was a desired goal. Not only did such a mentality divide Polish-American Catholics structurally and create repeated episodes of conflict among

Poles who remained united with the American Catholic church, but it conveyed a whole range of negative messages to Americans in general.

As generations of Polish-American Catholics matured in their faith, especially after the 1920s, and became aware of the mixed blessing that their perspective on church life carried, their adherence to a Polish kind of faith and their membership in national parishes underwent some change. Adjustments to their expressions of national and ethnic loyalty were made after World War I, as new and dangerous waves of nativism prompted even the Catholic hierarchy to become more insistent upon Americanization. Intermarriage caused attrition in the membership of national parishes. In still other cases, changes in attitude within national parishes mitigated the strictest observance of tradition. If dissatisfaction with the authoritarian ways of their elders grew too great, younger Polish Catholics might begin new national parishes in suburban areas. Some second generation Polish Catholics shifted to nonnational parishes. In a few more difficult instances, moreover, the special status of a national parish was terminated by episcopal command, as occurred in Iron City, Michigan, in 1924 and in Chicago five years later. Sometimes the example of German-Americans whose American status had been irrevocably changed by world events moved Poles toward less explicit ties with their national parishes.

Despite these trends, however, the vast majority of Polish-American Catholics remained within the secure setting of the national parish. Aware that they had succeeded in combining the elements of faith, national feeling, and ethnic culture within the structure of their American parish community, they developed a sense of pride over their achievements as Polish-American Catholics. When observed by other Catholics, moreover, their attentiveness to and fostering of their ethnic Catholicism had begun to be appreciated as an important contribution to the shaping and strengthening of the American Catholic church.

CHAPTER
8
The Separate World of Eastern Europeans

*B*esides the Polish-Americans, there were other groups from the sprawling empires of eastern Europe who chose to emigrate *en masse* to the United States in the decades at the turn of the century. In the new setting, they re-created their distinct styles of Catholicism. As with the Poles, for each of these groups the preservation of language and culture was of fundamental importance. For this reason, a guarantee that they could continue to express their Catholic faith through cherished religious traditions became an essential goal; it also formed the basis of their willingness to adapt to the American Catholic church. The lack of that assurance, on the other hand, provided the focal point for dissatisfaction and dissent. Because these immigrants related to both the church and its leaders differently than the majority of American Catholics—even the Polish—their particular practice affected American Catholic practice. The degree to which the alternative expectations, views, and goals of eastern European immigrants were appreciated by majority Catholics determined the degree to which ethnic Catholics of central and eastern Europe shaped the Church in the United States.

Compared to the approximately three million Polish-Americans who had settled in the United States by 1920, other Eastern European immigrant groups, mainly Slovaks, Hungarians, and Lithuanians, may have appeared less significant numerically. Collectively, they probably totaled no more than Polish Catholics. Like other unskilled immigrants, moreover, the vast majority found themselves at the lowest socioeconomic strata of American society, their men working alongside Polish-Americans in northeastern or midwestern factories, mines, and steel mills, their wives and daughters involved mostly in domestic service, boarding-house chores, or factory work. Smaller numbers followed the pattern set by Czechs, emigrating farther west to the farming areas, especially of Nebraska or Texas. Among the Slavic groups, many affiliated with the Roman Catholic church; but some held on tenaciously to Byzantine, or other Eastern rite, traditions. By the 1920s, despite a certain ethnic kinship, three of the Slavic groups, namely, the Slovaks, the Ruthenians (each numbering some 500,000), and the Czechs (350,000) had all developed distinct traditional patterns within separate national parishes. The same was true of the more than 300,000 Lithuanian immigrants, who rejected their religious ties with the Poles once they had settled in the United States—despite the fact that most were able to speak the Polish language. Similar independence of religious development characterized the less numerous groups, especially those who had also been the victims of political oppression: the Hungarians, Croats, and Slovenians. Yet even in their scattered American settlements, each group in its own manner managed to affect the shaping of the Catholic church in the United States. Like the Poles, these ethnically diverse immigrant Catholic communities insisted upon expressing their faith in a distinct style, one that would ultimately complement the Polish perspective and underscore the American Catholic reputation for cultural pluralism. And as had been true with the Poles, much of the influence of these less numerous groups would be exercised through the parish. Within immigrant enclaves of their own making, pastors and parishioners set to work to maintain old-world values and to champion those republican values that would insure their continued autonomy.

By the 1880s, large numbers of Eastern European immigrants had already settled in the northeastern sections of the United States, especially New York, New Jersey, Pennsylvania, and Connecticut. In the Midwest, in the areas around Saint Louis and Omaha and in cities such as Cleveland, Chicago, and Detroit, they also developed self-sufficient ethnic communities. Predominantly in the urban areas, where separate accommodations could be made for them, clerical and lay leaders acted as intermediaries between community, church, and society. Following the basic pattern set by other Catholics, each group banded together to begin negotiating with the new world. Sometimes the previous settlement of one group precipitated moves by other groups. Thus, the Slovak community's success in church organization on the east side of Bridgeport, Connecticut, in the late 1880s pushed Hungarians, who had been their neighbors in Europe but who had arrived in the city later, to relocate *en masse* on the west end. Although churches were usually begun in cooperation with immigrant clergy, lay pioneers were always intimately involved in the initial plans. Lay leaders, for example, were the first to start the mutual-aid or other fraternal societies out of which most of the parochial institutions were developed; they also helped to gather together the faith communities and to raise the money to purchase property for church purposes. Single-mindedness characterized the first formalization of their relationships with American church officials. Unlike the middle-class Irish-Americans who wanted to blend into American society, however, most of Slavic, Hungarian, and Lithuanian immigrant groups preferred to develop parishes that maintained their separateness from other American institutions.

In the words of the Hungarian prelate Ottokar Prohaszka, who had visited fellow Hungarians in the United States, the national parish bound these immigrants, just as it had the Polish-Americans, "together like hoops on a barrel or the links in a chain."[1] It symbolized the religio-ethnic solidarity of the specific group. Sometimes imitating ornate baroque or Byzantine styles in stone, more often in simpler frame buildings, each church celebrated a people anticipating acceptance on their own terms. Usually located close by territorial parishes and side by side with other national parishes, each church incorporated special features of faith and piety: the hewn wayside crosses of the Lithuanians, the revered icons of the Ruthenians, the Marian shrines of the Czechs and Slovaks. Devotion to Christ in his Passion or to the Mother of God or to patron saints, such as Cyril and Methodius or John Nepomucene, bound the faithful spiritually in liturgical events and devotional services. Christmas and Easter, Lent and Advent remained the highlights of the social and religious year. Each group gathered within its own churches to celebrate these events and to ritualize the expression of faith. There, dramatic and choral presentations, feast-day celebrations, and processions and pilgrimages all proclaimed creative adaptations to the new land. So central were these devotions to the life of the ethnic parishes that the vitality of a parish was in part measured by the level of community involvement in the spiritual exercises offered by the congregation.

By the turn of the century, the pattern of leadership among these other Catholics in their accommodation to the American church was clear. Again, it imitated the Polish model. Those minority clergy who had retained the backing of their congregations found themselves in extremely influential situations even with diocesan leaders, who depended greatly upon them for loyalty and advice. Occasionally they even gained prestige within official diocesan circles, serving as diocesan consultants or in other advisory capacities. One Slavic priest,

Reverend William Coka, for example, forged such a good reputation in terms of parish development that he was appointed vicar-general of the Omaha diocese; at the death of the bishop in 1890, Coka was named interim administrator of the diocese. Because of the demands of their own congregations, however, and because diocesan officials depended more upon their leadership among their fellow ethnics, most of these immigrant pastors were not considered for positions that would have moved them beyond the limits of their pastoral service. Unless they lost favor with their bishops because of particular aspects of discipline, they usually enjoyed continued support from the diocese and a sense of independence from its restraints—especially if the parishes they directed were developing on sound financial bases. Prestige remained theirs, but usually only on the local level. There they were deferred to, both by their bishops and their people, on matters concerning the moral well-being of their parishioners; there a patriarchal spirit, which was familiar to both priest and people from their Old World experiences, insured faithful participation.

This special way of being Catholic in the American setting continued to dominate among Eastern European minorities well into the twentieth century. The dominance of the immigrant clergy and the initiative of lay people in the establishment of parishes remained, with parishioners and pastors trying to accommodate to one another within the confines of the parish while also satisfying the requirements of the diocese. Where this failed, the same kind of divisiveness that could disrupt Polish-American parishes might undo the best efforts of clergy and parishioners. "Isn't it true," wrote one prospective Lithuanian missionary to the United States, "as has been rumored, that in response to what the priest says in the pulpit, people persecute him, fire bullets through his windows, submit untruthful remarks to newspapers, sever parishes in two?"[2] Central and Eastern European immigrant clergy understood the background that prompted such questions. Riots seriously damaged the early career of Slovak pastor Gaspar Panik in Bridgeport; harassment continually upset the endeavors of another Slovak-American priest, Matthew Jankola, both as a curate in Pennsylvania and as pastor in Bridgeport. Troubles reached the diocesan level because of the demands of the parishioners of Saint Wendelin's in Cleveland and Saint Cyril's in Minneapolis. Dissension often discouraged the activities of creative Lithuanian pastors, like Alexander Burba of Pennsylvania or Joseph Zebris, the pioneer Lithuanian missionary to New England. They so disrupted Byzantine, or Eastern-rite, Catholic parishes in Connecticut, New York, New Jersey, and Pennsylvania that they precipitated a second wholesale defection of Slavic Catholics and the rapid growth of the Orthodox church in the United States.

Undoubtedly, Eastern Europeans still sought an ideal way of relating to the American Catholic church. Where their parishes were able to develop uninterruptedly along the lines of a corporate vision, they seemed satisfied that they were doing their best, and personal ambitions did not seem to take the same toll as they did among the Poles. For one thing, Eastern Europeans seemed less interested in gaining access to positions of prestige within the American church—especially the ranks of the Irish-dominated episcopate. There were notable exceptions, of course. Reverend Joseph Kossalko was very active in a national Slovak league, agitating for representation on the episcopal level. The Ruthenians, or Byzantine-rite Catholics, successfully argued for the right to name an episcopal leader with separate jurisdiction over their affairs. In a manner somewhat analogous to Polish and Ruthenian immigrant strategy, moreover, Hungarian-American Catholics promoted the idea of special delegates to represent their needs. For the most part, however, Slovak, Ruthenian, Lithuanian, and Hungarian immigrant Catholics seemed to content themselves with the notion that separate parishes and jurisdictions within the American church were sufficient to prevent interference in the development of their faith and their culture. In their pursuit of this limited goal, they generally had the cooperation of their bishops, once the bishops were convinced of the good will of both pastor and people.

Perhaps because they lacked massive numbers, Eastern Europeans sought ties with communities that were simultaneously developing in other parts of the nation. Such moves were often spearheaded by immigrant clergy, many of whom enjoyed national prominence as a result. Although they realized that their primary obligation was to serve those to whom they had been assigned as pastors, in reality, many priests preferred to work in the larger ethnic context. In fact, the interaction that developed between pastors and parishes in different parts of the country did strengthen ethnic solidarity. Pioneer clergymen like Stefan Furdek and Matthew Jankola developed Slovak self-consciousness as they worked in several midwestern and New England ethnic areas, serving as pastors, educators, directors of personnel, editors of journals, and authors of news articles or poetry. The immigrant pastor Joseph Zebris who established six Lithuanian parishes in Connecticut, founded at least eight other Catholic communities in Massachusetts, New York, and New Jersey. He also disseminated information nationwide on Lithuanian causes. Stephen Chernitzky, the Hungarian pioneer priest who created a model parish at Saint Stephen's in Bridgeport, Connecticut, brought a sense of importance to Hungarians nationwide. Because of the work of such immigrant leaders, dispersed communities of Lithuanians, Hungarians, and Slavic immigrants, became united to one another through the bonds of family and parish. The various communities of ethnic Catholics were also integrated through separate national organizations, composed of both priests and laity, that functioned on a social or cultural level and that incidentally ensured an almost instant communication of significant information involving the membership.

With the tacit acceptance of American bishops, therefore, eastern European leaders had found a number of ways of strengthening their immigrant communities. Within separate spheres but often in close proximity, each group conveyed a clear message about their particular way of developing within the American Catholic Church. Even the decision to provide schooling manifested differing perspectives and aims. Among Slovaks, for example, the establishment of schools seems to have been especially important. According to their spokesmen, this was because of the allegedly antireligious atmosphere in the public schools. In Stefan Furdek's words: "The saving of souls was more important than a good secular education."[3] Another early Slovak priest, Matthew Jankola, valued the religious education of Slovak children so much that he labored throughout his life to find ways of maintaining their cultural traditions. Agonizing over the lack of qualified teachers to educate children "without, however, destroying the national character and their cultural traditions," he worked to organize "our very own Slovak Community of religious teachers."[4] The community he helped to found, the Sisters of Saints Cyril and Methodius, became accomplished educators in many areas of the northeastern United States where Slovaks had developed separate Catholic parishes. Wherever possible, Slovaks established schools and acquired the services of religious women to staff them. By the 1930s, more than half of all Slovak parishes had schools; when these were unavailable, Slovaks were as eager to send their children to non-Slovak parochial schools rather than expose them to the secular values of the public schools. Because they believed that schools had the capacity to improve the quality of life, moreover, the Slovak community was notable for its development of specialized schools and academies and for the encouragement it gave its children to acquire college and university degrees. In Bridgeport, Connecticut, for example, the pastor of Saints Cyril and Methodius parish, Stephen Panik, established a commercial high school during the 1930s, and from this school an impressive number of Slovak youth went on to "normal" schools or four-year colleges.

Although the development of schools was less prevalent among other European minorities, religious education was an important goal for them as well. Some Lithuanian and Hungarian religious congregations of women were recruited from Europe or founded here specifically to provide a variety of educational services. The history of the Lithuanian Sisters of Saint Casimir reveals the desire of Lithuanian immigrants for teaching sisters, as well as the initial reluctance of one bishop to approve the idea. "They may fail," wrote Bishop John W. Shanahan of Harrisburg (1846–1916) to Father Anthony Kaupas in 1906, "and the Lithuanian people would be humiliated and probably scandalized." And to Mother Cyril, major superior of the Sisters Servants of the Immaculate Heart of Mary congregation in Scranton, Pennsylvania, who trained the fledgling community, he put it in more graphic terms. "My principal objection," he wrote in 1907, "is the downright 'cussedness' of the Lithuanian people. We don't know what moment they may put a stick of dynamite under the Convent, and blow the Sisters into Kingdom Come. Then a schism, a fight, or a row, is likely to occur, anytime, in a Lithuanian Congregation, and one faction may turn the Sisters into the streets."[5] The bishop's predictions proved vastly inaccurate. In later years, he grew to be one of their strongest supporters, and the Sisters of Saint Casimir were well received in their widespread apostolate.

The ministry of the printed word was another apostolate that seemed to be especially attractive, particularly to those ethnic leaders whose membership was both small and widely dispersed. This strategy certainly caught the imagination of Lithuanian-Americans. In fact, early pioneers among the Lithuanians seemed to value written communication as much as the Irish-Americans preferred sermons and other forms of public address. The content of Lithuanian publications also suggests that they pursued publishing in order to raise the ethnic consciousness of a people who had been unduly influenced in Europe by Polish secular values and now were being exposed to Protestant American values. Well documented is the fact that the experience of living in Russian-occupied Lithuania and seeing their language suppressed through the muzzling of the press had first fired the minds and hearts of those involved in the educational ministry. It certainly animated the zeal of such immigrant clergy as Alexander Burba, who published weekly scriptural readings and essays as early as 1896; Joseph Zebris, the pioneer of New England Lithuanian Catholicism, who edited his own newspaper, *Rytas*, between 1896–1898 and later was a constant contributor to Lithuanian newspapers; Anthony Kaupas, who served several Pennsylvanian Lithuanian communities and in 1909 became editor of the Chicago newspaper *Draugas*; Antanas Milukas, who was considered the most prolific publisher of Lithuanian periodicals and books in America; and Antanas Staniukyunas, who wrote for the Lithuanian press, translated and prepared series of readers for Lithuanian schools, and published commentaries on the New Testament.

To a number of congregations of religious men and women who

came to serve the immigrant population of the American church, this ministry of the printed word was also important. One congregation whose ethnic ties were deeply rooted in both Lithuanian and Polish traditions, the Saint Casimir Province of the Marian Fathers, developed such a reputation in that apostolate that they were commissioned by Cardinal Mundelein in 1919 to take full charge of *Draugas*, a Lithuanian newspaper for which they had already been working for several years. The philosophy of this religious community was that the apostolate of the pen was a marvelous opportunity for unleashing "a new weapon for their fight against the irreligion threatening the unadjusted immigrant Lithuanian."[6] Congregations of women could also join in the effort. When Sister Maria, the founder of the Sisters of Saint Casimir, first discussed her intention to enter the convent of the Nazareth Sisters in Chicago (a Polish teaching congregation), she was encouraged by a priest-friend to consider instead the apostolate of the Lithuanian Catholic press. Assistance in publications formed one of the major apostolates of the Marian Sisters of Thompson, Connecticut, when they were established in the United States during the late 1930s. For them, the printed word was the means of evangelization and instruction in the faith as well as the best means of clarifying the singular identity of their fellow Lithuanian immigrants.

Besides different emphases regarding ministries, there were other subtle means by which Eastern European immigrants demonstrated their particular style of relating to the Catholic Church in the United States. It was a widely accepted fact, for example, that each immigrant group tended to display a different way of confronting problems between themselves and church officials. The Slovaks, for example, prided themselves on their *Tauben-Blut*, or "dove-blood," which they explained as their ability to withstand their oppressed status with equanimity and which allowed them to approach bishops and other church leaders in a manner calculated to defuse tension and achieve success. In fact, they sometimes hinted that their history paralleled the Irish experience of persecution. As Matthew Jankola worded it, the Slovak story best resembled that of the Ireland's exiles; thus, the Slovaks were, in fact, the "Irish of the Hungarian kingdom."[7] Wherever possible they sought a peaceful way to avoid the escalation of their struggles with church authority on both the local and diocesan level. Still they were as capable of protests, including ransacking rectories, threatening bodily harm, and engaging in shouting matches against those who would deprive them of their "rights." While the Hungarians could also loudly defend themselves against alleged injustices and racial slurs, they were also often even more able than the Slovaks to adjust to the options presented them. Perhaps this was because, even before they came to the United States, many of their associates had become members of Hungarian-Reformed Protestant churches. For whatever reason, in the new world, their tolerance for religious diversity and their assimilating power seemed all the more remarkable. In fact, some of the immigrant clergy who came to serve them charged that Hungarian Catholics seemed prepared to join any Christian church, regardless of denomination. Like the Italians, the Hungarians also appeared more willing to accept non-Hungarian priests to minister to their spiritual needs.

In the end, it was one minority Slavic group, the Ruthenians, or Rusins, a Byzantine-rite Catholic people from one section of the Austrian-Hungarian Empire, who were to provide the most dramatic example of a confrontational style when challenged by American Catholic leaders. Even before 1900, these Catholics had strongly objected to their treatment by church leaders, who not only seemed insensitive to their need for special consideration on the basis of ritual differences but were even more intolerant of their tradition allowing clergy to marry. To be told by a liberal bishop, John Ireland, that he could not be incardinated in the archdiocese of Saint Paul so infuriated Father Alexis Toth that both he and his congregation joined a Russian Orthodox parish in Minneapolis. His case became a *cause célèbre*, forcing other American bishops to express their disapproving views of Eastern rite customs in general. Attempts at rapprochement were equally depressing, usually carrying warnings similar to the one expressed by Ireland in 1906 during an attempted reconciliation. "Of course you easily understand," Ireland wrote at that time, "that the priest coming to Minneapolis must be celibate. The presence of any other would be the occasion of great scandal . . . and I should feel obligated to protest against it."[8]

In the presence of such a shortsighted approach to ethnic difference, the Ruthenians—like certain Polish-Americans before them—decided to follow the path of schism. In their case, however, the issue for both priests and congregations was not so much one of their prestige or hierarchical representation within the church as it was a fear of losing their ancient and treasured ethno-religious traditions. Even the appointment by Pius X in 1913 of Stephen Soter Ortynsky, O.S.B.M., as the first Ruthenian bishop in the United States, an appointment that gave him full and ordinary jurisdiction over all the faithful and clergy of the Byzantine-Slavic rite in the United States, did not stem the tide of dissatisfaction. The reason for rejecting Ortynsky was based largely on ethnic concerns. Over one-third of these immigrant Catholics would eventually leave the American Catholic Church over the major issues of rite and married clergy, joining Greek or Russian Orthodox churches in entire congregations.

In the long run, their belief that the American Catholic church represented the Church of Rome was sufficient to retain the loyalty of most of these "other Catholics." Gradually more and more of the American Catholic bishops came to appreciate the strategy of accommodation—even to the point of allowing married immigrant clergy to continue to function as pastors, albeit unobtrusively, in some dioceses. This can be seen especially with respect to the Slovak, Hungarian, and Lithuanian minorities. For the most part, the predominantly Irish-American episcopate found the aims of these isolated immigrant groups congenial. In fact, they saw their demands as far less threatening than those presented by other, more aggressive immigrant groups. This may have been due to the fact that these minorities did not pose the same numerical threat as did the Poles or Italians and were more widely dispersed than some of the other immigrants.

To be sure, factionalism did take its toll. Sporadic riots, especially in certain Middle Atlantic and New England parishes, were obvious reminders of how tenuous could be the balance between Irish leaders and these immigrants from many European lands. Yet, if language, customs, and culture were permitted expression within national parishes, confrontations with church authority on the part of immigrant minorities seldom escalated to the extreme degree of acrimony that devastated Polish-American parishes. As a result, these minority groups did not exert the same kind of negative psychological pressure upon church officials as did other immigrants. Some would wonder if their very docility had, in the long run, worked against their best interests—as well as those of the church. Others would see the blessing in this approach for both minorities and the church. These Central and Eastern Europeans were, for the most part, able to maintain their faith, customs, and religious traditions within the ambiance of a protecting church.

What had really been achieved by these Eastern European immigrants in their attempt to become full-fledged members of the American Catholic church? They had, in fact, brought a rich and steadfast faith from Europe and persistently nourished it here within the confines of ethnic parishes. They understood what corporate participation in the life of the church really entailed, and they were willing to live by its standards. They provided a rationale for separatism that protected the newest members of the American church. Although their perspectives were advanced by the more numerous or more confrontational immigrants, the reinforcement provided by this motley variety of other Catholic traditions underscored the importance of valuing each portrayal of culture in the context of faith. Whether faith found expression in an Eastern ritual of solemn splendor, as was true of the minority Ruthenians, or was nurtured within a far more elaborate Latin rite than the Irish-dominated American church was accustomed to, its warm and appealing transmission proved important to the development of American Catholicism. Finally, just as the Germans had influenced earlier generations with their rich musical and artistic adornments of the faith, so too would these Slavic, Lithuanian, and Hungarian Catholic immigrants contribute to the elaboration of baroque forms of beauty in both their liturgical and devotional life.

American Catholic leaders understood that Eastern European immigrant congregations possessed an impressive group solidarity that could almost be viewed as an immigrant counterculture. Developed according to separate ethnic needs, these cultures had the capacity to enhance the faith of all those who appreciated what they had to offer. The diversity of expression and independence of thought challenged the myopic tendencies among Irish-American church leaders, making sensitivity to other traditions an important dimension of pastoral ministry within the context of the American Catholic community. Most important, the experience of these minorities pointed to a fundamental need among Catholics for identification as a religious community within American society. What these European immigrants wanted for themselves and for their children was analogous to the German- and Polish-American goal: that the cultural and religious values they shared—not the national ties which, in some cases, had been thrust upon them—be the decisive test of their Catholicism within the United States.

CHAPTER
9
The Italian Challenge

*P*erhaps as many as four million Italians arrived in the United States between the years 1880 and 1920. At least three-quarters of these came from the Mezzogiorno, east and south of Rome; they represented the most desperately poor of the Italian peninsula. In the United States, they joined small resourceful colonies of Italians who had settled in port cities and were the scattered diaspora of northern Italian immigrants who had begun arriving in the 1820s. The migration that grew from trickle to stream to flood-tide in the decades following the Civil War would eventually make the Italian-American population as widespread as the Irish-, German-, or Polish-Americans. The Italian-Americans are the largest ethnic Catholic group today. Fully half of the Italian immigrants ultimately returned home. Even more made numerous trips between the continents. Not until the post–World War I era would most decide that America was to be their permanent home.

Mostly male and single, the first contingents of immigrants were often described as "opportunists" or "birds of passage." Often they replaced the Irish in the most strenuous jobs in big-city construction, industry, or commerce; they were builders of bridges, tunnels, and subways, longshoremen and factory workers. Americans did not easily take to these more "swarthy" and illiterate people. Protestants viewed them as almost pagan in their concept of the Sabbath and disdained their boisterous religious celebrations. Many more were frightened by their talk of socialism and political anarchism or by their clannish displays of family loyalty. Most Catholics concurred in these assessments; to a great extent, they found it difficult to defend the Italian way of relating to either church or nation. In particular, the anticlericalism that some of the more educated Italians seemed to support offended the Irish, whose reverence for the clergy had already become legendary. When, in the 1850s, for example, Italians joined antipapists in the ceremonial burning in effigy of the papal visitor during his visit to the United States, some Irishmen became convinced that, in reality, the Italians wanted to join with the Protestants against them. Nor did Irish fears abate in the latter years of the nineteenth century. By then, anticlericalism had become widespread. To prove their point about the Italians, Irish writers simply pointed to the prevalent view as offered by one radical: "I hate proud and vainglorious men, liars, hypocrites, impostors; . . . but the men that I hate the most, and those whom I abhor and despise above the rest—are the priests."[1] Irish-American Catholics had other objections to the Italian immigrants as well. A typical comment was that pastors to the Italians "would starve to death" if they had to depend, as more than one priest did, "upon the beggarly Neapolitans" to support them.[2]

But Italians were equally disturbed—by these and other images that certain Catholics conjured up about them. Many Catholics, they argued, belonged "to that race of most intolerant Catholic fanatics whose priests teach them that we Italians keep the pope prisoner and make him sleep on a lurid straw cot." "From this," one observer wrote, "stems the inveterate hatred nourished by the priests of the Irish toward the Italians."[3] For their part, the Italians could not help but wonder how their Irish peers could be so attached to the Pope that they would ply him with money or run to him when beset by problems. Although Italian immigrants may not have always given the impression that they particularly aspired to become Americans, they were a loyal people who did not want to fail their church or new homeland. They were willing to accept the paternalistic overtures of the church, often demonstrating their docility through their cordial relationships with certain bishops, members of chancery offices, and the Italian-speaking Irish priests who were sometimes appointed as their pastors. In many respects, therefore, Italians did make efforts to adapt to American society; but little seemed to come of it. Thus, their experience would be extremely different from that of the Irish, whose "exiled" mentality helped them to think in more permanent terms about their involvement in the church's governance, structure, and life. Nor did Italian-Americans resemble the German or Eastern European minority Catholics, whose background as religiously persecuted Catholics had exaggerated their defensiveness against those who might deprive them of their "old-world" faith. That Italian immigrants remained faithful to their religion here really cannot be explained in terms of their being understood or well-treated either by American Catholics or Americans generally.

Today accounting for 20 percent of American Catholics, the status of Italian-Americans within the church still reflects their difficult historical experience in the United States and among the nation's Catholics. Having become members of the church at the very time that it began to take on a pronounced Hibernian cast, their lack of influence upon the contemporary church in terms of personnel and prestige is understandable. Given the minority status to which they were consigned along with other Catholic immigrants, they had few options concerning the role they would play in the shaping of American Catholicism. They could have imitated the Irish, using the church as a vehicle of personal advancement in American society; had they followed this course they might have been more able to influence church attitudes or policy. Or they could have ignored many of the institutional decisions and ideological directions which the church was making under the guidance of its Irish-American leadership. This separate path was the one that French-Canadian and Polish-American Catholic leaders had apparently chosen. Regarding the American church as a cold, remote, and puritanical institution that did not have their best interests at heart, the vast majority of the first generations of Italian-Americans gravitated toward the latter alternative. Remaining deeply attached to their Catholic faith *suo cuore*, they nourished their traditional religious ways within whatever framework was provided them—but in their own way. But they were far less afraid than some other groups to move beyond the national parish setting, integrate with American society through marriage or profession, or assume a greater role in church affairs. Unlike the Polish-Americans they saw little reason to cling tenaciously to presentations of the ritual or the doctrines of the church that reflected an ethnic modality.

The first parish founded for the Italians was Saint Mary Magdalene de Pazzi. Established in Philadelphia by Bishop John Neumann in 1852, its beginnings reveal something of the background of the earlier Italian immigrants, and its continuing history is illustrative of the typical pattern of expansion within the American environment. The parish's first pastor, Antony Cauvin, had been a tutor of Count Camillo di Cavour's family. His assistant was Gennaro de Concilio, a Neapolitan who arrived in 1860; his career also reflected an elevated social status, one shared with other of the earlier Italian clergy and laity. (Among de Concilio's accomplishments were his academic position at Seton Hall, New Jersey, where he was professor of logic, a noted scholar, and a chaplain; his contribution to the preparation of the Baltimore Catechism; and his role in the founding of two Italian parishes.) This original Philadelphia settlement proved an important magnet for Italian immigration. But the social and cultural background of the newer, turn-of-the-century immigrants was not be the same. The newcomers reflected the more desperate economic conditions that drove southern Italians to emigrate. As time passed, the overwhelmingly impoverished and unskilled immigrants who found their way to American shores were perceived in a different way, both by Catholics and by Americans generally.

By 1900, there were at least 50,000 Italians residing in Philadelphia alone, and Italians had displaced the Irish as the largest foreign-born group in the city. As would be true in other cities, many suffered from the prejudices of Protestants and fellow Catholics alike. Some became estranged from the church because of vulgar epithets or disrespectful treatment. In at least one of the so-called Irish churches they were subjected to the rantings of prejudiced pastors. Occasionally they were saved from this humiliation in more congenial Catholic settings. Sometimes they were even allowed to worship separately, often in basement chapels; there they nourished their faith through devotions, processions, and festive expressions of their faith. But the pattern of economic mobility was also clearly discernible. Over the next generation, Philadelphia again proved its capacity to lead; fifteen Italian national parishes would be established in the city; some others were founded in the suburbs, while many of the territorial parishes were altered by the Italian presence. This variety of initiatives and responses by Italian-Americans in just one American setting gives evidence of their capacity for adaptation to changing situations.

Other cities from coast to coast also became quickly populated by Italians. The settlement happened in much the same way and for many of the same economic and sociocultural reasons. In each of these areas, similar patterns of accommodation to the massive immigration developed. In such immigrant enclaves as New York, Newark, Boston, and, to a lesser degree, San Francisco, Italian immigrants simply joined existing Catholic parishes, where they worshipped with largely Irish congregations, were relegated to basement chapels, or accepted *de facto* status in changing neighborhoods. An example of this last accommodation was Saint Anthony de Padua parish in lower Manhattan, which originally included both Irish and Italian parishioners; by the 1890s, it began to take on a distinctive national character. Perhaps the most successful New York Italian parishes emerged from the Missione Italiana della Madonna di Loreto, begun in 1892 by Father Nicholas Russo, and the Congregazione del Monte Carmelo della 115ma strada, begun in East Harlem in 1884 by the Pallottine Fathers and raised to the status of an official Italian shrine-sanctuary in ceremonies celebrated in 1904. Other important Italian parishes included Saint Leo's in Baltimore, which early received the support of Cardinal

James Gibbons. First served by the Redemptorists, this parish later became a rich source of ethnic pride under the direction of the Pallottine Fathers.

Sometimes Italian immigrants were specifically asked to dispense with old-world regional differences in the formation of Italian parishes; they were even encouraged to join with other foreign-language speaking groups. In the case of Saint Ambrose in St. Louis, Missouri, a parish that consisted of Italians who emigrated from Lombardy or Sicily, the request to join forces proved troublesome; only the dynamic leadership rendered by church leaders and sympathetic secular institutions made this combination of disparate Italian groups workable. Despite the tensions that might be expected these strategies were typical responses to the press of immigrants. In Paterson, New Jersey, Italian Catholics were first asked to worship with Franco-Americans at Our Lady of Victories; in nearby Passaic, they were ministered to by an Italian-speaking Slovak priest. The original parish assigned the Italians of the San Francisco area was Our Lady of Guadalupe, a church specifically designated for Spanish-speaking immigrants. Archbishop Joseph Alemany appointed an Italian assistant to the parish and granted it a special dispensation so that services for the Italians could be provided. Only when increasing waves of unskilled Italian workers began to arrive in San Francisco after 1880 was the Church of San Pietro founded just for the Italians. Interestingly, the title given to the new parish was deliberately chosen, not to commemorate a saint to which the Italian community was devoted, but as a sign to anticlerical factions of this congregation's allegiance to the pope and the universal church.

By the turn of the century, two basic concerns influenced the decisions of most Catholic leaders relative to Italian immigrants. Some churchmen continued to worry over the abstract "Roman question" and its anticlerical implications, especially with regard to Italian attitudes toward papal authority. Others expressed concern over the more practical "Italian problem" generated by the rapid influx of southern Italians and exacerbated by the lack of reliable immigrant Italian priests. As early as 1884, the question of what to do with the impoverished and "neglected" Italian immigrants had been of concern; it was one of the topics introduced that year at the Third Plenary Council. It was then downplayed, because of the sensitivity with which it was met in Roman circles. In the words of the bishop of Wilmington, Thomas A. Becker (1832–1899), it was "a very delicate matter to tell the Sovereign Pontiff how utterly faithless the specimens of his country coming here really are." Yet, even Becker seemed able to assess the complexity of the problem and recognize the responsibility of the church to provide spiritual care. Although religious ignorance and "a depth of vice little known to us yet" were reasons for the accumulating problem, he submitted, the immigrants themselves were not to blame; rather, it was their clergy, who were "sadly remiss in their duty."[4] As immigration increased, the realization that something must be done for Italians if their religious heritage was to be saved was constantly on the lips of Irish spokesmen. If at times they expressed shock over the irreverent and blasphemous language of Italian radicals and fretted over these radicals' capacity to subvert the masses, they realized their need to face the immediate predicament: overwhelming numbers of desperately needy Italian immigrants who looked to the American Catholic church. From diocese to diocese, some bishops and clergy sought ways to impress the Italian newcomers with the responsibilities that had to be shouldered by both American Catholics and the immigrants themselves.

This special "Italian problem" was often discussed in ecclesiastical reviews and diocesan newspapers. The need for a closer look at the basic realities of immigrant life was often a focus of these articles; analyses of the problems were facile. According to many of the authors, a large part of Italian immigrants' troubles stemmed from the *padrone* system. Because of it, they argued, the people were "always and constantly led by designers, who use and abuse them in money matters as well as in religion."[5] But their illiteracy, narrow "village" mentality, and explosive emotionalism were also cited as factors hurtful to their spiritual and temporal well-being. In 1899, the editor of Milwaukee's *Catholic Citizen*, Humphrey J. Desmond, published another view of the problem. In his tract *The Neglected Italians: A Memorial to the Italian Hieracy* (sic), he expressed dismay that "Catholic Italy, with her rich church endowments, her surplus of priests and her virtual control of the revenues of the Catholic world" had not looked after its own problems.[6] As the years passed, many would argue even more emphatically that this was, in actuality, the "biggest Catholic question."[7]

Still another concern often mentioned in articles and essays was the apparent "apathy" with which Italians seemed to meet the obligations of their faith. It was an attitude that astonished most Catholics, who had hoped that a change would come with the arrival of the wives and children of Italian immigrants and their settling down in numerous "Little Italy" enclaves. But Italian men continued in their previous habits of religious disinterest, as Patrick Corrigan, the author of *What the Church Most Needs in the United States* (1884), observed. Living in "perfect indifference to the affairs of their Church, and to the ordinary practice of their religion," Italians seemed, he noted, to transfer their religious obligations to the women of the family.[8] Moreover, unlike the Irish, Germans, and Slavs and other eastern

Europeans—all of whom persisted in their efforts to seek out priests from their own villages or cities to serve them—few Italian immigrants seemed to look back to the old country for their religious leaders. Instead, displaying a certain degree of exasperating docility, they appeared to prefer a passive attitude toward church affairs. Only the rites of passage and the celebrations of their festivals compelled both interest and activity. Apparently, because their wives and children continued to attend church faithfully—some figured that over 70 percent of all Italian churchgoers were women—they maintained a pattern of aloofness. Worse, Italians in general did not seem at all interested in the education of their children in parochial schools, especially if the education was according to the pattern set by the Irish. For this reason, it was feared, the religious education of Italian adults and children would be undermined. Ironically, this apparent religious apathy and lack of interest in institutional involvement by Italian-Americans created as much a problem for American Catholic leaders as had the stubborn upholding of their traditions of faith by Eastern European immigrants.

Complicating the issue, according to American Catholic observers, was the Italian immigrant response to the blatant endeavors made by Protestants to convert them. Like many Catholics, Protestants had noted the apathy and "unchurched" demeanor of Italians. They seemed to understand that the present religious status of Italian immigrants had been made worse by prejudice on the part of Catholics— that, for example, much of the disaffection felt by Italians stemmed from the lack of welcome often extended them by bishops and pastors. But they were also aware that Italians seemed disinterested in the institutional development of the church under the aegis of the Irish-American hierarchy. From this, they deduced that these immigrants, in particular, would be receptive to evangelization, and they prepared to take advantage of the strained situation. According to one Catholic editor, every Protestant church developed missions among the Italian immigrants. In fact, the Methodists, Baptists, and Presbyterians together financed more than three hundred churches and missions in Italian neighborhoods and assigned some two hundred ministers to evangelize. Even Episcopalians and Congregationalists developed plans to missionize them, as Philip Rose, pastor of the First Italian Congregational Church in Hartford, testified in his 1922 monograph, *The Italians in America.*

Not surprisingly, this unprecedented development did occasion a strong defensive response from U.S. Catholics. As the official newspaper of the Chicago archdiocese, *The New World,* observed, "designing societies with deluding names are forth to proselytize. Sinister social settlements abound and are laying foundations broad and deep for the decay of faith." According to another commentator, the settlement houses and social centers where evangelization was going on had become the "sectarian dens of these human spiders." In particular, they were incensed over the use of English language classes, sewing instruction, nurseries, musical bands, and other welfare and social programs as means toward missionary ends. Protestants, they complained, were well on their way to detaching "the immigrants from the Mother Church."[9] What these worried Catholics failed to emphasize, however, was that the Italians had few scruples about taking advantage of Protestant overtures. The fact is that this energetic proselytizing and its acceptance by Italian immigrants both intimidated and embarrassed the Irish-led church. Just how, indeed, could they explain to Roman officials that Italians were the only group of immigrant Catholics being successfully lured by these "misguided soul-chasers" from their ancient religious traditions?[10] Something, indeed, had to be done to ward off the alarming advance of Protestants among the nation's newest Catholic immigrants.

Finally, the Italian penchant for both anarchism and anticlericalism, which sometimes manifested itself in violent behavior, remained a focus of discussion and concern. Some argued that it was this tendency more than any other that characterized the "Italian problem," sullying the reputation of the church by implication. Thus, when an Italian anarchist shot and killed a priest as he was distributing communion in Denver, Colorado, in 1908, not only was the nation horror-stricken, but the American Catholic community was compelled to voice its concerns. As far away as Chicago, one Irish priest predicted the worst. "There is no denying," wrote Edmund M. Dunne, then pastor of Guardian Angel parish, that the "lives of Chicago priests are endangered by recent anticlerical agitation." Convinced of ensuing tragedy, priests said mass under police protection, especially in Italian parishes, while newspapers fed the paranoia with reports of real or expected violence. Granting that the Italians were "in the mass a law-abiding and deeply religious people," the Chicago Catholic paper stated the position quite clearly: "Among them are to be found coteries of evil minded and foul hearted men who are banded together for the purpose of disseminating principles that make for social and religious unrest . . . and . . . goad unfortunates . . . to terrible crimes." Subsequent events would prove that hysterical xenophobia, especially regarding Italian immigrants, could easily sweep across the nation, exciting even the Catholic population and producing comment in church circles.[11]

One underlying question recurred for the church leadership: what was to be done about the unique Italian situation? Being willing to solve the problem was, in itself, a sign of growth. It meant that the leaders of the church admitted that they had to come up with an acceptable plan with respect to the Italians. In so doing, Catholic leaders began to realize that not only did they have to define the specifics of the Italian situation, but they had to go beyond Italian problems to discern whether the norms and standards of discipline and practice that they had devised were really appropriate for every Catholic. Specifically, were their attitudes toward the expression of faith in the United States patronizing toward Italians? Were they really in a position to speak of the typical Italian celebrations as bizarre or superstitious? Were they free to ridicule their love for the Sousa bands, the aroma of grilled sausage and fried green peppers, the lantern streamers and the Madonna statues covered with the donations of penitent marchers—all of which often seemed more important to Italians than liturgical celebrations? Finally, was it right for Irish-American leaders to publicly criticize the behavior of Italians, to refer to their plight as the "Italian problem" or as "our biggest Catholic question" and, worse, to complain in private about their manners, their ignorance, and their apathy?[12] In the face of so many disturbing questions, many began to agree that it was time to investigate and remedy the source of these negative attitudes as well.

By 1913, the Paulist priest-author Joseph McSorley lamented the obvious: that the Italian population had, indeed, "run beyond us; [had] grown so fast as to confuse us; [had] made demands which under the pressure of other work . . . [have] tempted many of us to believe that the task of adequately meeting these demands is clearly impossible,"[13] Sometimes Italian priests offered their own jeremiads as well. With attendance at church services down to, perhaps, only 5 percent of the Italian population, one immigrant pastor, Salvatore Cianci, bemoaned the "kind of anemia of the soul" that prevailed and the behavior of his people, who regarded their faith as "nothing more than a halo which glorifies our cradle to disappear after first communion and be conjured back again at our last moments to hover over our coffin."[14] In the long run, the Italian situation became almost a litmus test for every other immigrant problem. Confronted with their own prejudices and the complexity of dealing with this particular "unchurched" Catholic group—and sometimes abetted by the concerns of Italian clergy—Catholic leaders had to face the immigrant problem in its most exaggerated form. In the end, they addressed the problems raised by Italian immigration with a far greater seriousness than they had afforded the problems of any other of the European immigrants. Precisely because Italian immigrants as a group looked to the American Catholic church for answers to some of the questions concerning Catholic identity more than did other immigrants, they had become the first group to force the American Catholic church to grapple seriously with the implications of ethnic diversity within the same cultural environment.

Challenged by the special circumstances presented by Italian immigration, many of the nation's bishops began to develop more sophisticated strategies for dealing with Italian immigrants in their dioceses; at the same time they doubled their efforts to locate clergy committed to the task of evangelizing immigrants here. Because of the multiple problems caused by the "apathetic" among the Italian immigrants, however, some new, creative approaches were initiated. New York's Archbishop Michael Corrigan, who had reported in 1884 that he believed that only 1,200 of his diocese's 50,000 Italians attended church, refused to let a series of disappointing first attempts keep him from searching for Italian priests. When an Italian bishop, Giovanni Batista Scalabrini, founded a college at Piacenza in 1887 to train priests to be missionaries in the Americas and, that same year, also began the Pious Society of Saint Charles Borromeo for this apostolate, Corrigan wrote almost immediately to him, "The Lord be praised a thousand times! Now I can breathe easy. . . . Up to now I could find no way to save them. Finally I am happy and assured. I commend to you my neglected Italians. I should like to have, if possible, two missionaries immediately."[15] In 1888, the first ten Scalabrinian missionaries were presented with mission crucifixes. That very year, several were already at work in Corrigan's New York.

In nearby Hartford, Connecticut, another bishop, Lawrence J. McMahon, had requested help from the same community only months after their arrival in New York. His first letter to Bishop Scalabrini, dated October 30, 1888, met with similar success. Almost immediately, two parishes were started by members of the new apostolic society in New Haven; a third was begun in Hartford. McMahon's successor, Michael Tierney, advanced the process one step further; in 1904, he sent the first two of several Irish-American seminarians from Hartford to study for the priesthood in the seminary at Piacenza. Later, under his successor, John J. Nilan, some of these graduates were assigned as pastors to Italian parishes in Connecticut. At the same time, not only were the services of the Scalabrinians used in innovative ways by the bishops of New York and Connecticut, but by the turn of the century this congregation had been called upon to take charge of more than twenty parishes in several dioceses throughout the United States. Especially strong in Chicago, New York, and New England, they already numbered more than fifty priests and forty brothers by the turn of the century and were dispersed in both North and South American mission fields. Because the Scalabrinians expanded their numbers to include non-Italian candidates, they also helped church authorities find solutions to other immigrant needs. Thus, when John Chimielinski, who had entered Scalabrini's Instituto Cristoforo Colombo in Piacenza, came to serve an Italian parish in Boston, it was not long before he was called upon to serve the neglected Polish population of the city, establishing eventually some of the first Polish parishes in the Boston area.

In a similar fashion, many American bishops lent support to proposals offered by Italian clergy working in the United States. For this reason, a number of Italian immigrant priests were able to render important services within their dioceses. One was the Italian Franciscan Leo da Saracena, a Civil War veteran. Da Saracena's vision for his Connecticut parish included the establishment of a congregation of religious men and women, a parochial school, and a boarding academy, which he founded in 1866 for "educated young ladies in the higher branches," as the school's advertisement stated. But he also served an important role in the diocese, functioning both as consultant to several bishops and as theologian to the Third Plenary Council. It is possible that it was da Saracena's good judgment and constant presence as adviser that convinced Bishop McMahon to persist in his efforts to locate other Italian priests to serve the diocese. Throughout his career da Saracena not only received the respect of the Catholic community but was also appreciated generally by the citizens of Winsted, Connecticut, where he served longest. In 1896, the Yankee town awarded him with a gold medal for his thirty-five years of community service. Another important immigrant priest-builder of the American Catholic Church was Nicola Odone, who arrived at Saint Paul in 1899 at the invitation of Archbishop John Ireland to take charge of the Roman Catholic mission among Italian immigrants in Minnesota. Although Odone met with great difficulties and eventual failure in his attempt to bring together several immigrant groups from culturally distinct regions of Italy, he did provide strong leadership during the first decade of his missionary work. Like other Italian priests, his main role became that of mediator between the immigrants, American society, and their church. Especially through his sermons and his quarterly journal, the *Guida Practica*, Odone provided his people with advice and even remonstrance to move them toward integration into American society.

Other early Italian clergy evangelized, with varying degrees of success, especially in the major eastern- or western-seaboard dioceses where most immigrants had settled. A more well-known clergyman, whose advice some of the nation's bishops particularly heeded, was Pacifico N. Capitani, pastor of the first Italian parish in Cleveland. When this immigrant priest developed a program to improve the Italian situation in the United States in a series of articles published in 1889 in the *Freeman's Journal*, his ideas were read and discussed.

Maintaining that the real blame for the loss of immigrants from the faith lay in the neglect of Catholic leaders both in the United States and in Rome, Capitani proposed the establishment of an Italo-American College in the United States for the preparation of missionaries to the Italians. According to his plan for the institution, the training of English-speaking Italian priests would be the major goal, since this was absolutely essential if the second generation was to find salvation. Although several important American prelates, including Cardinal Gibbons, gave support to Capitani's appeal, nothing came of it. Yet, what was demonstrated by the attempt was the concern and willingness of the bishops to find constructive ways to improve the lot of Italians.

Until other programs similar to the college proposal could be developed, the bishops continued to call upon religious congregations, like the Scalabrinians and the Italian Franciscans and Jesuits, to found parishes in their dioceses and to help them locate other congregations who could join them in the task. In San Francisco, for example, the Italian Jesuits stationed at Saint Ignatius College, whose headquarters were in Turin, Italy, were asked to care for their fellow immigrants throughout the city and, later, to establish the first Italian parish, Saints Peter and Paul. Within a few short years, however, the need for more priests became so urgent that Archbishop Patrick W. Riordan (1841–1914) sent a second petition to the Italian Jesuit headquarters for additional priests. Having no priests to spare, the Jesuit superior turned the matter over to Turin's Salesian community. In 1897, four years after Riordan's petition, the first members of the Salesian community arrived in San Francisco to take over the parish. This congregation was later involved in the establishment of a second parish for Italian and Irish parishioners, and the congregation's activities spread beyond the California diocese. In an interesting wrinkle in the usual pattern of European missionizing in America, what assisted the Salesians in expanding into the second San Francisco parish was the presence of four candidates from Ireland who had joined their Turin community and could then be sent to the mixed Italian-Irish parish in the United States.

Since the American bishops were painfully aware of the need to find missionaries who could address the basic human needs of the impoverished, they turned their attention to locating religious congregations of women. In the 1880s, the first of a prodigious line of women religious was recruited for the American mission, the result of the same New York-Rome communications line that had brought the Scalabrinians to the United States. The first stage of this unfolding drama was the redirection that Leo XIII gave to the mission of Francesca X. Cabrini, guiding her away from her desire to work as a missionary to China toward a commitment to Italian emigrants to the United States. The next stage was the prodding that Bishop Scalabrini gave to the archbishop of New York concerning the availability of the new community founded by Mother Cabrini. The fruit of these endeavors came on March 19, 1889, when the bishop of Piacenza presented mission crucifixes to Mother Cabrini and her first six sisters, Missionary Sisters of the Sacred Heart. Within a month after their arrival in New York, these sisters were operating an orphan asylum and otherwise providing health and social services to immigrants. Within three years, they were in charge of a hospital as well. Under Mother Cabrini and under the Salesians, who had also been invited by Archbishop Corrigan during this period, again under the advisement of Bishop Scalabrini, parishes and institutions to help the desperately poor of New York were organized.

Before her death in 1917, Mother Cabrini had shared in the organization of sixty-seven institutions, including schools, day nurseries, hospitals and orphanages. Her Missionary Sisters, who had come to number more than 2,300 members, quietly worked in missions throughout the Western Hemisphere. At the same time that Mother Cabrini's community was expanding, a number of other Italian-based congregations had become involved in ministry to Italian immigrants. In 1895, Scalabrini himself had founded a congregation of sisters, the Missionaries of Saint Charles. Because of Italian initiative and the encouragement of American Catholic bishops, there were over two dozen Italian religious orders caring for Italians in America by 1920. Once again, the archdiocese of New York was in the forefront of innovative projects. In the early decades of the twentieth century, for example, Archbishop James Farley adapted the Capitani challenge to his needs by giving over an old diocesan seminary in Troy to the Salesian Fathers for the purpose of training Italian-American boys for the priesthood. He also saw to it that a diocesan bureau, specially organized to care for Italian immigrants, was begun in 1912. Finally, not only did he encourage Italian priests to develop a program, called the Apostolato Italiano, to preach missions to Italians, but he also asked the Italian clergy to join him in dialogue over new ways to help the immigrant.

In other dioceses, supportive bishops developed distinct policies and programs with the needs of the Italian immigrant children in mind. Much of what they proposed could be considered unprecedented. The diocese of Hartford provides an interesting example. In 1914, Bishop John J. Nilan called upon diocesan clergy to head a core of Catholic public school teachers (most of whom were Irish-Americans) in organizing special religious education programs for Italian immigrant children. According to his plan, which was published in both the diocesan and secular press, the teachers were to urge their Italian pupils to attend mass and Sunday school. They were also to work with the clergy, especially with regard to encouraging Italian pastors to develop regular programs of religious education. If they discovered that the children were receiving no formal instruction, they were to form classes themselves and were "not to be interfered with by the Italian pastor until the priest whom I shall place in charge of certain centers shall see fit to place them under his direction." "In other words," Nilan concluded, "all doors are to be opened to the Italians and the disinterested and earnest work of all the priests of the diocese is sought in the effort to save to the church some of the tens of thousands who come to us without instruction and with little love for priest or church."[16] Local programs were begun in other dioceses with the assistance of religious sisters, brothers, or lay persons with varying ethnic backgrounds and training. The Sisters of Mercy, whose roots were in Ireland, and the Sisters of Charity from Cincinnati were among many established American congregations called upon to work among Italians. In the West, the Sisters of the Holy Family became well known for their involvement in the religious instruction of immigrant Italian children.

Especially in those sections of the United States where the largest Italian communities had settled, episcopal initiatives were proposed and developed during the first decades of the twentieth century. In Chicago, "the bishop of the immigrants," James E. Quigley (1854–1915), worked at trying to save the next generation of Italians. His proposals were often structured around education—bringing Italian children into existing parochial schools or founding schools specifically for them. In the process of establishing some dozen Italian parishes in Chicago, Quigley recruited both the Servites and Scalabrinians and assigned a number of diocesan priests for this purpose. In Newark, Bishop Winand M. Wigger (1841–1901) pursued similar strategies. He both founded schools and encouraged the development of catechetical programs. In neighboring Trenton, Bishop Thomas J. Walsh (1873–1952) began school programs and located Italian sisters to staff them. Several of the Pennsylvania dioceses produced similar programs. In Philadelphia, Archbishop Patrick J. Ryan (1831–1911) encouraged and financially aided the Missionary Sisters of the Third Order of Saint Francis so that they could begin kindergartens and day nurseries to assist Italian immigrant mothers; efforts were made to provide the same kind of services in Pittsburgh. Bishops of Syracuse and Rochester, New York, and Kansas City, Missouri, cooperated with Scalabrinians and other Italian congregations in the founding of schools. Under Bishop Thomas F. Hickey (1861–1940), for example, vacation schools for Italian children were opened at Rochester in 1916;

his successor, Bishop John O'Hern (1874–1933), also developed programs for Italian immigrants.

Although formal expansion of institutional services for immigrants had to begin at the offices of bishops, one must not underestimate the contributions of diocesan clergy and the congregations of religious, whose support for almost 600 parishes throughout the nation and whose assistance in schools, immigration bureaus, and mission offices made continuing success possible. As one historian of the Italian experience, Giovanni Schiavo, remarked about these efforts: "To give credit where credit is due, the Italian immigrants owe a great debt of gratitude to quite a few American priests, mostly Irish, with a sprinkling of German . . . who spared no efforts to help the immigrant both in his religious and civic life."[17] Nor can the work of individual lay people and the organizations they sponsored be ignored. Settlement houses in Chicago, Rochester, and New York, for example, were renowned for their assistance to hundreds of thousands of Italian immigrants. So too were the hundreds of mutual-benefit associations, such as the Maria Assunta Society of Berwick, Pennsylvania, acknowledged as precursors of parochial development or social-service centers. When a spirit of cooperation between Italian immigrants and church representatives developed through such means, the best aims of all were achieved, and the question of the "indifference" of Italians was rendered meaningless. But resistance to the suggestions of these groups could produce effects as disastrous as those seen by Eastern European immigrants.

By the 1920s, then, a loosely coordinated pastoral plan had been created across the dioceses of the nation for Italian immigrants. To a large extent, it functioned relatively smoothly and proved to be more ambitious than any plan developed for other ethnic groups. No long lasting schisms or scandalous episodes occurred to embarrass either Italians or church leaders. While the earlier phase of assistance to the Italian immigrants may have been prodded into existence by Rome, the second phase indicates that both church and immigrant groups had begun to value mutuality as the better relationship between immigrant and church. From the somewhat paternalistic stance taken earlier by bishops and accepted by Italians evolved gradually a greater cooperation between both groups. This subtle change gave new energy to the Italian community and added new dimensions to the ethnic shaping of the American Catholic church. The clearest sign of this new phase was new Italian-American initiatives regarding their role in the institutional church. Diverging from the path taken by Polish-Americans and French-Canadians, Italian-Americans preferred to maintain their national parishes, develop schools, yet remain socially integrated with other Catholics.

The Italian-American immigrant community was greatly affected by World War I. The decline in immigration during the war, the effect of the war upon their homeland, and especially the rising xenophobia of the nation, which was often directed against them and which culminated in the immigration restriction laws of the early 1920s, made many finally face the inevitable: that they would have to forsake their dream of returning to Italy. Having accepted this, they began to show a shift in attitude and a change in their way of relating to American institutions. One of the most obvious changes was in the level of financial support and commitment to the parish; such support was now offered in earnest. Because they had come to believe that their parish and their church would best sustain and advance them in the American setting, the Italians finally put their money where their faith was.

This new development became discernible in Italian-American communities from coast to coast. The three Italian parishes in Rochester, New York, for example, registered major increases in contributions after 1915. During the consecutive years following 1915, contributions in those parishes rose 37 percent, 74 percent, and 234 percent. In the interwar years, furthermore, one of these parishes built a new church, purchased a convent for the teaching nuns, and converted its old combination sanctuary-school into an exclusively educational facility. At the Salesian parish of Saints Peter and Paul in San Francisco, the growth of the parish was slow, developing according to a similar chronology. In that parish, a variety of associations had created the vital center of parish life for the first generation of immigrants. But well-structured and firmly supported organizations had their first substantial growth only after 1910. The need to educate immigrants and youth became a greater concern; English and citizenship classes as well as recreational and sports clubs were started in earnest. Finally, during the 1920s, the construction of the parish church, a project authorized by Archbishop Riordan in 1908, was started. On land acquired for them at the time of the approval to build, the steel structure was begun in 1922. Only two years later, the stately Romanesque structure was finished, and in another three years a fourteen-room school for boys was completed.

From such collective endeavors, undertaken from Connecticut to California during the years following the First World War, came the Italian-American Catholic parochial complex with which mid-twentieth century American Catholics were familiar—this despite the fact that efforts to build up the parish plant had been urged by pastors and bishops since the turn of the century. It was the acceleration of building programs among Italian-Americans in general that characterized Italian-American Catholicism for the next several decades, not only distinguishing Italians from most other immigrant American communities at this time but actually providing a remarkable contrast to the number of postponed building projects of the depression years. Revenues in Italian parishes, in fact, even multiplied during these decades, and long-standing debts were paid off. That changes in church policy did encourage Italian initiatives concerning their commitment to the American church must be taken into consideration in explaining this unique phenomenon. But the degree of difference that the Italians manifested indicated changes within the ethnic community itself. Italian-American accomplishments during this time served as a reminder to American Catholic leaders that the pastoral approach to immigrants must always be seen in the context of diversity.

Well into the middle of the twentieth century, this dynamism and prosperity, which had eluded Italian-American parishes for decades, continued. As Italians viewed the church in a more benevolent way, so too did the church adjust its somewhat confused perception of the Italian community. A kind of reciprocal respect developed. The opportunity to celebrate traditional values within the new social context began to excite the imagination of Italians. For many Italians, the American church finally became more comprehensible; what it had to offer seemed more appealing. For the first time, they saw that it could act as mediator between traditions and new expectations, that it could be both nurturer and socializer. Now they used the church to help them look forward in a land of promise, to provide them with an avenue of openness to new religious and cultural options, and to give them a source of identification and power. For church leaders, on the other hand, it was a time to realize that they must refrain from comparing or judging all immigrants by the same standards. It was a time to reevaluate the need to "Americanize" or homogenize. It was a time to understand the importance of different approaches to evangelization and pluralism with regard to the needs of individual immigrant communities. Above all, their association with Italian-American Catholics had taught church leaders that they must direct their efforts more seriously toward the creation of a more comprehensive pastoral plan for the American Catholic church. One can almost argue that it was primarily because the Italian-American immigrant community had challenged them to consider this particular obligation of ministry within the American setting that church leaders really began to construct policies and strategies for its immigrant members in general.

There was much that the Italian-American experience had done to shape the American Catholic church. By persistently expressing their need for assistance and by their willingness to accept what was offered them as gracefully as possible, the Italian-Americans served as the model upon which a pastoral plan regarding immigrants within the American multicultural context was first developed. Their continued trust that the American church would reflect the same universal qualities with which they had long been familiar remained the best challenge that the U.S. Catholic Church could expect from any of its members. According to their distinct style, Italian-American Catholics forced the American church to see itself as a pluralistic people of God.

CHAPTER
10
French-Canadians Plead for *Survivance*

❧❧❧

*D*escendants of the explorers and settlers who came from France during the seventeenth century to establish New France, the French-Canadians who migrated from the Canadian province of Quebec became a distinct—even from others of French descent—group within the American Catholic church. Between the years 1845 and 1895, more than 300,000 of these Quebecois settled in the United States; at least a quarter million more came and soon returned to Canada. Nearly two-thirds of those who chose to remain settled in the six New England states; the rest spread across the country in smaller groups as far west as Montana. French-Canadians in the United States today number about one and a half million. By no means as numerous as other immigrants, they were so unified in the ways in which they related to American culture and, especially, to the American Catholic Church that it is important to look separately not only at their experience but also at its effect upon the shaping of American Catholicism.

As members of a territory that was an eighteenth-century conquest of the British, French-Canadians were accustomed to the experience of being a minority in a Protestant land. Despite their status, they had developed a rich religious culture that had given them a special sense of ethnicity. It was not because of religious oppression that they had decided to migrate to the United States. Plagued by continual economic crises, especially after 1840, they had "gone to America" by lumber wagon, baker's cart, stagecoach, even on foot, to seek temporary relief from their financial troubles. As did the Italians, the French-Canadians saw their trek south and west only as an expedient. They were, in fact, classic examples of a migrant people, or as one historian has referred to them, "bewildered cultural strangers" in the new land.

But the alluring pull of economic opportunities began to work against their instincts to return to Canada. For the deeply religious French-Canadians, their church had always been as significant to their well-being as their family. In Quebec, the parish had been their hearth. Moreover, their priest was at the center of their lives, the source of their spirit and their guide to salvation. He had performed a multiplicity of tasks; as their confidant, director, lawyer, teacher, social worker, architect, contractor, financier, banker, and labor mediator, he had been the one who had helped them maintain their faith and culture in a hostile land. If they were to remain in the United States, French-Canadians realized they would still require the twin pillars of church and clergy.

For the first several decades of migration, French-Canadians seemed caught between two worlds. They clung tenaciously to their religious past as they developed their skills, mostly in America's mills or factories, and attempted to make decisions about the future. In Canada, the sacred and the secular had been united in the ebb and flow of customs and traditions; they looked to recreate the same religious culture in the new environment. They took heart in any advances made by American bishops to assist them, as, for example, the establishment of Saint Joseph in Burlington, Vermont, as the first French-Canadian parish in New England headed by a French-Canadian pastor and the appointment in 1853 of the French-born vicar-general of Cleveland, Louis de Goesbriand (1816–1899) as the first bishop of the Burlington diocese. They also found the presence of French-speaking clergy in New England dioceses comforting. Provided that their practice of Catholicism could be as beautifully celebrated within American parishes as it was in Canada, they considered permanent relocation. Where they felt barred from this experience, they were likely to return home. Ultimately they tended to base their decisions upon the degree to which some kind of religious community that supported their way of practicing their faith could be established. Like Polish-Americans, the parish remained an essential element in the setting up of their ethnic world in the new land.

As employment continued to lure French-Canadians across the border during the second half of the nineteenth century, more and more migrants began to test the American environment to see whether it could support their religious dreams. From the time of the English conquest of Canada, they had endured the prejudice of Anglo-Americans; in the land of the Yankee they wondered if they could escape this hostile, Protestant environment. It came as no surprise, for example, to be described in negative terms as the "Jews of New England" or the "Chinese of the eastern states." Even their own clergy had publicly ridiculed them as self-seeking materialists because of their migration to the United States. "Let them go; it's the rabble that are leaving," was a typical sentiment expressed by their fellow countrymen. One missionary working with the French of Waterville, Maine, summarized the pre-1870 attitude of Quebec's clergy toward the New England *habitant* when he wrote the following to his bishop:

> They are unjust, sensual, libertine, profoundly corrupt, lazy, indolent, querelous [sic], possessive, liars, drunkards, calumniators, blasphemers, and braggards [sic], thinking they know everything knowing nothing.[1]

Fellow Catholic immigrants did not disguise their dislike for this Quebec invasion and the fact that they felt extremely threatened by their presence. Irish-American workers joined native-born Americans in hurling insults, accusing them of "scab" techniques that further jeopardized the tenuous economic existence that both groups were attempting to improve. During the recurrent strikes, especially at the century's end, violent episodes between the immigrant Irish and French-Canadians were a common occurrence. Stung by the insults from Canadians and wearied by the assaults of strangers, French-Canadians realized that if they were to survive in the United States they would have to band together in faithfulness to their religious aims. In the new land, they must fight for *survivance*.

Unlike the more docile Italian migrants, whose need for their own priests and parishes seemed less intense, French-Canadians became more and more confrontational and demanding as they worked to improve their religious environment. Mutual-aid societies, such as the ones begun as far back as 1848 in Saint Albans, Vermont, and Detroit, Michigan, became models for these later organizational efforts. In the East, especially where general conventions of such societies had met since 1865, these groups served as precursors to the formation of parishes. Through these ventures, French-Canadians were prepared to present, even to demand, what they needed for religious survival. In addition to secular social clubs and societies, French-Canadians also began to organize themselves in more specific Catholic communities along the lines of the *fabrique* (trustee) system that had worked well for them in Canada. Sometimes forming lay trustees groups, known as *marguilliers*, they took active part in pre-parish government arrangements, gaining experience in independence and local control—all this in anticipation of the arrival of one of their own *curés*. Grateful that the 1869 prohibition by the Canadian episcopate that forbade their clergy from remaining permanently in the United States had been lifted, they set themselves to the task before them—this even though their continued reliance upon their clergy was to win them the dubious reputation of being "priest-ridden." Undaunted by this charge and convinced that their future in the United States as Catholics depended upon sympathetic clergy, they continued to ask for priests throughout the difficult transition decades. Wherever they could find an American bishop who understood their needs, they developed solid French-Canadian parishes. But regardless of the religious personnel or institutions made available to them within American dioceses, they continued to argue for special consideration on the basis of their being French-Canadian, for the sake of "la foi, la langue, et les moeurs," that is, their faith, their language, and their customs.

Despite their best attempts to plan their future in the United States, however, economic and natural crises often kept French-Canadians on the move between the United States and Canada, and sometimes from one state to another, throughout much of the last quarter of the nineteenth century. This complicated their settlement pattern and, especially, their ability to establish viable Catholic communities. The population of some border towns rose and declined with the times— albeit always retaining a distinct air of Quebec. A few towns, like Biddeford, Maine, were transformed; by the 1880s, for example, it was already 80 percent French-Canadian. Despite this mobility, town after town began to bear French-Canadian traits as new migrants found work and settled at least temporarily. Although work shifted between mills, quarries, factories, and manufacturing or mechanical shops, more and more French-Canadians persisted in their efforts to find work that could provide a decent livelihood. Centers like Worcester, Fall River, and New Bedford in Massachusetts; Lewiston and Waterville in Maine; Manchester and Nashua in New Hampshire; Woonsocket, Rhode Island; and Willimantic, Connecticut, continually attracted new groups of French-Canadians, especially during boom years, when new contracts were negotiated with New England's industrialists. If by 1870 the employees of eighteen communities were two-thirds French-Canadian, by the 1880s between 20 percent and 50 percent of all New England's cotton mill workers, brick and tile makers, furniture workers, and sawmill employees could claim French-Canadian background. Well into the middle decades of the twentieth century, manufacturing and mechanical industries beckoned. By then there was little doubt that the French-Canadians could find work. But one matter remained unclear: would their accommodation to the American church work out satisfactorily for both French-Canadians and American Catholic leaders?

By the turn of the century, French-Canadian priests had joined the migration. Their presence within American parishes was to make a decided difference in determining the future of *survivance*. Some clergy immediately became involved in the formation of distinctly French-Canadian parishes; their success motivated church leaders to recruit other French-Canadian priests to serve in parishes where their countrymen predominated. Especially in northern New England, bishops attempted to appoint French-Canadians or French-speaking pastors to such parishes. In this way, many territorial parishes became de facto French national parishes. By the end of the century, new national parishes were also established. Thus, "Little Canadas" with impressive cathedral-like churches, built under the guidance of missionaries and financed largely through the sacrifices of their parishioners, became a part of the New England scene. From the start, Maine French-Canadians fared especially well; they seldom lacked priests or parishes. Farther to the south, in Fall River, Massachusetts, the two parishes that had been founded to serve immigrants before 1872 continued to be served by French-Canadian clergy; both parishes confounded Yankee prejudices in the 1880s as magnificent churches rose to dominate the Fall River skyline.

When the call for French-Canadian priests could not keep up with the demands posed by rapid immigration, several American bishops recruited French-speaking clergy from Europe. For the diocese of Hartford, Francis Patrick McFarland (1819–1874), had initiated such recruitment as early as the 1860s, when he managed to persuade a professor headquartered at the American College in Louvain, Father Florimond DeBruycker, to become a pastor to the French-Canadians of Willimantic. DeBruycker successfully divided his energies among all the French-Canadians scattered in eastern Connecticut mill towns. Satisfied with his ministry, McFarland made further requests of Louvain, managing to acquire eight more priests, the first of a series of graduates to work in the Hartford diocese. Until the 1890s this policy was continued by his successor; it proved an excellent source of French-speaking clergy. Archbishop John J. Williams (1822–1907) also used this tactic. In 1869, he procured the services of Abbe Paul Romain Louis Adrien de Montaubricq to become first pastor of the French-Canadians of Fall River. In Boston and Hartford, however, subsequent bishops turned to Canadian priests once they were available.

Other New England bishops also concentrated their efforts on acquiring French-Canadian priests and sisters. In Portland, Maine, Bishop James Healy (1830–1900) recruited French-Canadian priests and nuns for work in parishes and schools after his appointment there in 1875. His persistence helped introduce dozens of Quebecois clergy to the Maine Catholic community. This interest in locating Canadian clergy apparently even seemed to make Healy too empathetic about certain Canadian perspectives. His apparent willingness to sympathize with those opposed to union tactics, coupled with his expressed sympathy with regard to certain of the French-Canadian demands was, in the eyes of some American Catholics, a sign that Healy lavished a disproportionate amount of time, energy, funds, and attention on them. Yet Healy also understood how both churchmen and civic officials could become exasperated with French-Canadians. When the bishop of Hartford, Michael Tierney, was experiencing great difficulty with a group of French-Canadians in Danielson, Connecticut, he penned a quick note to the harried bishop with the advice that Tierney should simply "stand to your guns and let them rave."[2]

Even though limited, the gains made by nineteenth-century New England bishops in recruiting both French-speaking and Canadian clergy to American dioceses actually meant that French-Canadian migrants fared better than most of their immigrant contemporaries. As with no other group, a rapidly increasing core of clergy and religious was available to help recreate the French-Canadian kind of faith within the American environment. Second generation French-Canadians also entered diocesan seminaries; growing from a dozen in 1870, to nearly 90 in 1890 and 138 in 1910, such vocations indicated that a new way of serving French-Canadians in the United States had begun. In both the archdiocese of Boston and the diocese of Hartford, for example, where during the first quarter of the twentieth century more than three-quarters of the seminarians were Irish-Americans, French-Canadian young men made up the second most numerous ethnic group to enter the seminary. And growth in American chapters of Canadian-based religious congregations of women, such as the Congregation of Notre Dame, the Sisters of Saint Ann, the Sisters of the Holy Names of Jesus and Mary, and the Sisters of the Presentation of Mary, as well as the Marianite Sisters of the Holy Cross, testified to the increasing attractiveness of vocations to French-Canadian women.

There were some 400 priests and 2,000 nuns active in New England by the early 1900s. By 1907, moreover, another French-Canadian, Georges-Albert Guertin (1869–1931), had been appointed bishop of Manchester, New Hampshire. With the cooperation of a few French-Canadian and a number of Irish-American bishops who were also active and successful recruiters of French-speaking clergy during crucial periods of growth, French-Canadians parishes became more able to respond to the educational and health-care needs of their people. The number of parishes where French-Canadians were either the most numerous or the only parishioners increased rapidly—much more so, in fact, than the parishes of European immigrant groups. In 1890, there were fifty-three French-language parochial schools in New England alone, with 25,000 children in attendance; by 1910, that figure rose to one hundred thirty-three schools, amounting to 41 percent of all parochial schools in that region. In Woonsocket, Rhode Island, 75 percent of French-Canadian children attended parochial schools; in other communities, like Holyoke, Massachusetts, more than half did. Overall, French-Canadians ranked third among Catholic ethnic groups in the establishment of schools.

Yet, there were still problems; these had surfaced in the 1890s and overshadowed what seemed to be the beginning of a remarkable success story. Perhaps a predisposition toward certain difficulties was reflected in their history as French-speaking Canadians. Having suffered discrimination in Canada, they had anticipated the freedoms enunciated in the American constitution, especially with respect to religious rights. These, they believed, would ensure them that their fate in Canada would not be repeated in the United States. When their requests for clergy or parishes met with resistance here, they were quick to react. Especially after the 1890s, when they often joined forces on the national and international level, they looked to authorities beyond the diocese to assist them. In 1892, for example, Antoine Racine, bishop of Sherbrooke, addressed a memorial to Rome, entitled "Mémoire sur la situation des Canadiens français aux Etats-Unis de l'Amérique du Nord." It was especially aimed at conveying the sense of degradation and hardship felt by immigrants to the United States. This document reflected the growing stridency of Canadian nationalism and showed that French-Canadians were capable of projecting their intentions when their religious rights were jeopardized. Intensifying the discontent were some Canadian immigrant clergy or lay leaders who had their own personal grievances against the American church. Especially in the decades following the memorial, unrest instigated by French-Canadians within the American Catholic church easily mounted; there were intense confrontations with bishops. In the long run, the effect was far from what the French-Canadians intended. Instead of helping to resolve the problems they presented, their complaints only seemed to lead to increased tensions, setting some French-Canadians even farther apart from the mainstream of American society and from the American Catholic church.

This narrowing of viewpoints and confrontational attitude on the part of French-Canadian spokesmen proved particularly disconcerting to those bishops who had attempted to provide properly for all newcomers. On one occasion, when he was accused of opposing the acquisition of French Canadian clergy for assignment in Connecticut, a discouraged Bishop McMahon defended himself by describing his policy even before his appointment to the diocese. "I know that your papers have published certain items on this point, but they are absolutely false," he wrote, "and to give you proof to the contrary, I was the first who built a Canadian Church in New Bedford, Massachusetts and I received two priests from Canada who aided me in the parish."[4] But even such pleas seldom prevented dissident communities from taking their concerns to the apostolic delegate in Washington, D.C., or even to Rome.

Within a decade of McMahon's defense, his successor Michael Tierney was embroiled in a *cause célèbre* over dissent in Saint James Parish, Danielson, Connecticut. Some of the members of that parish, who had been influenced by a fellow parishioner and "ardent patriot," Dr. Charles Leclaire, began to argue that their Irish pastor had failed them in a number of ways, emphasizing his failure to keep his promise that French would be used in school instruction. What particularly enraged them as the battle continued was that Bishop Tierney's solution was to commission two religious congregations from France (the LaSalette Fathers and the Sisters of Saint Joseph of Chambéry) to address the language problem properly. It was a reaction that dumbfounded Tierney; equally shocked were the apostolic delegate and Roman officials, who understood the goodwill behind the bishop's move. When two appeals to the delegate failed, the dissidents persisted in seeking a sympathetic hearing. Eventually they sent a personal delegate from Canada to Rome to plead their case. Even some secular newspapers commented on the scandal and sided with the aggrieved bishop. All of the complainants' measures ultimately failed, and some degree of peace was restored. But the memory of the adamant refusal of the French-Canadians to come to an amicable solution remained to haunt the New England Catholic leadership.

Other, minor incidents reflected similar tensions, tensions that led more than one bishop to question the willingness of the French-Canadians to accommodate to the American church. Sometimes the French-Canadians wondered why they were being so unjustly treated. In Fall River, Massachusetts, Bishop Thomas F. Hendricken (1827–1886) and the French-Canadians of Notre Dame parish became locked in a struggle over the naming of a suitable pastor. The impasse lasted two years, during which time the parish was interdicted by Hendricken; the intervention of Archbishop Williams of Boston only made matters worse. During the struggle, both bishop and parishioners traded insults publicly and, on several occasions, were involved in shouting matches. A maze of communications complicated the settlement; daily reports of the ongoing dissension in both English and French newspapers exacerbated the struggle. Eventually, only the intervention of Cardinal Giovanni Simeoni, Prefect of the Sacred Congregation of the Propagation of the Faith, who found himself "weary

. . . without end" over the incessant letters, would settle the matter. A face-saving compromise was finally achieved with the appointment of an Irish pastor and a French curate. To this day, memories of the intransigent behavior of their bishop influence the attitude of Fall River French-Canadians to their church.[5]

The French-Canadian parish of Biddeford, Maine, provided similar examples of parochial recalcitrance and authoritarian behavior on the part of a cleric, in this case the later bishop of Portland, Louis S. Walsh (1858–1924). By reorganizing one parish to their distinct disadvantage, by enforcing a ban that prohibited ethnic societies from performing at liturgical and other societies, as well as by challenging some aspects of the national parish's finances, Walsh reinforced French-Canadian fears that their traditions would not be honored. When Walsh attempted to acquire church property as the sole owner, however, he stirred up their deepest resentments. Catholics fought one another over these issues. For generations after the rancor begun during his administration had died down, Biddeford's Irish and French ethnic neighborhoods still relived the disputes through internecine struggles, brawls, and name-calling. Whatever originated the disputes between the bishop and French-Canadian congregations, however, the ethnic communities continued to insist upon one particular point. Reminding their Irish-American leaders that they approached their religion through their culture and their language, they felt justified in demanding priests who would appreciate this difference and help them preserve their expression of faith within the haven of their parishes.

To many observers, the strength of French-Canadian complaints or defiance raised serious issues. What was at the heart of this need for special treatment? Why had this happened to a group of migrants whose ancestral roots dated back to colonial American times and who were so much a part of development of the Catholic faith in both Canada and the United States? Why had a people whose deep faith and hope was so evident become caught up in episodes of rancor and rage? What, they wondered, had reduced the French-Canadians, who had so much to bring to the U.S. church, to the same situation as that experienced by immigrants from Southern and Eastern Europe?

In their search for answers, it became quite clear that the conflicts that erupted in French-Canadian parishes after the 1890s were often an aspect of nationalism, now fueled by the same resentment and fears that were experienced by any transplanted people. Yet the problems were not over pride of nation. Dominated by the Protestants in Canada, they now discovered that even their church had betrayed them in the United States. What French-Canadians said they now had to endure in the United States was an Irish-American hierarchy and an Irish-American church whose ideas of Catholic practice and tradition left no room for the celebration of French culture. More, they were confronted with church leaders and members who only occasionally took the time either to listen or to respond to their deeply felt needs. This feeling on the part of French-Canadians that their "American status" was being overlooked and that they were being consigned to the same inferior place within the American Catholic church as other immigrants, may have done much to bring on the bitterness and vindictiveness that proved at times scandalous. Thus, in the early twentieth century, when it was really not too late for French-Canadians to utilize some of the more positive aspects of their immigrant experience, many opted instead to develop their faith in the more protective environment of the national parish setting. For the most part, they rejected Americanization and assimilationist strategies, choosing to cultivate their special kind of Catholicism within the American church.

With increasing determination during the first quarter of the twentieth century, therefore, some French-Canadians joined the more strident voices of nationalists, especially in their insistence on the need for special consideration in the U.S. Catholic Church. Disregarding evidence that other ethnic groups, such as the Germans and the Italians, were becoming assimilated, these French-Canadians stepped up their campaigns for *survivance*. More in the style of Slavic or other Eastern European immigrants, who continued their campaigns for proper representation during the first three decades of the new century, some French-Canadian leaders redoubled their efforts to demonstrate that it was necessary for them to transplant their faith not only for their own good but also for the sake of American Catholicism. Even more, they rivaled the Polish-Americans in becoming vocal critics of the American Catholic hierarchy with regard to immigrant policy. Arguing that they had been victimized by an unfeeling clergy and hierarchy, they especially insisted upon greater control over their own parochial affairs.

In the long run, the French-Canadians who mounted these campaigns would have to share some of the responsibility for the dissention, division, and sense of separateness that became characteristic of certain French-Canadian parishes, especially in the dioceses of New England. The strife emanating from the complaints and demands of the wronged French-Canadians continued well into the 1920s in certain areas. In Providence, Rhode Island, it became the basis of the *Sentinelle* affair, one of the most publicized disputes. Arguing once again that American bishops intended to strip them of their ethnic culture by requiring them to support diocesan building projects, the leaders of this dissident group, named after the newsletter of the larger federated Canadian-American mutual-aid associations, once again argued for control of parish property, more national parishes, and bilingual schools. When, in 1928, their appeals both to Rome and to the Superior Court in Rhode Island resulted in opinions holding that the bishop's method of procuring funds for diocesan needs was legitimate, the Sentinellist faction was required to capitulate. In many ways, however, this affair became the swansong of any concerted French-Canadian resistance to the American Catholic church.

By the mid-twentieth century, only the remnants of French-Canadian protest remained. French-Canadian outlook became more open and more positive. As the traces of bitterness subsided, the more positive aspects of Catholic cultural distinctiveness would begin to be perceived by defensive American church leaders. No longer by demands and quarrels, but by drawing wisdom from previous struggles, would the questions of ethnicity be posed. Through their parishes, their schools, and their many social clubs, in which they had developed and preserved a vibrant and distinct Catholicism, French-Canadians were finally able to point out their contributions and expect to be heard. At their best, they had highlighted what the immigrant Catholic church of the United States should continue to be: a pluralistic community that respected the distinctiveness of its special membership. The acquiescence on the part of church leaders to the unequivocal French-Canadian stand that distinctiveness was at the heart of Catholicism meant that twentieth-century American Catholicism had, indeed, been shaped by the French-Canadians in its midst. The significance given to the parish, the respect for the gift of pastoral care, the understanding of the value of solidarity attained through Catholic organization—these had not been disregarded as French-Canadians kept the traditions of their faith in a way that transcended national borders. Their insistence upon these particular aspects of their faithfulness was the outstanding legacy of French-Canadian Catholicism in the United States.

CHAPTER
11
Lost Hopes for Black and Hispanic Catholics

*D*espite the fact that both Hispanics and blacks could trace their American roots back longer than many European immigrants, their experience within the American Catholic church tended to be even more painful than that of most European newcomers of the post–Civil War period. Members of each minority had to accept the segregated place set for them by society in general; in much the same way, they found themselves separated from other Catholics. And as industrialization continued to bring teeming masses of new immigrants to the United States from Europe, these two groups began to find themselves in worse circumstances within both church and society.

Still, for a brief period after 1865, the hopes and expectations of black Catholics ran high. There were signs that the Catholic Church might become the church most responsive to their pastoral needs. During their years of slavery, some blacks had experienced the concern and care of clerical and lay Catholics. There had already been some impressive—albeit paternalistic—moves toward blacks, especially in those areas where free black Catholic communities could gather. In New York, for example, black Catholics were able to worship side by side with other Catholics. But although the Haitian-born black philanthropist Pierre Toussaint managed to gain prominence as a religious leader among New York Catholic lay men and women, the typical experience of black Catholics in the North was often as difficult and as humiliating as it was for their brothers and sisters in the South.

In the South there was, of course, even less ambivalence concerning blacks. The "peculiar institution" had already split Protestant denominations. Although this did not happen among Catholics, practices and policies clearly indicated that Afro-Americans were treated in much the same manner as in Protestant churches. Even from colonial days and well into the early republic, wealthy Catholic planters and religious congregations of men and women owned slaves. The Jesuits held about three hundred slaves on their farm lands until the 1830s; among women religious in the South the same kind of acceptance of slavery had prevailed. The novices who were first received into the Carmelite monastery at Port Tobacco, in southern Maryland, came with their slaves; and the Sisters of Charity of Nazareth in Kentucky still owned thirty slaves as late as the Emancipation Proclamation. Still, there were some Catholic clergy who worked with small, active communities of free black Catholics in Maryland. The Sulpicians ministered to a Baltimore group whose members had for the most part migrated from Haiti. In New Orleans, where blacks could worship in church alongside whites even into the twentieth century, the black Catholic community of the Sisters of the Holy Family was founded in 1842.

Contrary to their hopes, post–Civil War developments provided few improvements for black Catholics. To be sure, some parishes were organized in Baltimore and Washington, D.C., in the final days of the war. Just as during the long history of slavery, the problems that developed regarding these "newer" members of the church were based not so much on whether they should be granted parishes, be treated kindly, or even be evangelized, but rather on whether they should be fully integrated into the church. Examples of the inability of American Catholic leaders to empathize with the plight of the black population or to take steps to develop black congregations are multiple. When the archbishop of Baltimore, Martin J. Spalding, suggested a policy for the pastoral care of the 150,000 newly emancipated black Catholics at the Second Plenary Council (Baltimore, 1866), his fellow bishops clearly indicated their narrow sense of justice and charity. They not only rejected his notion that there was "a golden opportunity for reaping a harvest of souls," but they collectively bemoaned the fact that freedom had not come, as "in regard to the serfs of Europe," in a "more gradual system of emancipation . . . so that they might have been in some measure prepared to make better use of their freedom, than they are likely to do now."[1]

The only positive measure taken by the assembled bishops at this time was to urge European-based religious congregations to take over the evangelization of the black population. As a result, in 1871, the Mill Hill Fathers from England became the first religious community to do apostolic work among the blacks in the United States in the postbellum era. Under them, two blacks had been ordained by the first decade of the twentieth century. Reorganized as the Josephites and still attempting to fulfill its mission to black Catholics, this religious society itself soon began to show some of the endemic effects of racism. By the 1920s the community had effectively excluded all blacks but an occasional mulatto from its college and seminary; in fact, the Josephites did not ordain another black candidate until 1941. Other congregations of religious men and women gradually entered the service: the Society of the Divine Word, the Society of Saint Edmund, the Spiritans, and the Society of African Missions among the men and Katharine Drexel's Sisters of the Blessed Sacrament for Indians and Colored People among women's congregations. By 1900 there were ten black parishes and sixteen black parish schools in the Southeast (every diocese in the Southeast, except Wilmington, North Carolina, had a black Catholic school); thirty years later, twenty-five parishes and thirty-five schools had been founded. But such figures are shockingly low by comparison with the achievements made during the same period by new immigrant groups. Generally speaking, whether in the North or South, every Catholic institution implicitly accepted segregation and secondary status as normative for blacks.

The inability to incorporate blacks into religious congregations founded by nonblacks clearly symbolized the pervasiveness of prejudice. To be sure, the renowned Healy brothers had made their own special mark upon the nineteenth-century American church. But these three famous churchmen were sons of an Irish plantation owner and a mulatto slave; furthermore, although born in Georgia, they had been able to receive their educations in northern schools, where their nonblack features allowed them to distance themselves from their heritage. Besides, their priestly lives had been spent serving the "white" American church, during which time little, or no, reference had been made to their black background. The most famous of the brothers, James Augustine Healy, became a bishop, serving the diocese of Portland, Maine, from 1875 to 1900, while his brother served as president of Georgetown University. Still, in the postbellum period, it was not until 1886 that the first ex-slave was ordained a recognized black priest. That year, Augustine Tolton, whose father had served in the Union Army and whose mother had gained freedom by crossing the Mississippi with her small children to freedom in Illinois, was ordained for the diocese of Alton, Illinois.

Despite his being sponsored by the Franciscan minister general and his prestigious Roman seminary training, Tolton was to experience great difficulty during his priestly career. For one thing, he was not immediately incardinated into any American diocese. Once assigned at Quincy, Illinois, moreover, he still found himself unacceptable in Catholic circles. Only his transfer to the archdiocese of Chicago allowed Tolton the opportunity to give himself tirelessly on behalf of the black Catholic community as preacher, teacher, orator, and author. Yet his early death, in 1897 at the age of forty-three, was a clear indication of the severe strains he had been under, strains that would most certainly be experienced by any black who chose priesthood within the American Catholic church. In Baltimore, two Josephites, Charles Randolph Uncles, ordained in 1891, and John Henry Dorsey, ordained in 1902, were the only other black priests to serve the church during this early period. Their ordeals were further evidence that traumatic psychological suffering and misunderstanding would be the lot of the black Catholic priest.

By the twentieth century, it was obvious that prejudice would continue to mar the Catholic attitude toward blacks. In Baltimore, Gibbons's advisers suggested that they would vote against the further ordaining of "colored" priests.[2] In other dioceses, an unwritten policy concerning the preparation of black men for the priesthood had the same effect. The agonized careers of the three black priests Tolton, Uncles, and Dorsey underscored the tragic reality. John R. Slattery, first superior general of the American Josephites from 1884 until 1903 and consistent spokesman for the advancement of blacks throughout his priestly ministry, argued that it was hierarchical prejudice and discrimination within the church that had occasioned the scandalous situation. Yet his Josephite community itself would soon fall heir to a similar myopia. Even Slattery grew so dissatisfied with Uncles and so concerned over several black students that he would adopt a more "cautious" approach to the training of blacks for the priesthood. After 1918, ordination as a Josephite would, in fact, become totally unavailable to blacks—a shocking reversal of aims that was not corrected until the 1940s. Had it not been for the commissioning in the 1920s of the Society of the Divine Word (SVD) specifically to train blacks for the priesthood (the first black priest trained by the society was ordained in 1934), there might have been not a single opportunity for Afro-Americans to advance to ordination within the American Catholic church during the first half of the twentieth century.

The continued exclusion of all but a handful of black men from the Roman Catholic priesthood in the United States well into the twentieth century both symbolized and helped perpetuate the second-class status of blacks within the church. Black sisterhoods, of course, rendered service, especially in the field of education, at diocesan supervisory positions, in federal programs, in day-care centers and intercommunity projects. Other communities of religious women assisted black congregations in their work. In 1915, Mother Katharine

Drexel was able to open a school, which later emerged as Xavier University, the only Catholic university for blacks in the country. It was her community that would be highly successful in developing leaders among the black Catholic community as well.

But from the start, it was the black laity that had to assume the heaviest burden of correcting the inequities to which black Catholics were exposed. Ignoring the implications of being without clerical leadership, lay blacks willingly took it upon themselves to improve their lot within the church. In fact, during the last decade of the nineteenth century, a number of Afro-American laymen returned to a practice that had begun as early as the 1830s, gathering renewed corporate strength through conventions or congresses that would plan strategies for self-help within the church. In this dramatic way, they proclaimed their solidarity as a group and detailed their concerns. One layman, in particular, made this strengthened direction possible: Daniel A. Rudd, born a slave in 1854 and reared a Catholic, became the spokesman for his people. Through a newspaper, the *American Catholic Tribune*, which he founded, as well as through the series of black Catholic congresses that he helped to organize, he singlehandedly presented the American Catholic Church with the challenge of developing a way to incorporate black Catholics on an equal basis within the Church. In fact, even more so than the few priests or the many sisters who labored on behalf of black Catholics and their church, Rudd stood out as a sign that their best hopes might be achieved. So convinced was he that the Catholic church could improve the bitter lot of segregated blacks—because it alone could break the color line—that he constantly developed this theme in his writings and through the conferences he sponsored.

Perhaps Rudd's most notable achievement was his convening, in 1889, the centennial year of the organization of the American Catholic church, the first national black Catholic congress. Held in Washington, D.C., at Saint Augustine's Parish, one of the oldest black parishes in the country, it produced amazingly positive results. Not only was it well attended—about one hundred delegates came from all parts of the United States—but members of the Catholic hierarchy and black Protestant ministers were also present. Even President Cleveland watched, later inviting some of the delegates to visit him at the White House. Filled with enthusiasm over the power present within the group, those assembled made bold to call for reforms, especially the establishment of parochial and industrial schools for blacks, the admittance of blacks to labor unions, and the end to poor housing and other social deprivations.

Influenced by Rudd, four more congresses were sponsored in key cities during the next five years, each becoming more specific as to the nature of Afro-American grievances, each suggesting ways to alleviate social crises. For a brief historic moment, good feeling and great hope ran high among black Catholics. At a meeting held during the Columbian Exposition in Chicago, one black speaker proclaimed: "Above all things, we rejoice that our church, the church of our love, the church of our faith, has not failed to stand by her historic record."[3] But optimism was soon dashed as a measure of stridency was introduced among black Catholics. There was only one more congress after the Columbian event. What Rudd and those who interacted during the five lay congresses had begun, however, was not lost; blacks had at least expressed a sense of identity, pride, and confidence as Catholics. A handful of blacks had emerged as a people conscious of their faith and devoted to a common ideal.

Unfortunately, in the waning years of the nineteenth century, as questions of Americanization grew more disturbing to church leaders, discussions of the "Negro Question" took another tack, and black Catholics generally felt isolated and unsupported. Like immigrants, they were seen as a minority to be dealt with, a problem to be solved. Liberal spokesmen headed the list of the well-intentioned who spoke in those terms; sympathetic churchmen, like Slattery, began to reinterpret the "Negro problem" as early as the 1880s; and John Ireland took up the cause when he addressed Afro-American meetings and Catholic congresses in the next decades. Many began to feel it more appropriate to counsel blacks to "be industrious, purchase homes, respect law and order, educate themselves and their children, and keep insisting on their rights," as Ireland did, than to suggest that other Catholics must develop more expansive attitudes.[4] Most of the positive statements seemed, unfortunately, nothing more than rhetoric. Certainly one of Ireland's suggestions—that blacks insist upon their rights—belonged to that category. Even John Slattery's convictions were only paper-thin in the long run. It was Slattery, for example, who cautioned missionaries that, while remaining identified with "the temporal interests of the colored race," they should not act in a way that would make blacks "disliked by the whites, for that would work injury" to their people. Reminiscent of other meliorist black leaders, including Booker T. Washington, Slattery suggested that perhaps it was best that the Afro-American "play the acorn."[5]

By the twentieth century, all the ambivalence of the American racial situation was reflected at every level of American Catholic membership. Caught in the web of generalized prejudice and distracted by concerns over how to handle the massive numbers of European immigrants, American Catholic leaders worked to accommodate prevalent attitudes with the aims of evangelization. As a result, the needs of black Catholics became more and more joined with those of the Indians and others who needed special care. Once again, John Slattery was heard speaking in terms of "the mission field" only within which the evangelization of blacks could occur. In his words, blacks were really a church within a church. "Neither by nature nor by traditional training can the colored people, taken as a body," he wrote, "stand as yet on the same footing of moral independence as their white brethren."[6] Ironically, the most blatant examples of racism and segregation ever to affect the American Catholic church occurred at a time when the church might have been in a position to respond in a different tenor.

As late as 1930, there were still only three black priests serving the American Catholic church. More successful were the black sisters, who continued to provide extraordinary assistance in education and social work: the Oblates of Providence, centered in Baltimore, who had reached over 120 members; the Sisters of the Holy Family in New Orleans, numbering 150; and a third, tiny community, the Handmaids of the Most Pure Heart of Mary, begun in New York with 11 members. In a paternalistic fashion, however, church officials seemed satisfied to turn to other Catholics to serve the needs of blacks. From Slattery's Josephites to Drexel's Sisters of the Blessed Sacrament, the energy of committed apostles together with the mite of the school child or the fortunes of benevolent millionaires continued to be put to the service of "colored people," as if they were no more than the objects of missionary endeavor.

The results of such an approach were predictable. In the North where blacks had begun to migrate after World War I and where some parishes had been organized for them, a mission atmosphere prevailed. Although differently moderated, northern black Catholic churches and schools reflected southern segregationist patterns. To be sure, their institutions did serve the somewhat more positive function of promoting a certain feeling of equality among blacks since, at least in this setting, blacks did not have to face discriminatory practices; they could also develop their own social clubs or parish organizations. In their own schools, especially, they could provide educational opportunities that were clearly being denied within the public school structure. Still, power remained with nonblacks: pastors, and often coworkers, were white; black ethnicity was not enhanced or championed; and the role that blacks were to play as Catholics in the largely non-Catholic black environment was not properly assessed or clarified. More, in both the North and the South, the bulk of evangelization was in the hands of missionary religious orders of men and women, such as the Spiritans or Blessed Sacrament Sisters, and a handful of diocesan priests who worked to assimilate blacks into modes of worship and practice to which whites had been long accustomed. Not surprisingly, only 2 percent of the total black population chose to identify with this approach. In 1928, there were still only some 200,000 black Catholics. The major dioceses with large black Catholic populations were New Orleans (35,000), Lafayette, Louisiana (60,000), Baltimore (22,000), New York (13,800), and Brooklyn (12,000). Among a population of almost twelve million blacks, of whom approximately half belonged to Protestant churches, Catholics appeared as merely a small fraction.

During these difficult years, the parochial mission to southern rural blacks grew increasingly compromised by prejudice. The scattered band of black parishes could not develop prestige or a positive image, as some of the national parishes of European immigrants in the North had been able to do. In fact, there are no remarkable biographies of founding pastors or tales of energetic interaction between bishops and congregations to testify to an equally productive history of the black experience within the church. Nothing more than minimum care—or worse, neglect—was apparent. Even the formation of the black parish in the more rural areas of the South was not usually at the initiative of blacks. Quite the contrary, the segregated black parish in the South was clearly for the sake of the white population. Only because they provided a haven from blatant acts of discrimination could they be seen as pastorally beneficial. Not surprisingly, southern black Catholics found little, in social terms, to be enthusiastic about concerning their Catholic heritage. Little wonder that most were more attracted to evangelical Protestant churches, or that there were few converts to Catholicism among southern blacks.

Yet, even in these straitened circumstances, southern laity often emerged as the backbone of black Catholicism. Reminiscent of their ancestors, they sometimes provided the commitment and vision that church leaders assigned to them failed to show. Perhaps because it required courage to accept further degradation within a southern society where they were already seen as inferior, southern black Catholics were all the more remarkable for their faithful efforts. In certain urban areas, especially, they initiated the establishment of their own parishes and schools. The Florida foundations of Saint Benedict the Moor in Saint Augustine (1911), Saint Pius in Jacksonville (1921), and Saint Mary of the Missions in Miami, which became Saint Francis Xavier (1938), were all begun at the insistence of black Catholics. Saint Benedict's was, in fact, the first independent black parish in what is now the diocese of Miami; it was not simply a mission of the cathedral. Moreover, black Catholics often reached out to ally with non-Catholic blacks, as well as with their white brothers and sisters. Although the ecclesial personnel who served them in these areas were members of all-white congregations—the Josephites and Adrian Dominicans were two congregations especially active in southern Florida—black Catholics still did more than their share in their own parishes. They created their own organizations and helped to initiate parishes. They became teachers of religion and, in some cases, educators in the grade schools which they supported. Because of such efforts, blacks were often highly visible in the life of the southern Catholic church.

Northern black Catholics became similarly involved. They too experienced varying degrees of assistance, paternalism, or neglect. As their numbers increased, however, northern blacks also demonstrated their own blend of initiative and organizational skills. Furthermore, since enforced segregation, per se, was not the northern norm, they were at times able to meet the challenge with a more enthusiastic and coherent sense of mission. This lent itself to racially integrated initiatives and greater activity, especially on the part of the priests who either volunteered or were assigned to work with blacks. As Harlem became more and more black, for example, it took on the appearance of one of the "mission fields" served by white clergy and religious. In 1912, Cardinal John Farley turned over one church, Saint Mark's, to the Spiritan Fathers. While nearby pastors gratefully directed black worshippers there—some personally providing the incentive as they stood on their own front steps pointing the way—Saint Mark's developed a vital congregation. By the 1930s, parish after parish in Harlem had been reorganized to serve black Catholics; by then, the once-fashionable academies had begun to be operated as integrated, parochial schools. Albeit in a somewhat diminished way, this new pattern nevertheless expressed energy and commitment under the direction of noteworthy priests and religious. By 1928, for example, the black Catholic population had grown to 26,000 in New York and Brooklyn. In New York City there were two major black parishes, Saint Benedict the Moor and Saint Mark, as well as six interracial churches. Twelve hundred black children were attending parochial schools within the archdiocese.

In most cases, however, the development of northern black Catholicism had occurred only because of the personal commitment and leadership of the white missionary. All too often, nonblack priests assumed the full task of conversion. Father William McCann, who became pastor of Saint Charles parish in New York, was one of the most prominent of these urban missionaries. He gained fame, in fact, as the first of a certain type who would develop the art of winning black converts. Throughout the 1930s and 1940s his parish added 200 blacks a year; instruction classes became a standard practice that served as a magnet for the parish. During the 1940s, McCann claimed that five thousand had "received the light of Faith and Baptism, and we have created a record unequaled in the country."[7] If a certain paternalism may have animated Father McCann's efforts, as well as those of a number of other priests who imitated him, it proved an agreeable change of attitude for many blacks. Evangelization remained not just an important and uncontested aim, therefore, but a major preoccupation and incentive for those who served black Catholics in the early twentieth century.

What had begun to animate New York black parish communities in the 1930s and 1940s also inspired black congregations in the areas further south and west. Often arising without the benefit of black leadership, the new spirit tended to involve a new consciousness and a more sympathetic clergy. The advance of piety and social justice became the major priorities of both clergy and laity. Sometimes organizations of clergy were started to aid missionary efforts for the education of blacks. In Newark, Mobile, Richmond, and Raleigh, local and regional clerical forums and groups united around issues of racial justice. In almost every large city there arose at least one charismatic priest committed to the advance of black Catholics in both church and society. In Philadelphia, it was Edward Cunnie, the pastor of Saint Elizabeth's, who turned that parish into a showcase of black Catholic piety. Between 1937 and 1955, the parish population grew to 3000 members, 90 percent of whom were converts; the school enrolled 900 pupils. A midwestern clerical conference, the Clergy Conference on Negro Welfare, was another example of such involvement; it was set up in 1938 as a support group for priests involved in the black Catholic apostolate.

A small community of intellectuals began to emerge in the first quarter of the twentieth century. Under them another lay organization, The Federation of Colored Catholics, dedicated to the pursuit of equality and justice, was launched. A Washington, D.C., organization, the Federation was started in 1924 by Howard University Professor Thomas Wyatt Turner; it was an outgrowth of an earlier group, the Committee Against the Extension of Race Prejudice in the Church, which had first addressed the role black people should play within the church. The interests of the Federation embraced both regional and national concerns. At one point, for example, it petitioned the archbishop of Philadelphia to secure the admission of blacks into the Knights of Columbus and the National Catholic War Council. The Federation held annual conventions during the 1920s and 1930s and sought to bring about a closer union among black Catholics. In particular, it hoped to raise the status of the blacks in the church and to stimulate black Catholics to a greater participation in racial and civic affairs. Like its predecessors, it continued to attract nationwide attention; but, like them as well, it was an idea "before its time." One of the major achievements of the Federation, however, was that it prompted black Catholics to question both the vision and the morality of the very religious institutions that purported to serve them. In this capacity of challenging a church that did not attempt to "summarily abolish the color line," it served as a watchdog organization on matters of segregation and discrimination.

Despite problems that eventually diminished its opportunities to lead the fight for racial justice, the Federation of Colored Catholics greatly influenced American Catholic perspectives and indirectly introduced the first major shift in emphasis among both black and white Catholics in their pursuit of improved status for black Catholics. Their insistence that the times were right for justice and equality was strongly endorsed by a small core of black social-justice proponents who had earlier organized as a laymen's union. Their key spokesman was John LaFarge, a Jesuit who had worked in the Negro missions in Maryland and had come to understand the necessity of educating all Catholics to social justice. One issue, however, kept the Federation and this union apart: whether or not social-justice organizations should develop along interracial lines. For some black leaders, the introduction of whites into their federation was tantamount to allowing themselves to be dictated to by whites. This difference between the Federation and LaFarge's group, which advocated interracial collaboration, eventually ended any opportunity for cooperation. After two years of uneasy liaison, the Catholic Interracial Council was formally launched. Almost 800 people—nearly half of them white—attended the first meeting of the Council on June 6, 1934, at the Centre Club, New York, during which a committee was formed to draft a constitution. Within months, the *Interracial Review* was also begun; its guidelines proclaimed:

> We shall guide our course in the light of the Catholic teaching, that all men are equal in the sight of God and equally entitled to the full measure of social justice. We shall at all times be vigilant in opposing bigotry, intolerance and discrimination of every kind and neither a prejudiced minority nor an indifferent majority will find justification in our columns.[8]

The aims of both the Council and the *Review* continued to reflect LaFarge's perspective. To his way of thinking, racial tensions were not the result of prejudice so much as of ignorance. Thus, he consistently argued, interracial cooperation must be promoted by those who could best achieve it, namely, "small groups of conscientious, educated, and intelligent Catholics of both races working together methodically and continually, under competent spiritual direction."[9] Through his speeches, writings, and especially his book *Interracial Justice: A Study of the Catholic Doctrine of Race Relations* (1937),

LaFarge continually drove home the one theme that attitudinal changes were necessary if racial harmony was ever to be achieved. By 1959, thirty-five councils were functioning in cities throughout the North and South, and John LaFarge continued as the key person in their organization and development, eventually becoming nationally known and respected for his promotion of racial justice.

This approach to black Catholic concerns gained wider support only during the 1940s, when it finally became the most powerful and influential church stance on behalf of racial justice. Influenced by its efforts were a cadre of priests and laypersons who led the way in announcing a strong Catholic emphasis on behalf of integration— years before such initiatives as the *Brown v. the Board of Education* Supreme Court decision and similar landmark moves were made by the federal government. In Saint Louis, two Jesuit priests, John and William Markoe, led the fight for racial justice. Pastor of the city's black parish from 1927 to 1941, William Markoe battled with Cardinal John Glennon (1862–1946), over the issue of equal rights. The breakthrough came in 1944, this time under the inspiration of another Jesuit, Claude Heithaus, when Saint Louis University admitted its first black students. Meanwhile, in the suburbs of Washington, D.C., in Selma, Alabama, and in many other fringe areas of the South, the Spiritans and the Edmundites, the Sisters of Saint Joseph and the Sisters of Notre Dame worked more quietly toward social justice. In such pursuits, parishes such as Our Lady Queen of Peace, in Arlington, Virginia, organized for blacks, slowly became integrated, territorial parishes and began to provide programs such as day-care centers or shelters for the homeless. Other bishops added compelling voices. In Saint Louis, Glennon's successor, Cardinal Joseph E. Ritter (1892– 1967), issued an edict in 1947 that demanded the integration of the parochial schools. Francis J. Spellman (1889–1967) in New York, Vincent S. Waters (1904–1974) in North Carolina, Patrick O'Boyle (1896–1987) in Washington, D.C., and Robert E. Lucey (1891–1977) in San Antonio were other episcopal advocates of racial justice who sponsored the integration of their dioceses.

In 1885, the editor of the *Boston Pilot*, John Boyle O'Reilly, had dreamed a marvelous future for blacks within the American Catholic church. Basing his hope upon what he perceived, he wrote enthusiastically:

> The negro is . . . the most spiritual of Americans, for he worships with soul and not with narrow mind. For him religion is to be believed, accepted like the very voice of God, and not invented, contrived, reasoned about, shaded, and made fashionably lucrative and marketable, as it is by too many white Americans.

> The negro is a new man, a free man, a spiritual man, a hearty man; and he can be a great man if he will avoid modeling himself on the whites. . . .

> God send wise guides to my black fellow-countrymen, who shall lead them to understand and accept what is true and great and perennial, and to reject what is deceptive and changeable in life, purpose, and hope.[10]

Unfortunately, all the efforts to achieve this end or to attain some semblance of equality for one group of minority Catholics within the American Catholic Church and within society generally remained grossly inadequate to the needs of blacks well into the 1950s. In an early optimism, a golden harvest had been predicted in 1866; a black laymen looked with expectation toward what the Church offered his people in the 1890s; and the Federation of Colored Catholics rekindled the hopes of blacks in the period of 1920s renascence. Yet, even in the mid-twentieth century, all too little seemed to have resulted. John Boyle O'Reilly's paean to the future of black Catholicism had indeed been swallowed up in a sea of prejudice, and the issue of the integration of blacks and the mainstream Catholic Church remained a secondary matter within the church. Only when American society as a whole was forced to take up the question of racial justice in the 1960s did American Catholics seem to listen more seriously to the concerns of black Catholics. Only then would what black Catholics have to offer the American Catholic church be seen for the rich gift that it is.

Mexican-Americans, a people whose Indian background and history of subjugation put them in an inferior position similar to that of blacks, experienced similar discriminatory treatment within the American Catholic church. The fact that they clung tenaciously to their religion did not prove to be any more of any advantage for them than it had been for European minorities, not any more than their history as inhabitants of the territory directly north of Mexico even before the establishment of the southwestern states had given them status over the Yanqui. To the contrary, their background often resulted for these deeply religious people in a more decided hardship, as their spiritual needs and practices ran counter to either the ideals of the conquerors or the expectations of those who were sent to serve them. With each passing decade, their impoverished circumstances, which bred ignorance, sickness, and the ills endemic to a deprived people, effectively prevented them from building common links with American newcomers. Their pattern of downward mobility—from landowner to unskilled laborer, shepherd, or farmer—did not change during the nineteenth century, nor did their difficult situation improve in the early twentieth century. When, by 1950, Hispanics had clearly become the second largest source of emigration to America, they still were viewed as a depressed minority in need of assistance—the object of social-justice-oriented Catholic mission bands, welfare groups, or Protestant evangelization. Like black Catholics, their economic status, as well as their cultural and ethnic differences, continued to serve them poorly. From the days when every hope of the industrial advance of the United States became tied to a policy of imperialistic Manifest Destiny even to the present, the Mexican-Americans remained more a people to be manipulated by avarice than a people to be cherished because of their Christian ways.

When Mexican migrants began to settle in the newly established Texas, New Mexico, and California territories, they found that the colonial missions, which had once given testimony to the shared faith of their missionaries and their ancestors, were already in shambles. To a certain extent, so too was the religious culture that many of the Mexicans had inherited. Still it was this distillate of native, Indian, and Spanish elements that had set their identity and provided their uncomplicated lives with meaning as they took up residence within the borders of the United States. Whatever missionaries came their way they were apt to receive with docility and welcome. When John Mary Odin (1801–1870), a Vincentian priest assigned as vice-prefect apostolic of Texas in 1840, landed on the Gulf coast to inspect the church committed to his care, he was amazed at the religious fervor which he found among the Mexicans who had settled there. Jean Baptiste Lamy (1814–1888), who arrived as the first bishop of Sante Fe in 1851, was immediately touched by the beauty of a people who had managed to remain attached to their faith, though he recognized that this faith mixed Catholic practices and folk traditions. A folk religion lingered on throughout the Southwest among these former inhabitants of Mexico; a believing people continued to baptize their own children, bury their kinfolk, and celebrate marriage without the benefit of clergy. Into this world American missionaries entered, attempting to reconcile the disparate models of the church. Their aim—to build an American church—was as strongly felt as it had been for those who evangelized the Northeast and Midwest.

Lamy's three-and-a-half decades of leadership at the head of the New Mexican church can be seen as illustrative of this perspective and of the consequent clash of cultures. His imposing presence, in fact, represented the meeting between a determined immigrant missionary builder of the church who endeavored to build an American ecclesial structure and a faithful people whose religious sentiments were more deeply rooted in the folk traditions of the ancient Mexican and Hispanic-American Catholic past. The interchange of cultures and practices could not help but cause personal and corporate distress. But it was also a source of growth. Thus, what Lamy tried to do for the New Mexican church cannot be dismissed because it proved disruptive, even divisive. To the contrary, it must be appreciated at least for its intention to contribute to the re-creation of faith along more universal lines, but within the context of American expectations.

Although it helped to shape the living faith of the New Mexican church, Lamy's career, as well as that of other missionaries of the Southwest, exacerbated the cultural crisis through which an indigenous people had to pass. Realistically, the constraints of Roman Catholic discipline that he was to impose upon the American church could not have been avoided. Nor could the explication of theologically sound doctrine be deferred. It must also be said that the aim of Lamy or other missionaries was probably neither to impose a European kind of Catholicism—despite his background or that of most of his personnel—nor to suppress the native religious culture. The hope of the prelates and missionaries of the Southwest was simply that the American faith, as verbalized and disseminated by the plenary councils, would be strengthened by closer ties with strong, central episcopal authority and purified of the abuses in governance and practice to which the neglect and ambition of earlier missionaries had subjected it. Their dream, it appeared, looked back upon tradition yet was future-oriented—just as the American environment dictated. The present strength of the Southwestern church suggests that the folk-oriented faith of the people was resilient enough to absorb such aims, regardless of whatever petty or overbearing elements arose to block the appropriate advance of Southwest Catholic culture.

Lamy's New Mexican church has been well-documented and described as a fitting example of what could occur when clearminded institutional expectations met established culture. The church he served had developed from a Catholic world in which both priests and people had learned to improvise in harsh conditions. It had been a church overburdened by the self-aggrandizement of clergy, yet made colorful through the imagery of the *santos* (carved statues or plaques) and the family collections of *dichos* (proverbs) and *cuentos* (pious stories). It fostered a ritually oriented, emotional environment dependent more upon devotionalism than upon liturgical celebration, a world in which penitents, through plays and processions, dramatized the sufferings of the Savior and pious groups of men and women gathered for all night prayer vigils (*velorios*). It was the faith of a people for whom the celebration of mass was a rare occasion and who, therefore, centered their religious activities around their confraternity (*cofradia*) rather than their parish, a people whose devotion to Mary was especially evident in the scapulars they wore, the rosaries they displayed around their necks, and the Gospel reenactments they performed in her honor.

But to Lamy's mind it was also a church in need of greater commitment to the Gospel that it both symbolized and celebrated. In particular, he was convinced, it was a church in need of aggressive hierarchical reform in order to bring its people forward into greater harmony with the message of the universal church, its policies and practices. In his capacity as head of the church of New Mexico, Lamy consistently struggled to reshape the religion that New Mexicans had crafted of their own liturgical style, sacred actions, and folk devotions into a visible structure of American practice. One of his first acts after arriving in New Mexico was to emphasize the most recent pronouncement of the American bishops. He had the 1852 pastoral letter issued after the First Plenary Council translated into Spanish, printed in quantities, and distributed throughout his new diocese, this despite the fact that few of the Catholic people of his diocese could read. Then Lamy issued his own pastoral letter, which outlined the expectations he had for the people and priests of New Mexico. Although he had no intention of deviating from the plan of the bishops, he did not calculate that his taking charge in this direct fashion would be as explosive as it proved to be. In Paul Horgan's words, it was like "a hot coal, touched to a short fuse," followed by an immediate explosion. He simply knew there was work for the American church to be done; if Sante Fe was to resemble other dioceses, he had to clarify the roles of the dozen priests who were then serving an estimated sixty-eight thousand Catholics scattered across an area as large as his native France. At the same time, he turned his attention to enlisting reinforcements from Europe and the United States, just as previous American Catholic bishops had done.[11]

At Lamy's invitation, other ministers did come to serve the church of New Mexico. Christian Brothers came from France, Sisters of Loretto from Kentucky, Sisters of Charity from Cincinnati. Most were involved in education. In fact, motivated by the threat of the Protestant advance that his fellow bishops insisted could only be stopped through the proper Catholic education of children, Lamy struggled throughout his administration to see to it that Catholic education was made available. He also attempted to make it attractive to his Mexican flock. Moving forward with his own parochial network of private and public schools, Lamy reflected an educational bias that was shared by most American bishops. This style of leadership would be repeated throughout the Southwest.

In Colorado, Texas, and other western territories, European-born frontier bishops, such as John Odin, who became bishop of the fledgling Galveston diocese, Projectus Joseph Machebeuf, who worked as vicar under Lamy in Sante Fe and later was named bishop of the Colorado Territory, or Thaddeus Amat (1811–1850) who served as bishop of Monterey, in southern California, labored to spread the faith in a manner that conformed to American Catholic policy. Each believed that he understood what needed to be done for the Hispanic Americans of the Southwest. By bringing a native church closer to other elements of the American Catholic church, they hoped to improve the social and economic conditions of their people as well. Often they traveled to Europe in the hope of recruiting other missionaries to serve the thousand-mile stretches of their own episcopal domains. Yet each was inspired by earlier experiences on the frontier; each strove to evangelize and educate a neglected population, building a church that was American in every detail.

In a world complicated by the social and cultural structures of past Catholic practice, moreover, these western bishops braced themselves against clerical factions or schisms that threatened to divide their people. Aided by the religious congregations and personnel that they were fortunate enough to secure, they worked to emphasize officially sanctioned devotions and practices, to assimilate those practices that seemed to conform to already accepted ones, and to settle cultural problems. Yet, also convinced of the need to discipline and to educate—regardless of the tensions such efforts produced—they were prepared to foster cultural and devotional changes wherever these were deemed necessary. In the process, especially in the face of recalcitrant clergy, they often resorted to the harsher methods of threatening those who disregarded the new directions with sanctions or excommunication. In an effort to maintain legitimate control over the Catholic people of their newly established dioceses, they alienated many of their flock. To the present day, hard feelings remain. For some, therefore, the contemporary church stands as a tribute to the faith and talents of both prelates and people developed in what were often the most trying of circumstances; for others it represents the suppression of the best aspirations of the Mexican-American people.

The growth of the Hispanic-American church was slow. In a report sent to Rome in 1881, Lamy reported that there were, for example, only 100,000 Catholics in his diocese, that the number of his churches and chapels had grown to 215, but that these were all constructed of mud brick, and that the archdiocese could still not boast of a cathedral of deserving grandeur. Nevertheless there was progress, especially because of the personnel that prelates had been able to recruit. Lamy's claim was that the church he built had been able to keep its sense of direction because of its personnel. The record in other dioceses seemed as clear. Many Mexican-Americans had been taught, ruled, preached at, and ministered to by French and later, Irish brothers, sisters, and missionary priests. But they had grown in faith and assurance of their own gifts as well. For the most part, the authentic accents, distinct tones, and vibrant rhythms of his Mexican people had been validated. As migration continued to swell the population of the dioceses of the Southwest, however, the socioeconomic plight of the people there often dictated a more gloomy picture for the Catholic church.

The newer immigrants of the twentieth century, in particular, were clearly different from those Mexican-Americans whose families had lived in the Southwest for generations. By this time, the more established Hispanic families might join in criticism of these newcomers, a phenomenon that led the discouraged Robert E. Lucey, bishop of Amarillo, Texas, to complain in 1941, "They are a people apart, ostracized and held in social and economic subjection."[12] By then, sensitized to the needs of Mexican-Americans, some Catholics had begun to extend a helping hand. Unfortunately, all too many of the American Catholic community acquiesced in the prevalent patterns of segregation and discrimination, thus escaping their responsibilities. Moreover, even when mission societies, such as the Catholic Church Extension Society, or mission bands, such as those composed of lay and religious volunteer catechists, focused on the needs of the most economically deprived Catholics, sometimes these poorest were not the first to be served. Thus, of the more than one million dollars contributed to the Catholic church in Texas by the American Board of Catholic Missions from 1925–1951, English-speaking parishes received three times the amount that Hispanic parishes did, this despite the fact that Mexican-Americans constituted the state's most needy Catholics.

Other problems confronted the Catholic church and the Hispanic population of the Southwest during the early twentieth century. The isolation of the farms where many Mexican-Americans worked or lived meant a continued lack of clergy and other church resources. A single parish might stretch hundreds of miles, encompassing as much territory as several dioceses in the populous Northeast. When one Franciscan took over Sacred Heart parish in San Angelo, Texas, in 1925, for example, he was told that he was to serve "a vast field like a diocese."[13] Such constraints could have blessings as well. Desperate over the need to supply pastoral care, bishops often recruited religious orders and gave parishes totally over to them. As a result, religious congregations, such as the Claretians, Oblates, Spiritan, and Holy Cross fathers and brothers were able to join Franciscans or Jesuits in the work of the church. Equally impressive were the religious congregations of women, including the Incarnate Word, Dominican, and

Mercy sisters, who developed educational and catechetical apostolates throughout the Southwest.

After World War II, however, some headway was made toward the development of a greater national commitment to the church of the Southwest. The major catalyst in the transition was Robert E. Lucey and the committee he fostered: the Bishops' Committee for the Spanish-Speaking. After some initial meetings, which underscored the need for an action-group to serve the needs of this region, Bishop Lucey, then archbishop of San Antonio, spearheaded the organization of the special committee. As its executive chairmen for the next twenty-five years, Lucey lead the crusade against social injustice in the Southwest, especially in Texas. This committee of the National Catholic Welfare Council sponsored catechism and child-care programs, established health clinics and community centers, and became involved in public housing and unionization efforts. By the 1950s, it had become the "virtual farm workers' organization"; its aim was to expose the migrants' plight and broaden the church's involvement in confronting injustice.

As was true with respect to their attitudes toward black Catholics, American Catholic leaders were not inclined to recognize the many cultural and spiritual gifts of Hispanic Americans or value their contributions to the American Catholic Church. But as was also true concerning the black community's response to the church, Hispanic Catholics did not wait around to be asked about what their role should be. They took it upon themselves to shape the Catholic church in the Southwest in what may seem to be subtle, but were nevertheless important, ways, especially with regard to devotional practice. Their commitment was evident in the resignation and long-suffering manifested by so many Hispanics; their hope has been witnessed to by their willingness to look to the church despite its apparent lack of interest in responding to their needs. And their deep love of Jesus, Mary, and the saints continues to be expressed through their devotional practices, which give testimony to the depths of their spirituality and the vitality of their religious enterprise.

PART THREE

The Postimmigrant Church

"We urge all Americans to accept the fact of religious and cultural pluralism not as a historic oddity or a sentimental journey into the past but a vital, fruitful and challenging phenomenon of our society. ("Cultural Pluralism in the United States," a paper of the Committee on Social Development and World Peace; chairperson, Bishop Stanislaus Brzana, Ogdensburg; National Catholic Council of Bishops, 1980)

This request, addressed in 1980, was an outgrowth of the wisdom and historical reality of ethnic Catholicism as experienced within the American Catholic church. But it was especially motivated by the postwar realities of the 1950s and beyond. The image of the immigrant church that had held so firmly until then—of separate kingdoms of Catholic culture—was undergoing transition. To a great extent the change was influenced by the lessons of the immigrant church, but the dramatic events that were reshaping American society and the Roman Catholic church in this postwar generation also did much to alter American Catholics' understanding of how the Catholic church could be identified. The church participated fully in this redirection and developed a greater breadth of vision as well. For the first time, the American Catholic minority within the Protestant-dominated majority began to feel warmed by the approval and the applause of fellow Americans. New concepts of the church as a diverse people of God and new emphases on the dignity and rights of humankind meant that Catholics not only might, but should, expand their expression of the faith.

In this period of rapid change and broadening growth, the only constant aspect of American Catholicism was the pluralism of its members. More, the post-1950s church remained a safe harbor for newcomers from Asia and Latin America. In the process of accommodating these newest immigrants, church leaders had to reexamine their previous approach to the incorporation of new members. In particular, they had to consider the consequences of separatism and decide which aspects of separatism should be maintained as the norm for future generations of immigrants. Just as in the past, they were reminded that any attempt to diminish differences for the sake of cultural or religious uniformity would not be satisfactory. In this modern world they had to weigh, once again, the most beneficial aspects of the reality that had faced them for the previous two centuries. In this postimmigrant period, they had to construct a design for the future that in many ways resembled the pattern of the past yet called for new ways of adjusting to pluralism. While celebrating the church's roots in ethnicity, they had to emphasize the pluralistic unity of the church.

In 1917, a Hungarian commentator described the American Catholic phenomenon in ethnic terms:

> Among the immigrants the English and the Irish are rapidly converted into "Yankees"; they participate fully. The Germans keep their national identity for one or two generations, strengthened by help from the motherland. The Swedish and Norwegians are also rapidly integrated. However, the Italian, the Slav, and the Magyar always feel themselves strangers in this land.[1]

This pattern of development had greatly influenced the growth of the American Catholic church; it was evident in the listings of parishes in the annual *Catholic Directory* of the early twentieth century. Before European immigration had been radically cut by the two immigration acts of 1921 and 1924, for example, the United States Bureau of Census's Religious Bodies statistics (1916) had already noted that there were 2,230 Catholic churches using foreign languages, with another 2,535 churches in which both English and foreign languages were spoken. Other statistics for this period pointed to the variety of ethnic patterns that characterized the Catholic church: that, for example, the Poles had established at least three times as many churches as the Italians; that the Czechs, who founded 54 parish churches, shared accommodations in 102 cases, while the Lithuanians, an equally small American Catholic minority, had many more churches than the Czechs for their own use (87) but shared facilities in only nine cases; that the Germans maintained only half the number of parishes that they had listed ten years before. If each group in its own way had used the national parish as an important means by which both leadership and membership could find a sense of identity within the church, new questions would emerge concerning the significance of national parishes after 1950. Would the more recent immigrants be incorporated into the Catholic church in this way? Would they want to relate to their church on this basis? If not, what policies and accommodations should be developed?

As they considered historical precedents in weighing contemporary responses to a perennial problem, church planners were able to see some of the inherent flaws in previous patterns of separatism. The advent of second-generation ethnic leaders who could help to bridge the separation between members of their own parishes and those who worshipped in mixed-ethnic congregations indicated that the need for special status was waning. Membership in the church need no longer be so closely associated with ethnic background. Intermarriage between Catholics of different nationalities provided another pattern of integration in both society and church. But, as church population expanded during the 1950s, some diocesan leaders complicated the process of incorporation with their method of dealing with demographic change and declining numbers. A backlash effect occurred that reemphasized the defensiveness of minority Catholics. Newly beset by the threat of losing claims to distinctiveness, some revived their advocacy for national parishes and representation of their ethnic group in the ranks of the episcopacy. Repeating the arguments of their predecessors, they pointed out that the root cause of their problems remained the same as ever. If they had been better integrated into the leadership of the church, they stressed anew, their need to be separate would be less pronounced and their ethnicity would not have been compromised.

By the 1960s, such complaints found new forms of expression, as Black Power advocates helped ethnic Catholics identify the sense of segregation that certain church policies with regard to the national parish had, perhaps unwittingly, tended to foster. With these new insights to guide them, Catholic ethnic minorities began to be less concerned with maintaining ethnic separateness *qua* segregation and more determined to effect integration on the leadership level, in order to promote equal treatment for all Catholics. This turn of events would signal the third phase of Catholic development in which ethnicity was to play an important role.

To achieve their aims, officials in the church, especially those influenced by episcopal commissions that studied the phenomenon, began to search for the best contemporary solutions to accommodating new immigration. Often they looked back to previous accomplishments in order to refocus their policies with regard to the newest waves of immigration. Aware that many of the national parishes that had been founded by their predecessors had promoted solid growth in their dioceses and that these parishes remained an essential factor in the fidelity of succeeding generations, some bishops continued to look to that model as relevant to present needs. To their minds, for example, the fact that some dioceses had successfully established networks of territorial and national parishes meant that a similar plan could be adopted in any diocese. (A case in point was the archdiocese of Chicago which had founded 200 parishes by 1915; in these, there were 30 German churches, 33 Polish, 10 Italian, 4 Croatian, 5 Slovak, 2 Slovene, 10 Lithuanian, 4 French and 1 each Dutch, Black, Syrian, Belgian, Chaldean, and Hungarian.) They noted as well that success was achieved there and in other dioceses because of flexible episcopal responses which relied upon ethnic parishes, schools, and organizations and immigrant clergy to meet the psychological, as well as spiritual, needs of the immigrants.

A review of ethnic developments in various dioceses also revealed that it had been the particular policies of the more enlightened church leaders, rather than the demands of immigrants who requested these accommodations, that had often been the prime reason for the smooth transition of immigrants into the church. While encouraging new ethnic initiatives and listening to demands, therefore, bishops in the 1950s were attentive to the historic record when it came to planning for new immigrants or refugees. Although accepting the concept of the national parish as a necessary phase of development, however, they began to experiment with other ways to accommodate the newcomers. They stressed those policies that would assist immigrants in making the transition into American society.

After the 1960s, episcopal leaders felt free to alternate between previously useful concepts of ethnic accommodation and those that moved beyond the older categories of assistance in more progressive directions. Both church and ethnic leaders were able to agree upon the problems of separatism and to work out measures to assist in preserving necessary aspects of immigrant culture while also addressing the issue of ethnic incorporation. Thus with the advantage of historical analysis and a social-justice orientation, many dioceses developed programs supportive of the needs of the present generation of refugees, immigrants, and migrants. Another sign of changing methodology and practice was the establishment of national church organizations sponsored by bishops for the purpose of assisting immigrants and developing coherent national policies in this regard. Among these were Catholic Relief Services, Migration and Refugee

Services, the International Catholic Migration Commission and a variety of Catholic-sponsored nationality associations that had also become involved in resettlement and assistance programs. Through these organizations, as well as through diocesan and parochial networks, church leaders were able to take strong measures on behalf of immigrants. The organizations represented the largest voluntary agency in immigration work.

Still another advance was the organization of church agencies to watch over legislative developments and to lobby for social assistance to the newly arrived. The plan had roots in the 1940s, when the bishops urged remedial legislation to provide for the migrant Mexican-Americans. During the enactment of both the 1952 McCarran Act and the 1965 Immigration Act, church leaders, working through the Immigration Bureau, renewed their argument that the problems of immigrants were problems of social justice, and that immigration must be seen as an issue to be balanced with problems of employment, foreign policy, and ethnicity. In the meantime, mission-minded religious men and women, clergy, and bishops worked to raise the consciousness of middle-class, urban-oriented American Catholics on these issues. Widespread support resulted from these efforts on such issues as boycotts for fair wages, reevaluation of immigration quotas, and other social-justice issues.

The pastoral dimension of evangelization of immigrants, which had first reemerged as a key concern in the postwar era, also received renewed consideration. In 1943, for example, the Catholic Action Department of the National Catholic Welfare Conference held the first regional Catholic meeting convened specifically to consider the plight of the Spanish-speaking people of the Southwest. In 1945, the Bishop's Committee for the Spanish-speaking was formed to provide for the religious, social, economic, educational, and cultural advancement of Mexican-Americans. To aid in the spiritual and pastoral care of migrants, the conference recommended assigning priests as chaplains and sending Catholic action groups to live and work among migrants. When in 1949 Father Donald McDonnell, with several other members of the San Francisco diocesan clergy, organized the first Priests' Conference on the Spanish-speaking, the aims of the conference proved compatible with the aims already set by their archbishop, John Joseph Mitty (1884–1961). In response to their report, a mission band was created; Mitty freed four of his clergy, including Father McDonnell, to work in the barrios of the archdiocese.

From the initial endeavors of these priests came a number of positive ways to help newcomers in the Southwest. In particular, McDonnell's encouragement of a young farm worker, Cesar Chavez, led to the formation of the Catholic-inspired National Farm Workers Association and to successful strikes against growers that culminated, in 1970, in the first of many contracts to protect the rights of migrant workers. Under other sympathetic bishops, including Aloysius J. Willinger, C.Ss.R (1886–1973), of Monterey-Fresno and Hugh A. Donohoe (1905–1981), who had served as auxiliary bishop in San Francisco and later as bishop of Stockton, the social justice questions regarding migrants were given necessary episcopal support.

Joint episcopal sponsorship also flowed from concerns first voiced after the arrival of Caribbean and Latin American immigrants in the postwar world. In 1955, the first conference on the spiritual care of Puerto Rican migrants was held in San Juan, Puerto Rico. Participants such as Ivan Illich and Joseph Fitzpatrick reviewed the cultural dimension of religious practice, the role of community, the types of parishes and structures best suited to the new arrivals, and the exchange of priests between the mainland and the island. What was at work here was the first discussion of new models for the integration of immigrants into the church in the United States. These efforts were joined by the Welfare Conference's committees, especially following the reorganization of the conference into the National Conference of Catholic Bishops (NCCB) and its working auxiliaries. At that point, Hispanic concerns came under the purview of the Secretariat for Hispanic Affairs, formally established in 1974; its predecessors had been offices maintained in San Antonio since 1945 and in Washington since 1968. A service called Pastoral Care of Migrants and Refugees was added in 1983.

Since the resolution that the entire body of bishops had adopted in 1976, titled "The Pastoral Concern of the Church for the People on the Move," the bishops have concentrated their attention on finding means to respond to the increasing immigration of workers and refugees and to defend the human rights and dignity of voiceless people. In 1977, this issue was again brought to light when American Spanish-speaking bishops issued their own pastoral letter; the bishops admitted that Hispanics had been afflicted by "institutional and personal racism both from within and without the Church," and they called for the consideration of new policies to address these issues. As a result, a major pastoral statement on Hispanics was released by the NCCB in November of 1983, which argued that more explicit steps must to be taken on behalf of Hispanics.

Throughout the 1970s, the bishops had, in fact, kept their concern for migrants, immigrants, and the displaced minorities to the fore in a variety of ways, issuing documents and lending sponsorship to both clerical and lay initiatives. In 1970, for example, they named a priest of the archdiocese of Washington, Geno Baroni, to direct program development for the U.S. Catholic Conference's Task Force on Urban

Problems. Because Baroni had experience in working with working-class ethnic Catholics, he was considered the right person to address the wider questions of their proper care. Baroni was not only to become the major force in the conception and organization of the Campaign for Human Development but, through the National Center for Urban Ethnic Affairs, established in 1971, he was also able to carry on his work of reinforcing neighborhoods, stimulating pride in ethnic origins, and providing for such needs as housing, credit unions, and associations that develop the sociocultural stability of people.

The stated purpose of the urban center, namely, to assist ethnic clergy, religious, and lay people in improving the quality of their lives, was itself an outgrowth of the evangelical aims of the hierarchy. The Bishops' Ad Hoc Committee on Priestly Life and Ministry had endorsed such activity in its 1971 statement. Addressing the vocation issue, the committee reminded Catholics of the importance of incorporating all nationalities and races within the leadership and membership of the church. The challenge was that

> the Christian message must take root within a people. Hence, there is a pressing challenge for the Church in the United States to encourage the people of each race and culture to develop their own clergy, liturgy and other elements of Christian life and to accept these developments. Imposition of norms and practices upon a people by persons of different background is contrary to a real Christian evangelization.[2]

Sensitivity to the needs of immigrants also resulted in specific plans of action on the part of individual bishops. Thus in 1966 Bishop Donohoe of Stockton appeared before a Senate investigating committee to give the endorsed opinion of California's Catholic bishops that the farm situation had created a moral problem and that farm workers had the right to form unions, should have access to labor organizers, and were justified in their desire to strike. In the East, Bishop Francis Mugavero (b. 1914) of Brooklyn, who defined his see as a "diocese of immigrants," organized its various apostolates in 1972 with immigrant groups in mind; his interest in immigrants led him to become the first bishop in that area to take a stand in favor of amnesty for illegal immigrants without documentation. And, in 1973, the bishop of El Paso, Texas, Sidney M. Metzger (b. 1902), also proved his solidarity with his migrant population by writing to every bishop in the United States asking support for a boycott against the Farrah corporation on behalf of Mexican-Americans.

Much of the episcopal emphasis in the initiatives seemed to have been on the Hispanic population, which the bishops would describe in their 1980 statement on pluralism, as "one of the oldest ethnic American groups." In lesser, but equally consistent ways, church leaders had also begun to respond, especially through the offices of the United States Catholic Conference, to other recent refugees and immigrants. This has been especially true with regard to the most recent immigrants from Asia. Especially since the Vietnam War, work with Asian minorities has been given some attention. As a result, for example, by 1985, about 150,000 Catholic Vietnamese had been resettled in Louisiana, Texas, California, Washington, the District of Columbia, and generally throughout the South and West, largely due to the sponsorship of the Migration and Refugee Services of the Catholic Conference. The consistency of the services rendered Vietnamese over the next ten years meant that some 230 Vietnamese priests, 320 religious women, and 170 minor seminarians were made available to care for the needs of the Vietnamese refugees by the mid-1980s. This infusion of personnel allowed for the establishment of over 130 Vietnamese Catholic community centers, functioning in 28 dioceses, as well as for the organization of 10 national parishes. One Vietnamese parish alone, located in New Orleans, could count a Catholic population of 10,000; and a Catholic Center in Orange, California, cared for more than 15,000. Mostly autonomous, these parishes and communities fulfilled the needs of Vietnamese according to the local situation and depended on the leadership of their own people.

Through the work of national migrant commissions, pastors were also located for the far lesser numerous groups of Hmong, Laotian, and Cambodian Catholics. Serious efforts were made, especially by diocesan Catholic Charities offices, to meet their needs. The diocese of Fresno initiated a program of catechesis for Hmong and Lao children that served as a model for other dioceses in the West; in the East, itinerant ministries served Cambodian communities in Maine, Massachusetts, the Bronx, Harrisburg, Philadelphia, and Annandale, Virginia. The same kind of ministry served more than 150 Hmong families in Rhode Island, as well as scattered families from Massachusetts to Georgia. Some services included pastoral resource centers, or Indochinese Centers, such as the one in the archdiocese of Chicago and those established for East Asian Catholic Charities offices in such far-flung states as Minnesota, Texas, and Washington. The dioceses of California have been particularly active in granting aid for these various Asian groups. National meetings were held in 1982 in Saint Paul, Minnesota, for the Hmong Catholics, in which representatives came from sixteen cities to discuss the problems of these minority Asians. In Chicago, one for the Cambodian, Hmong & Lao Apostolate was held in 1985, in which the mission-team approach was established. From all these groups, study groups, on both the conference and diocesan level, have been formed to develop new pastoral models. Diocesan pastoral institutes have also been initiated to promulgate pastoral letters that aim at heightening the awareness of Catholics to the needs of immigrants and to their responsibilities in that regard. And diocesan offices have been reorganized specifically to include the needs of new ethnic minorities. In some cases, new experiments with parochial structures, including modified personal parishes, pastoral centers, and multilanguage parishes, have been attempted.

If considerable action has been taken by Catholic officials, social workers, members of the clergy and religious orders, and laity to assist political refugees or migrants from Asia or Latin America in the postwar era, the same is not as true with reference to the nation's black Catholic community. In fact, there has only been a gradual unfolding of interest and response to the plight of black Catholics on the part of Catholic leaders. Not until the 1960s would any concerted response to the needs of this minority within the church be given systematic consideration. As if caught in the vicious pattern of racism that lasted beyond the 1950s, black Catholics had to wait their turn until the era of civil rights: from the time of the Civil War, the Catholic church, to which approximately 100,000 blacks belonged on the eve of Emancipation, had foundered in the same hopeless mire of segregation and meek acquiescence to American societal values. Few bright episodes of enlightened ministry occurred; those that did were the result of the insights of Catholics, regardless of race, who opposed the degraded system. Numbering approximately 350,000 Catholics in 1950, blacks continued to be largely exposed to the dictates of segregation. In the North as well, the Catholic church all too readily imitated the American pattern. Bitter memories still remain—of being turned away from church or of having to receive the Eucharist last. These memories meshed easily with the daily experiences of dehumanizing racism experienced by blacks throughout the United States and conveyed the sense of the inferior place to which black Catholics had been consigned in the American church.

To be sure, black Catholics had remained quietly faithful, practicing a faith passed down from the days of slavery. In the southeastern and south central portion of the United States, as well as in the key cities of the nation, they worshiped in their own de facto segregated church. By the mid-1970s, their presence was cumulatively strongest in two dioceses of Louisiana (160,000), Chicago (75,000), Washington, D.C. (71,000), New York (50,000), and Los Angeles (45,000). But Catholic worship during these years continued to be difficult, perhaps even galling as blacks observed the actions of the church with regard to other, more recent Catholic arrivals in this country. There had been official statements by the bishops that suggested that there was sympathy at the highest level. In pastorals issued in 1943 and 1958, the bishops pointed to the moral evil of racism. Moreover, there were overtures by individual Catholics. First in Saint Louis and soon after in Washington, D.C., serious steps were taken to desegregate schools as early as the 1940s.

Despite the solidarity of white clergy and religious women who marched side by side with the Freedom Fighters in Selma, Birmingham, or Chicago, the long years of oppression from the official institutions of state and church took their toll on black Catholics. During the early 1970s, 250 black seminarians withdrew from American seminaries; more than 60 percent of black sisters left their religious congregations. The years of impressive conversions and civil rights rhetoric notwithstanding, it seemed that all too many blacks began to admit that Jim Crow was alive in Catholic institutions. Incredibly, many blacks stayed faithful to the church, and certain national black organizations began to counteract the prejudiced trend. The National Office of Black Catholics was founded in 1970; its adjuncts, the National Black Catholic Clergy Caucus, the Black Sisters' Conference, and the Black Catholic Lay Caucus did much to initiate measures to counteract any further erosion of respect for the church on the part of black Catholics. The positive thrust was perhaps best verbalized by the Benedictine historian Cyprian Davis, O.S.B., in an article written in the *Journal of Urban Ministry* in 1980: "It is significant that in a certain respect Catholicism is the fourth largest Church for Blacks in this country." The potential, he suggested, as Daniel Rudd had done a century before, was there for black Catholics to come to the aid of both the church and their own people in a unique and powerful way.[3]

Perhaps challenged by an awareness of their collective strength, as well as by the reality of their own particular situation within the American Catholic church, the ten black bishops of the United States issued a pastoral, "What We Have Seen and Heard," in 1984. Cognizant that the promotion of so few blacks to the ranks of the episcopate was but one of several significant signs of the lack of recognition of black Catholics in the life of the American church (until 1988, when Eugene A. Marino, S.S.J., was named archbishop of Atlanta, the only black to become ordinary had been Joseph L. Howze, bishop of Biloxi since 1977), they addressed the progress of their own people as well as the deficiencies of the American Catholic church in assisting its black minority. Presenting their arguments within the context of the history of oppression, the bishops pointed out to their own people the responsibilities that they had to their oppressors—wherever these were to be found.

From the beginning words of their pastoral, the bishops invited their people to a new awareness of their power. "Within the history of every Christian community," they explained, "there comes the time when it reaches adulthood. This maturity brings with it the duty, the privilege, and the joy to share with others the rich experience of the 'Word of Life.' " The bishops then proceeded to introduce the purpose of the pastoral: "We the ten Black Bishops of the United States chosen from among you to serve the People of God, are a significant sign among many other signs that the Black Catholic community in the American Church has now come of age." They went on to say: "We write to you, Black brothers and sisters, because each one of us is called to a special task. The Holy Spirit now calls us to the work of evangelization." In the course of the pastoral, the bishops presented a picture of the experience of black Catholics in America, stained as it is by racism. Yet they called, not "for separation but a pledge of our commitment to the Church and to share in her witnessing to the love of Christ" Just as "the Good News of the gospel has been enmeshed in our oppression and pain," so too, they argued, the time has come to accept the call to proclaim that news to a nation in need of forgiveness and redemption. Admitting that the way to a fully indigenous clergy and religious life has been blocked by an attitude that can be considered both paternalistic and racist, they encouraged their own people to pass on the truths of the Catholic religion and the spiritual values of their African heritage. In fact, they asked the entire black Catholic community not to "passively wait for directions or even an invitation from the clergy" but "to seize the opportunity for initiative and creativity in place of complaining about what can not be done." And they concluded with a challenge: "Because we as a people have been a deeply religious people, we as Black Catholics are in a special position to serve as a bridge with our brothers and sisters of other Christian traditions."[4]

The ethnic factor in the American Catholic church has indelibly marked the church as diverse. But it has also greatly enriched it. Analysis of how it has affected the church positively is all the more essential for those who must guide the future growth of the church. A number of present church leaders have already proposed third-stage policies for the postimmigrant era of the American church. These convey the perception that today's Catholic church in the United States continues the tradition of the past two hundred years. Acknowledging the identity of the church as involving the stranger in the land and recognizing both the achievements and problems of the past, church leaders have called for policies that will incorporate new membership with the same sensitivity and ability to alter structures in ways that formerly permitted the inclusion of nationality groups. For example, one of the suggestions presented by those who direct the current effort involving immigrants is that parishes that are personal, de facto, or de jure foreign-language parishes be encouraged, because they can offer today's immigrant the same context for the cultural expression of faith, the development of bonds of solidarity, and enhanced self-assurance that they once did. But a contemporary innovation has been to encourage planners to keep new parish structures as flexible as possible, so that they can better relate to the faster pace of population dispersal and avoid the trap of perpetual legal provisions in rapidly changing neighborhoods.

Learning from the lessons of history, church leaders have also suggested certain alternative policies for accommodating immigrants. Thus, they have suggested that consideration be given to organizing parishes that specifically serve more than one nationality as temporary centers for worship. Although historically such multilanguage parish communities have seldom worked, this was largely because they were ill-conceived, were based on mistaken perceptions of cultural affinities between groups, or were inadequately financed. Planners now suggest that, if ethnic groups can accept the concept of dual-purpose parish centers (based upon the notion that religion will bind the ethnically diverse newcomers), they can have the advantage of shared resources and information while at the same time they can solve an immediate logistical problem for church authorities. But this innovation is only possible if it develops along with strategies based on theological insight and if it engages in a partnership with a laity sympathetic to the design. Furthermore, it should involve leaders among priests, sisters, deacons, catechists, and liturgical activists. In this way, evangelization will reach into the community in the style and immediacy of present communication, then move out to the larger ecclesial community and society. Resources and time given to support the growth and organization of immigrant leaders can then act as an investment for the church in the next generation. Once again, the historical example can be the guideline as long as one of the essential works of American Catholics continue to be the care of immigrants.

These tentative suggestions are but one approach to the future, the result of studying the development of the church in its ethnic American context. They remind us that by building upon the historical precedent, American Catholics have much to offer the present church and that, in fact, the American church is in a strong position to lead the world church, especially in its need to recognize the value of the stranger in its midst. In the light of what previous American church leaders and members have accomplished, moreover, it would seem that the American Catholic church can point the way with regard to its policies concerning immigrants, migrants, and refugees. The third century, in which the factor of ethnicity must be tested again, is upon us.

Notes

Introduction

1. Moses Rischin, "The New American Catholic History," *Church History* 41 (1972):227; see also Harold J. Abramson, *Ethnic Diversity in Catholic America* (New York, 1973).
2. Among ethnic scholars who have contributed seminal works on immigrants and the Catholic Church are Colman J. Barry and Philip Gleason (German-Americans); Lawrence J. McCaffrey and Thomas N. Brown (Irish-Americans); Silvano Tomasi, C.S., (Italian-Americans); Anthony J. Kuzniewski (Polish-Americans); and William Wolkovich-Valkavicius (Lithuanians). Monographs and dissertations have followed on a regular basis; doctoral studies that have been used in the preparation of this book, some of which have been subsequently published, are June Granatir Alexander, *The Immigrant Church and Community: Pittsburgh's Slovak Catholics and Lutherans, 1880–1915* (Pittsburgh, 1987); Frances Campbell "American Catholicism in Northern New Mexico: A Kaleidoscope of Development, 1840–1885" (Graduate Theological Union, Berkeley, Calif., 1985); John Joseph Parot, *Polish Catholics in Chicago, 1850–1920* (Dekalb, Ill., 1981); Richard S. Sorrell, "The Sentinelle Affair (1924–1929) and Militant *Survivance:* The Franco-American Experience in Woonsocket, Rhode Island" (State University of New York at Buffalo, 1975); Robert Orsi, *The Madonna of 115th Street* (New Haven, Conn., 1985).

Part I   The Early Immigrant Church, 1790–1860

1. Theodore Maynard, *The Story of American Catholicism* (New York, 1941), p. xii.

Chapter 1   Identification and Structure of the Immigrant Church

1. Theodore Maynard, *The Story of American Catholicism* (New York, 1941), p. ix.

2. James Hennesey, S.J., *American Catholics: A History of the Roman Catholic Church in the United States* (New York, 1983), p. 37.
3. Ibid., p. 73.
4. Ibid., p. 79.
5. Quoted in Thomas T. McAvoy, C.S.C., *A History of the Catholic Church in the United States* (Notre Dame, Ind., 1969), pp. 124–25.
6. See Maynard, *Story of American Catholicism*, p. 234, and McAvoy, *History of the Catholic Church*, p. 130.
7. Hugh J. Nolan, ed., *Pastoral Letters of the United States Catholic Bishops* (Washington, D.C., Vol. 1, 1984), *1792–1940*, p. 90.
8. Ibid., p. 173.

Chapter 2   Frontier Evangelizing and Organizing

1. Mathias M. Hoffmann, *The Church Founders of the Northwest* (Milwaukee, Wisc., 1937), p. 23, quoted in Robert McNamara, "Church of the United States" (Rochester, N.Y., n.d., Mimeoscript).
2. Thomas O'Brien Hanley, S.J., ed., *The John Carroll Papers* (Notre Dame, Ind., 1976), vol. 2, *1792–1806*, quoted in Jay P. Dolan, *The American Catholic Experience: A History from Colonial Times to the Present* (New York, 1985), p. 107.
3. Samuel Mazzuchelli, O.P., *The Memoirs of Father Samuel Mazzuchelli, O.P.*, trans. Maria M. Armeto, O.P. and Mary J. Finnegan, O.P. (Chicago, 1967), p. 298.
4. Philip Gleason, ed., *Documentary Reports on Early American Catholicism* (New York, 1978), pp. 208–211.
5. Vincent M. Eaton, S.S., "Sulpician Involvement in Educational Projects in the See and Province of Baltimore," *United States Catholic Historian* 2, (1982):9.
6. Patricia Byrne, C.S.J., "Sisters of St. Joseph: The Americanization of a French Tradition," *United States Catholic Historian* 5 (1986):248.
7. George Pare, *The Catholic Church in Detroit: 1701–1888* (Detroit, Mich., 1951), pp. 317–18.
8. Richard Shaw, *John Dubois: Founding Father* (Yonkers, N.Y., 1983), p. 118.
9. Ibid.
10. Ibid., p. 156.
11. Ibid., p. 173.
12. *Record of a Hundred Years: History of St. Mary's Parish, Tiffin, Ohio, from Its Foundation to the Present Time, 1831–1931. A Memorial of the Centenary and the Consecration of the Church, May 19, 1931* (privately printed), pp. 36–37, 39.
13. Theodore Maynard, *Great Catholics in American History* (Garden City, N.Y., 1957), p. 179.
14. Ibid., p. 173.
15. Adele K. Donchenko, "Slovene Missionaries in the Upper Midwest," in *The Other Catholics*, ed. Keith P. Dyrud, Michael Novak, and Rudolph J. Vecoli (New York, 1978), pp. 1–21.
16. Maynard, *Great Catholics*, p. 145.
17. Joseph N. Tylenda, S.J., *Portraits in American Sanctity* (Chicago, 1982), pp. 146ff.

18. John Bernard McGloin, S.J., *California's First Archbishop: The Life of Joseph Sadoc Alemany, 1814–1888* (New York, 1966), p. 363.

Chapter 3   Organizing Strategies for the Urban Church

1. Hugh J. Nolan, ed., *Pastoral Letters of the United States Catholic Bishops* (Washington, D.C., 1984), vol. 1, *1792–1940*, p. 147.
2. Ibid., p. 107.
3. James Parton, "Our Roman Catholic Brethren," *Atlantic Monthly* 21 (April 1868):432–51.
4. Nolan, *Pastoral Letters*, p. 152.
5. James Hennesey, *American Catholics: A History of the Roman Catholic Church in the United States* (New York, 1983), p. 73.
6. Bishop Benedict Joseph Fenwick, S.J., *Memoirs to Serve the Future*, ed. Joseph M. McCarthy (Yonkers, N.Y., 1978), p. 156.
7. Ibid., p. 152.
8. Ibid., pp. 145ff.
9. James H. O'Donnell, *History of the Diocese of Hartford* (Boston, 1900), p. 116; see also James Fitton, *Sketches of the Establishment of the Church in New England* (Boston, 1872), p. 204.
10. Florence D. Coholan, *A Popular History of the Archdiocese of New York* (Yonkers, N.Y., 1983), pp. 53–84.
11. Henry A. Szarnicki, *Michael O'Connor: First Catholic Bishop of Pittsburgh, 1843–1860* (Pittsburgh, Pa., 1975), p. 50.
12. Ibid., p. 81.
13. Ibid., p. 111.
14. Robert Leckie, *American and Catholic* (New York, 1970), pp. 90ff.
15. Theodore Maynard, *The Story of American Catholicism* (New York, 1941), p. 246.
16. Patrick Carey, *An Immigrant Bishop: John England's Adaptation of Irish Catholicism to American Republicanism* (Yonkers, N.Y., 1982), p. 23.
17. Ibid., p. 236.
18. Ibid., p. 146.
19. Ibid., p. 158, quoted from *U.S. Catholic Miscellany*, September 7, 1832.
20. Parton, "Our Roman Catholic Brethren," pp. 432–51.
21. Fitton, *Sketches*, pp. 197–98; and *Record of a Hundred Years: A History of St. Mary's Parish, Tiffin, Ohio from Its Foundations to the Present Time, 1831–1931. A Memorial of the Centennial and the Consecration of the Church, May 19, 1931* (privately printed).
22. Leo R. Ryan, "Pierre Toussaint, 'God's Image Carved in Ebony'," *Historical Records and Studies* 25 (1935):128.
23. Ibid., p. 58.
24. Walter Hammon, O.F.M., *The First Bonaventure Men: The Early History of St. Bonaventure University and the Allegany Foundations* (Saint Bonaventure, N.Y., 1958), p. 29.
25. Ibid., p. 39.
26. Ibid., p. 40.
27. W. J. Howlett, *Life of the Right Reverend Joseph P. Machebeuf, D.D.* (Pueblo, Colo., 1908), p. 400.

28. John Bernard McGloin, S.J., *California's First Archbishop: The Life of Joseph Sadoc Alemany, 1814–1888* (New York, 1966), p. 363.

Part II The Second Stage of the Immigrant Church

Chapter 4 The Ethnic Church Develops, 1860–1950

1. *Sermons Delivered During the Second Plenary Council of Baltimore, 1866 and Pastoral Letter of the Hierarchy of the United States Together With the Papal Rescript and Letters of Councils: A Complete List of Dignitaries and Officers of the Council* (Baltimore, Md., 1866), p. 11; see also pp. xxiii–xxxvi.
2. *Connecticut Catholic*, 16 Dec. 1876; see also *Catholic Directory* (Milwaukee, Wisc., 1900).
3. *Memorials of the Third Plenary Council of Baltimore: November 9–December 7, 1884* (Baltimore, 1885), p. 168.
4. *Connecticut Catholic*, 3 Mar. 1884.
5. Anthony J. Kuzniewski, *Faith and Fatherland: The Polish Church War in Wisconsin, 1896–1918* (Notre Dame, Ind., 1980), pp. 43, 68.
6. Jay P. Dolan, *The American Catholic Experience: A History from Colonial Times to the Present* (New York, 1985), p. 223.
7. Kuzniewski, *Faith and Fatherland*, p. 8.
8. Daniel S. Buczek, *Immigrant Pastor: The Life of the Right Reverend Monsignor Lucyan Bojnowski of New Britain, Connecticut* (Waterbury, Conn., 1974), p. 17.
9. Quoted in Theodore Maynard, *The Story of American Catholicism* (New York, 1941), p. 511.
10. Andrew Greeley, *The Communal Catholic* (New York, 1976), p. 149.

Chapter 5 The Irish Take Charge

1. Andrew Greeley, *That Most Distressful Nation: the Taming of the American Irish* (Chicago, 1972), pp. 38, 118.
2. Bernard Smith Papers, Propagation of the Faith Collections, Archives of University of Notre Dame (microfilm), originals in the archives of the Benedictine Abbey of Saint Paul's Outside the Walls.
3. *Boston Pilot*, 6 June 1863; see also R. A. Burchell, *The San Francisco Irish: 1848–1880* (Los Angeles, 1980) p. 3.
4. *New York Times*, 7 May 1875; quoted in Leland Cook, *St. Patrick's Cathedral: A Centennial History* (New York, 1979), p. 58.
5. *Memorials of the Third Plenary Council of Baltimore: November 9–December 7, 1884 (Baltimore, 1885)*, passim.
6. Ibid.
7. John L. Spalding, *The Religious Mission of the Irish People* (New York, 1880), introduction; see also pp. 61ff.
8. Ellen Skerrett, "The Irish Parish in Chicago, 1880–1930," Working Papers Series, series 9, no. 2 (Spring 1981), Charles and Margaret Hall Cushwa Center, University of Notre Dame; see also James Hennesey,

S.J., *American Catholics: A History of the Roman Catholic Church in the United States* (New York, 1983), p. 178.

9. Timothy Meagher, "Why Should We Care for a Little Trouble or a Walk Through the Mud," *New England Quarterly* 8 (March 1985):5–26; see also Donna Merwick, *Boston Priests, 1848–1910: A Study of Social and Intellectual Change* (Cambridge, Mass., 1973), p. 7.
10. Helen Angela Hurley, *On Good Ground: The Story of the Sisters of St. Joseph in St. Paul* (Minneapolis, 1951), p. 225.
11. James Hennesey, S.J., *American Catholics: A History of the Roman Catholic Church in the United States* (New York, 1983), p. 177.

Chapter 6   German-Americans Make the "National" Difference

1. Jay P. Dolan, "Philadelphia and the German Catholic Community," in *Immigrants and Religion in Urban America*, ed. Randall M. Miller and Thomas D. Marzik (Philadelphia, 1977), p. 76.
2. Jay P. Dolan, *The American Catholic Experience: A History from Colonial Times to the Present* (New York, 1985), p. 162.
3. Henry A. Szarnicki, *Michael O'Connor: First Catholic Bishop of Pittsburgh, 1843–1860* (Pittsburgh, Pa., 1975), p. 70.
4. See Stephen Joseph Shaw, "Chicago's Germans and Italians, 1903–1939: The Catholic Parish as a Way-Station of Ethnicity and Americanization" (Ph.D. diss., University of Chicago, 1981), and Kristeen Brown, "The Multi-Ethnic Parish: Assimilation, Organization and Devotionalism" (Paper delivered at the Bay Area Catholicism Conference, San Francisco, Calif., June 1986).
5. Colman J. Barry, O.S.B., *The Catholic Church and German Americans* (Milwaukee, Wisc., 1953), p. 36.
6. Dolan, *American Catholic Experience*, p. 36.
7. Barbara Brumleve, *Nineteenth Century SSND Innovative Educators* (Saint Louis, Mo., 1983).
8. Henry B. Leonard, "Ethnic Tensions, Episcopal Leadership, and the Emergence of the Twentieth-Century American Catholic Church: The Cleveland Experience," *Catholic Historical Review* 71 (July 1985):398.
9. Ibid., p. 403.
10. Quoted in James Hennesey, S.J., *American Catholics: A History of the Roman Catholic Community in the United States* (New York, 1983), p. 195.
11. Barry, *Catholic Church and German Americans*, pp. 46, 52.
12. Ibid., p. 64.
13. Ibid., p. 53.
14. Ibid., p. 85.
15. Ibid., p. 248.
16. Ibid., pp. 119–20.
17. Ibid., p. 271, n. 52.
18. Philip Gleason, *The Conservative Reformers: German-American Catholics and the Social Order* (Notre Dame, Ind., 1968), p. 62.
19. Ibid., p. 63.
20. Ibid., p. 62.
21. Barry, *Catholic Church and German Americans*, p. 269.
22. Ibid., p. 85.

Chapter 7   The "Polish Kind of Faith"

1. Mary Cygan, "Ethnic Parish as Compromise: The Spheres of Clerical and Lay Authority in a Polish American Parish, 1911–1930," Working Papers Series, series 13, no. 1 (Spring 1983), p. 12, Charles and Margaret Hall Cushwa Center, University of Notre Dame.
2. Ibid.
3. Quoted in Charles Shanabruch, *Chicago's Catholics* (Notre Dame, Ind., 1981), p. 95.
4. John Joseph Parot, *Polish Catholics in Chicago, 1850–1920: A Religious History* (Dekalb, Ill., 1981), p. 67.
5. Daniel S. Buczek, "Three Generations of the Polish Immigrant Church: Changing Styles of Pastoral Leadership," in *Pastor of the Poles: Polish American Essays Presented to Right Reverend Monsignor John P. Wodarski in honor of the Fiftieth Anniversary of His Ordination*, ed. Stanislaus A. Blejwas and Mieczyslaw B. Biskupski (New Britain, Conn., 1982), p. 24.
6. Anthony J. Kuzniewski, *Faith and Fatherland: The Polish Church War in Wisconsin, 1896–1918* (Notre Dame, Ind., 1980), pp. 45–46.
7. Ibid., p. 46.
8. William J. Galush, "Faith and Fatherland: Dimensions of Polish-American Ethnoreligion, 1875–1975," in *Immigrants and Religion in Urban America*, ed. Randall M. Miller and Thomas D. Marzik (Philadelphia, 1977), pp. 87–88.
9. Kathleen Urbanic, "A Matter of Convictions: The Origins of the Polish National Catholic Church in Rochester, New York" (Paper delivered at Polish National Catholic Conference, Rochester, New York, 1985), pp. 9–12.
10. "Report of Parish-Fund Accounts kept at St. Stanislaus Church, Meriden, Connecticut, April 7, 1893, *Parish Annual Reports*, Archives of the Archdiocese of Hartford.
11. Kuzniewski, *Faith and Fatherland*, pp. 103–105.
12. Ibid.
13. "I Polacchi negli Stati Uniti dell'America del Nord," 28 June 1920, Archives of the Archdiocese of Hartford.
14. Ibid.
15. Ibid.
16. Dolores Ann Liptak, R.S.M., "The Bishops of Hartford and Polish Immigrants," in Blejwas and Biskupski, eds., *Pastor of the Poles*, p. 57.

Chapter 8   The Separate World of Eastern Europeans

1. Stephen Torok, "Hungarian Catholics and their Churches in America," part 2 of *The Other Catholics*, ed. Keith P. Dyrud, Michael Novak, and Rudolph Vecoli (New York, 1978), p. 4.
2. Reverend Vincent Gierdziunas to the Lithuanians of New Britain, Connecticut, 21 February 1898, Archives of the Archdiocese of Hartford.
3. Quoted in Jay P. Dolan, *The American Catholic Experience: A History from the Colonial Times to the Present* (New York, 1985), p. 281.

4. M. Emerentia Petrasek, *Brief History of the Congregation of SS. Cyril and Methodius Told in Five Decades* (Danville, Pa., 1959), preface.
5. Quoted in Maria Kaupas, *The Founding of the Sisters of St. Casimir* (Chicago, 1981), pp. 32–33.
6. P. Paul Gabris, *The Past Fifty Years* (Chicago: Marian Fathers, 1964), p. 26.
7. Matthew Jankola to Bishop John Nilan, 27 Jan. 1914, Archives of the Archdiocese of Hartford.
8. Keith P. Dyrud, "The Establishment of the Greek Catholic Rite in America as a Competitor to Orthodoxy", part 6 of Dyrud, Novak, and Vecoli, eds., *The Other Catholics*, p. 207.

Chapter 9 The Italian Challenge

1. Quoted in Rudolph J. Vecoli, "Prelate and Peasants: Italian Immigrants and the Catholic Church," *Journal of Social History* 2 (Spring 1969):223.
2. Carl D. Hinrichsen, "The History of the Diocese of Newark, 1873–1901" (Ph.D. diss., Catholic University of America, 1963), p. 319.
3. Vecoli, "Prelates and Peasants," p. 227.
4. Quoted in James Hennesey, S.J., *American Catholics: A History of the Roman Catholic Community in the United States* (New York, 1983), p. 174.
5. Hinrichsen, "History of Newark," p. 318.
6. Quoted in Vecoli, "Prelates and Peasants," p. 246.
7. *America*, 21 Mar. 1914.
8. Quoted in Hinrichsen, "History of Newark," p. 317.
9. Quoted in Vecoli, "Prelates and Peasants," p. 251–52.
10. Ibid., p. 252.
11. Ibid., p. 225.
12. Ibid., pp. 247–50.
13. Quoted in Richard M. Linkh, *American Catholicism and European Immigrants* (New York, Center for Migration Studies, 1975), p. 65.
14. Ibid., p. 40.
15. Quoted in Dominick Mondrone, S.J., "A Man Called John," part 2 of *Scalabrinians: A Century of Services 1887–1987* 6, no. 1 (Summer 1984):15.
16. *Hartford Daily Times*, 14 Dec. 1914.
17. Giovanni Schiavo, *The Italian Contribution to America* (New York, 1949), p. 477.

Chapter 10 French-Canadians Plead for *Survivance*

1. Quoted in Michael J. Guignard, *La Foi—La Langue—La Culture: The Franco-Americans of Biddeford, Maine* (privately published, 1982), p. 5; see also pp. 49ff.
2. Ibid., p. 51; see also James Healy to Michael Tierney, 4 Jan. 1896, Archives of Archdiocese of Hartford, and William Leo Lucey, S.J., *The Catholic Church in Maine* (Francestown, Maine, 1957), pp. 228–33.

3. A. D. Dolbec et al., "Rapport du comité nommé par la deuxième convention de l'état du Connecticut," *La Travailleur*, 9 Sept. 1887, Archives of Archdiocese of Hartford.
4. Ibid.
5. Philip T. Silvia, Jr., "The Flint Affair: French-Canadian Struggle for Survivance," *Catholic Historical Review* 66 (April 1980):430.

Chapter 11   Lost Hopes for Blacks and Hispanic Catholics

1. Cyprian Davis, O.S.B., "Black Catholics in Nineteenth Century America," *U.S. Catholic Historian* 5 (1986):11.
2. Martin A. Zielinski, "The Promotion of Better Race Relations: The Catholic Interracial Council of New York, 1934–45" (M.A. diss., Catholic University of America, 1985), p. 35.
3. Quoted in Davis, "Black Catholics," p. 15.
4. John R. Slattery, "The Catholic Church and the Colored People" (pamphlet, 1896), pp. 8–9.
5. William L. Portier, "John R. Slattery's Vision for the Evangelization of American Blacks," *U.S. Catholic Historian* 5 (1986):32–34.
6. Ibid., p. 36.
7. Jay P. Dolan, *The American Catholic Experience: A History from Colonial Times to the Present* (New York, 1985), p. 367.
8. Zielinski, "The Promotion of Better Race Relations," p. 57.
9. Ibid., p. 62.
10. John Tracy Ellis, ed., *Documents of American Catholic History*, 2d ed. (Milwaukee, Wisc., 1962), pp. 428–32.
11. Frances M. Campbell, "American Catholicism in Northern New Mexico: A Kaleidoscope of Development, 1840–1885" (Ph.D. diss., Graduate Theological Union, University of Berkeley, Calif., 1985), pp. 67–71.
12. Dolan, *American Catholic Experience*, p. 374.
13. Ibid., p. 375.

Part III   The Postimmigrant Church, 1950–

1. Quoted in Stephen Torok, "Hungarian Catholics and their Churches in America: Tracing the History of the First Twenty-Five Years," in *The Other Catholics*, ed. Keith P. Dyrud, Michael Novak, and Rudolph J. Vecoli (New York, 1978), p. 11.
2. Bishops' Ad Hoc Committee, *Priestly Life and Ministry* (Washington, D.C., 1971).
3. Cyprian Davis, O.S.B., "The Catholic Church in the Black Community Today: A General Overview," *Journal of Urban Ministry* 2 (Summer 1980):35.
4. *What We Have Seen and Heard: A Pastoral Letter on Evangelization from the Black Bishops of the United States* (Cincinnati, Ohio, 1984).

Index